THE JFK
ASSASSINATION
DEBATES

THE JFK
ASSASSINATION
DEBATES
Lone Gunman
versus Conspiracy

Michael L. Kurtz

UNIVERSITY PRESS OF KANSAS

Published by the University Press of Kansas (Lawrence, Kansas 66049), which was
organized by the Kansas Board of Regents and is operated and funded by Emporia
State University, Fort Hays State University, Kansas State University, Pittsburg State
University, the University of Kansas, and Wichita State University

Library of Congress Cataloging-in-Publication Data

Kurtz, Michael L., 1941-
   The JFK assassination debates : lone gunman versus conspiracy / Michael L. Kurtz.
     p.   cm.
   Includes bibliographical references and index.
   ISBN 0-7006-1474-5 (cloth : alk. paper)
    1. Kennedy, John F. (John Fitzgerald), 1917–1963—Assassination. 2. Oswald, Lee Harvey.
3. United States. Central Intelligence Agency—History—20th century. 4. Organized
crime—United States—History—20th century. 5. Conspiracies—United States—
History—20th century. I. Title.
  E842.9.K89 2006
  364.152′4—dc22   2006019969

British Library Cataloguing-in-Publication Data is available.

Printed in the United States of America

10 9 8 7 6 5 4 3 2 1

The paper used in this publication meets the minimum requirements of the American
National Standard for Permanence of Paper for Printed Library Materials Z39.48-1984.

Contents

Contents

Preface

In the past six decades, three events so altered the course of American history that everyone old enough to recall them can remember exactly what they were doing when they first heard the news of their occurrence: the Japanese attack on Pearl Harbor on December 7, 1941; the assassination of President John F. Kennedy on November 22, 1963; and the terrorist attacks on America on September 11, 2001. This book covers the second of those events, the Kennedy assassination. Like Pearl Harbor and the terrorist attacks, the assassination came as a stunning surprise, so unexpected, so shocking, that it continues to fascinate the American people four decades later. The assassination proved to be a watershed, separating an era of popular trust and confidence in the institutions and leaders of American government from one of deep distrust and cynicism. Although many other events—Vietnam, Watergate, revelations of CIA-sponsored assassination plots against foreign heads of state, Iran-Contra, fundraising scandals—clearly contributed to a precipitous decline in popular confidence in government over the next four decades, the failure of a presidential commission to provide a convincing explanation of Kennedy's murder and the government's massive cover-up of the relevant information about that crime formed the first of the events that undermined the historical faith that the American people had traditionally placed in their political leaders.

Before the issuance of the Warren Report in September 1964, it is no exaggeration to state that most Americans trusted their leaders to tell them the truth. J. Edgar Hoover was considered probably the most respected person in America, and even Lyndon Johnson could call upon a very high degree of popular trust in his leadership, at least during the early stages of his presidency. Initially, the Warren Commission's conclusion that Lee Harvey Oswald had acted alone in killing Kennedy received considerable support among the public, and as late as June 1966, polls showed nearly two-thirds of the American people expressing confidence in their government. But coinciding with Johnson's escalation of American involvement in Vietnam into a full-fledged war, combined with continual dissembling about that conflict by high-ranking members of his administration, books published by critics of the Warren Report in 1965, 1966, and 1967 convinced a very large number of Americans that their government had lied to them, and that the assassination had indeed resulted from a conspiracy. For all his faults, New Orleans district attorney Jim Garrison in 1967 touched a popular nerve when he hurled accusations against the Johnson administration and the CIA of covering up the truth about the assassination. Efforts by the national press and news media to denounce Garrison and defend the lone assassin theory failed to stem the growing public disillusionment with what had by then developed into a concerted effort by high government officials to prevent full disclosure of what really happened in Dealey Plaza.

By 1976, the barrage of public criticism, given new impetus by the public airing of the Zapruder film on national television the previous year and by Senate Intelligence Committee disclosures of assassination plots against the life of Fidel Castro, some entailing an unholy alliance of the CIA and the Mafia, persuaded the United States House of Representatives to establish a Select Committee on Assassinations to conduct a new investigation into the murders of John F. Kennedy and of Martin Luther King Jr. The publication of the Warren Report in 1979, which concluded that the Kennedy assassination "probably resulted from a conspiracy," did little to assuage public opinion. Furthermore, the House Select Committee's insistence on conducting the bulk of its investigation and analysis of evidence in secret, together with its classifying all of its unpublished materials until the year 2029, only reinforced an already deep-rooted and totally justified suspicion of a massive cover-up. Throughout the 1980s, this suspicion grew deeper, as the great majority of the new studies of the assassination supported the arguments expressed by the earlier researchers that the assassination resulted from a conspiracy.

It took an unlikely individual, controversial Hollywood movie producer and director Oliver Stone, to force the issue of government concealment of many facts about the assassination into the open. Stone's movie, *JFK*, partially based on Jim Garrison's 1988 book, *On the Trail of the Assassins*, unleashed a torrent of highly critical publicity, some published even before the December 1991 release of the movie. Accusing Stone of deception and of distorting historical truth in the interest of sensationalism, numerous members of the establishment vigorously attacked his theory of an assassination conspiracy. The denunciations of Stone came primarily from the mainstream press and media, which had always endorsed the Warren Commission's lone assassin–no conspiracy version of the assassination. From Dan Rather to Anthony Lewis to George Will to William F. Buckley Jr., renowned members of the eastern seaboard press and media establishment from both the right and the left assailed Stone and attempted to persuade the public to accept the commission's account. Their efforts proved futile.

Whatever the shortcomings of *JFK*, both as a work of art and as a factual account of a historical event, through his masterful cinematic techniques, Oliver Stone did succeed in bringing the issue of government secrecy and cover-up to the attention of the general public, and the support that he generated among ordinary Americans persuaded Congress to pass and President George H. W. Bush to sign the President John F. Kennedy Assassination Records Collection Act of 1992. That act mandated the presidential appointment of an Assassination Records Review Board to "identify, secure and make available all records relating to the assassination." After President Bill Clinton appointed the board in 1993, the panel, comprising one judge, one archivist, and three historians, disclosed that a massive cover-up had indeed taken place. An estimated four million pages of material relating directly or indirectly to the Kennedy assassination had been withheld from public availability and scrutiny for a decade and a half to three decades. During its five-year existence, the review board held public hearings and took depositions, laboring mightily against time constraints and bureaucratic intransigence to identify and make public those records that had been suppressed. Although the release of these materials did not reveal the "smoking gun" so eagerly anticipated by legions of conspiracy theorists, it did provide plenty of information confirming their long-stated claims of a massive government cover-up and outright distortion of evidence, and provided the advocates of conspiracy with plenty of additional material with which to reinforce their views.

In the four decades that have passed since the tragedy in Dallas, countless studies of the Kennedy assassination have been published. Ranging from thoughtful, insightful analyses to works of outright speculation and sensationalism, these works, both fiction and nonfiction, have generated an endless debate over whether the assassination resulted from the deranged action of a lone gunman seeking an outlet from his frustrations with a society that had rejected him in an act of violence against its leader, or from that of a group of conspirators—mobsters, Cubans, renegade CIA operatives—exacting revenge against Kennedy for certain actions that he had taken during his presidency. These general theories have been divided into innumerable subtheories, but they all fall back on the central question of whether there existed a conspiracy to kill the president. From popularized works to specialized journals, from television documentaries to Web sites, the assassination has prompted countless interpretations of that event.

The Kennedy assassination has certainly attracted its share of lunatics anxious to expound the most bizarre of explanations, from the actions of alien invaders to the diabolical vengeance of the Antichrist. It has been depicted in poems, novels, plays, movies, art, television dramas and documentaries, and works of investigative journalism and academic inquiry. In recent years, it has entered the realm of cyberspace and has claimed a place as one of the most frequently visited topics on the Internet. It remains the subject of fierce debate in public forums and lectures. It has, in short, had a mesmerizing effect on those who have studied it and continues to maintain a magnetic hold on their attention. Many Americans not alive when Kennedy was killed still demand to know the truth behind his murder, as I have discovered through innumerable conversations in person and over the telephone, as well as mail and e-mail communications. In hundreds of lectures, panel discussions, and seminars that I have presented on the Kennedy assassination to audiences ranging in size from five to one thousand, I have discovered a common thread running through the myriad theories that I have heard: the desire to know the truth.

The Kennedy assassination occurred at the beginning of profound cultural changes in American society. The so-called counterculture that the decade of the 1960s spawned reflected in some respects the profound disillusionment that many younger Americans experienced with the blatant prevarication and dissembling of their political leaders over the true causes of Kennedy's death. Other events of the decade—including Vietnam; the assassinations of Malcolm X, Martin Luther King Jr., and Robert F. Kennedy; and racial violence in Los Angeles, Detroit, Washington, D.C.—certainly contributed to the development of this cultural phenomenon. But it is no exaggeration to assert that the shock of Kennedy's death and the bungling efforts by government agencies to conceal the truth about it was the first of those events that so rocked the traditional foundations of society that they resulted in profound changes to the political system itself. The very notion that such men of respect and renown as Lyndon Johnson, J. Edgar Hoover, and Earl Warren would connive in a massive concealment of the facts behind the murder of a president of the United States came as a profound cultural and political shock to a generation of young Americans.

Name-calling, mudslinging, and character assassination have characterized the debate over whether Kennedy's death resulted from a conspiracy. Many print and media journalists, as well as most academics, tend to lump all conspiracy theorists together into a category that they would term irrational or paranoid. Even before the release of *JFK*, Oliver Stone was denounced and berated for what his critics called his descent into the depths of irrationality. Those who maintain the conspiracy side of the argument tend to consider the proponents of the lone assassin version part of a vast government-directed plot to conceal everything from the truth about the assassination to what really happened in Roswell in 1947. After the publication of his *Case Closed,* which argued persuasively for the lone assassin interpretation, Gerald Posner found himself and his family subjected to highly personal attacks and harassment by irate conspiracy advocates. It is no exaggeration to state that personal animosity ranks as high as the desire to know the truth among many assassination researchers. Having personally witnessed such venomous animosity between a leading conspiracy theorist, Mark Lane, and a leading lone assassin theorist, David Belin, that the two refused to appear on the same panel together, I have often wondered at the true motivation of many individuals who claim to seek the truth.

The result is an impasse. With the interminable controversy over whether the Kennedy assassination resulted from the action of a lone assassin or from a conspiracy showing no indication of abating, and with the lack of sufficient evidence to prove conclusively that one or the other side is correct, it is time for a dispassionate account of the facts, as opposed to partisan conjecture, about that crime. That is the purpose of this book. It will not engage in the lone assassin or conspiracy debate. Rather, it will cover the main areas of both consensus and conflict, describing both what we do know and what we do not know about the murder of President Kennedy. Its approach is thematic, and its chapters will discuss the present state of our knowledge or ignorance about such topics as the events of November 21–24, 1963, the theories of both the proponents of the lone assassin version and those who maintain the conspiracy side, Lee Harvey Oswald, Jack Ruby and organized crime, and American intelligence agencies. This volume will, I hope, provide the basis for future volumes that treat each of the major topics in detail, offering the most comprehensive series of secondary source materials on the assassination.

This book does not claim to offer a new or definitive account of the assassination, nor does it claim to offer compelling, sensational new evidence about the case. It does, however, make use of the latest materials available, including an extensive selection of the voluminous materials made available for researchers by the Assassination Records Review Board. It will offer new interpretations of existing areas of controversy, and it will present much new evidence based on more than three decades of research into the assassination. It will give credit where credit is due, to both the defenders and the critics of the Warren Commission, and it will refrain from engaging in the vitriolic attacks so characteristic of the prevailing literature on the subject. This is a scholarly work, not a partisan one, and I suspect that it will arouse criticism from both sides, not so much because of the inevitable errors it will contain but because it fails to champion their cause.

Four decades after it occurred, the assassination of President Kennedy remains a story that will not die. Virtually everyone alive at the time can still recall precisely what he or she was doing when they heard the news of the gunfire in Dallas. In my fourth decade of teaching a JFK assassination course at Southeastern Louisiana University, I find that young people, some born two decades after Kennedy was killed, remain fascinated by that event, as do many Americans who can recall the events of late November 1963 in vivid detail. The fascination derives not merely from the well-documented public curiosity about anything relating to the Kennedys, but also from the desire among ordinary Americans to know the truth about what really happened to their slain president. That their government has made a systematic effort at concealing that truth from them has contributed enormously to the cynicism and skepticism about government institutions and leaders so prevalent in our society. This book will not resolve their frustrations, nor will it give them an answer to the most fundamental question of all: Who killed JFK? But it will provide them with a solid basis of information upon which they can construct their own studies and make up their own minds.

Those who have read my earlier work on the assassination, *Crime of the Century*, will recognize many significant changes in my interpretation of that event. The reason is simple: new evidence or recent interpretations of old evidence has convinced me to offer a new analysis. Anyone, especially historians dedicated to uncovering and revealing the truth about the past, must approach their research with an open mind, ever ready to make revisions and to respect differing interpretations. What has not changed is my original conclusion that a conspiracy existed in the Kennedy assassination. Indeed, some of the newly released materials, especially involving the medical evidence, have reinforced that conclusion. In addition, I have finally succeeded in collating the material from numerous personal interviews and conversations that I conducted over the past four decades. This material adds a considerable amount of evidence to the evidentiary base, and it reinforces my long-held belief in an assassination conspiracy. In particular, these interviews shed new light on the still mysterious role of Lee Harvey Oswald, confirming the suspicions of many that his double life reflected that of someone being used by the intelligence community for purposes that remain unclear. Although I treat the views of both lone assassin and of conspiracy theorists fairly and objectively, I find that the evidence clearly lends credence to the latter.

The book begins with a chapter outlining the actual events of the assassination, the ensuing murders of Officer J. D. Tippit and of Lee Harvey Oswald, together with the aftermath of these events. In the second chapter, I discuss in some detail how the evidence so commonly cited by both sides often cannot be considered credible because of the care-less disregard for the fundamental rules of evidence gathering. In the third and fourth chapters, I present a synopsis of the main arguments of the lone assassin and conspiracy theorists, respectively. In Chapter 5, I try to reconcile the ongoing disputes over various areas of factual concern. In the sixth chapter, I add a new interpretation to the life and legend of the accused assassin, Lee Harvey Oswald. Chapters 7 and 8 provide analyses of the two most important conspiracy theories: the intelligence and organized crime connections. In Chapter 9, I present my conclusions and point to the new areas of research that remain.

The story that this book tells is one of deceit, deception, and dis-sembling about the murder of a president of the United States. Long-suppressed documents reveal for the first time the depth and extent of the cover-up. Interrogated under oath, the chief autopsy patholo-gist admitted that he destroyed not only the original autopsy report, but also critical notes he made at the postmortem examination. Other documents disclose that Warren Commission member Gerald Ford deliberately distorted the true location of a bullet wound in President Kennedy's back by elevating it to his neck in order to manipulate the medical evidence to force it to conform to the commission's contro-versial single bullet theory. Other documents disclose that commis-sion member John McCloy did not believe that the report he signed and publicly endorsed proved either that Lee Harvey Oswald fired all the shots or that all the shots came from behind the president. Newly uncovered witnesses testified under oath to the existence of autopsy photographs that depict positive medical proof of shots fired from in front and behind Kennedy.

This is not an enjoyable book to read, for it details the excesses and abuse of power by those anxious to conceal the truth behind the murder of President Kennedy. I hope that in reading it, Americans will learn that only an educated, alert citizenry can prevent the kind of cover-up that took place from occurring again.

Acknowledgments

Some people may be surprised to find their names on this list. Directly or indirectly, they influenced the writing of this book. I have met many; others I have never laid eyes on. Nevertheless, whether they agree or disagree with this analysis, I have relied on their work in one manner or the other. Yet this is my work, and these individuals are not responsible for it. I have listed them in no particular order:

Gary Aguilar; Robert Sam Anson; Harold Weisberg; David Wrone; David Mantik; David Lifton; Mark Lane; Sylvia Meagher; Ben Wecht; Cyril Wecht; Jeff Morley; Henry Hurt; Jim Fetzer; Roland Zavada; Robert Shaw; Charles Gregory; George Burkley; Robert O. Canada; Hunter C. Leake; Consuela Martin; Henry Morris; Sidney Johnston; Robert A. Maurin Sr.; Dale Myers; Seymour Hersh; Don DeLillo; Oliver Stone; James Ellroy; Patricia Lambert; Anna Marie Kuhns-Walko; Larry A. Sneed; Walt Brown; David Belin; Zachary Sklar; Gaeton Fonzi; G. Robert Blakley; Henson Moore; Russell Long; T. Hale Boggs; Jim Bishop; Jim Moore; Jim Garrison; Jack Anderson; Jerry Policoff; Robert Dallek; Jim Giglio; Herbert Parmet; Richard Reeves; Stephen Ambrose; David Scheim; Gerald Posner; Anthony Summers; Robert Tannenbaum; Noel Twyman; Harrison Edward Livingstone; Dick Russell; Jeremy Gunn; Seth Kantor; Richard Billings; Charles Crenshaw; Jim Marrs; Richard Trask; Gary Cornwell; Richardson Preyer; Robert Brent Toplin; Robert Groden; Michael Baden; Henry Lee; Peter Dale Scott; Howard Roffman; Warren Hinckle; Richard D. Mahoney; Milton Brenner; Patricia Lambert; Stephen Tyler; Jim DiEugenio; William Davy; Dave Reitzes; Max Holland; Vincent Bugliosi; Paul Hoch; Gerald McKnight; Gary Savage; Rusty Livingston; Edward Jay Epstein; William Alford; Arlen Specter; Marion Johnson; Kermit Hall; Warren Hinckle; Barbie Zelizer; William Manchester; John Davis; Chip Shelby; Joseph Dolce; Norman Mailer; John K. Lattimer; John McAdams; Ken Rahn; Debra Conway; Clint Bradford; Lisa Pease;

Stewart Galanor; William Gaudet; William Turner; Evan Thomas; John Tunheim; Anna Nelson; Ron Helper; Jack White; Vincent Palamara; Douglas Horne; Tom Samoluk; Gary Mack; D. B. Thomas; Fred Cook; Robin Winks; Bennett H. Wall; Henry Kmen; LeMoyne Snyder; William Eckert; Luis Alvarez; Josiah Thompson; Bud Fensterwald; Charles G. Wilber; Robert Artwohl; George Lundberg; Lou Russell; Roger Feinman; Robert Rosenstone; Marcus Raskin; Michael Rogin; Anthony Lewis; Dan Rather; Walter Cronkite; Roger Craig; Jesse Curry; Leon Jaworsky; Abraham Fortas; Jim Olivier; Jim Engster; Helen Forrest; Martin Shackleford; Paul Peters; Saundra Spencer; Carol Orr; Peter Schuster; J. Larry Crain; Thad Kilpatrick; Ralph Wiebelt; Hunter Durham; Ben Eberle; Sam Wilson; "Black Cat" Lacombe; Morey Sear; Henry Mentz; Hamilton Johnson; John Pastorek. My apologies to those I have inadvertently omitted. A special thanks to Mike Briggs for his inexhaustible patience and encouragement.

1

The Assassination and Its Aftermath

On Thursday, November 21, 1963, Lee Harvey Oswald decided to depart from his usual routine of staying in his room at a boarding house on North Beckley Avenue in Dallas during the workweek. Instead, he asked his fellow employee at the Texas School Book Depository, Buell Wesley Frazier, if he could ride with Frazier to his residence in Irving, a Dallas suburb. Frazier asked Oswald why he wanted to ride to Irving on a Thursday, instead of waiting until the weekend, and Oswald replied that he needed to get some curtain rods for his room. Since he started working at the Depository six weeks earlier, Oswald had usually ridden with Frazier to the home of Linnie Mae Randle, Frazier's sister, with whom Frazier lived. Randle lived just down the street from Ruth Paine, at whose home Oswald's estranged wife, Marina, and their two daughters, June, aged two years, and Rachel, aged five weeks, had lived for the past two months. Typically, Oswald spent the weekend at the Paine home and rode back to work with Frazier the following Monday. This day, however, Oswald appeared eager to visit Marina and the children, so Frazier obliged. As they rode back to Irving, Frazier noticed that Oswald carried nothing with him.[1]

When he arrived at the Paine home that Thursday, Oswald spent an uneventful evening. He played with his two-year-old daughter on the front lawn, watched television, ate supper, and went to bed. Neither Ruth nor Marina noticed anything unusual about his behavior. In fact, the only time Oswald was out of their sight came when the two women went into the bedroom to prepare the children for bed. After that, Ruth went outside to her garage and noticed that someone had turned the light on. Certain that she had not left it on, Paine assumed that Lee had gone to the garage to do some work. The next morning, Lee overslept, but Marina heard the alarm and told Lee to get out of bed. Lee dressed and told Marina to use the money he had left to buy whatever she needed. Then he departed. After Marina had arisen, she noticed that Lee had left her $170, and that he had left his wedding ring in a demitasse cup on the bureau. She had never known him to go anywhere without the ring.[2]

At about 7:15 on the morning of Friday, November 22, Linnie Mae Randle stood near her kitchen sink. As she glanced out of the window, she observed Oswald crossing the street, heading toward the carport. He carried a brown paper bag slightly over two feet long, holding one end of it by the fingers and thumb; the other end of the package almost touched the ground as he walked. Randle believed that the texture of the paper appeared heavier than that of an ordinary paper bag from a store. A few minutes later, Buell Wesley Frazier stepped outside and saw Oswald, wearing a jacket, standing next to his car. As Frazier entered the car, he noticed a paper bag, roughly two feet long, lying across the back seat. "What's in the package, Lee?" Frazier inquired. Oswald responded, "Curtain rods." Frazier, who had previously worked in a department store and packaged curtain rods as part of his duties, paid little attention to the brown-paper-wrapped package that Lee had put in his car.[3]

After a quiet drive to work, Frazier parked his car in the Depository parking lot about two blocks from the building. He told Oswald that he would remain there while he revved up his engine to ensure that the battery retained its charge, so he told Oswald to go on to work. Oswald said that he would remain, but Frazier insisted that he go ahead. As Oswald walked toward the Depository building, about fifty feet in front of him, Frazier noticed that he held one end of the package cupped in his right hand, with the other end resting under his armpit, in such a position that from behind, Frazier could not tell if Oswald even carried a package. When Oswald entered the building at the rear entrance, an employee, Jack Dougherty, saw him but did not notice any package.[4]

After spending the night of November 21–22 at the Texas Hotel in Fort Worth, President John F. Kennedy arose on Friday morning, attended a breakfast at the hotel, and gave a brief speech to a crowd assembled in a nearby parking lot. The president and his entourage then traveled to the airport, where they boarded *Air Force One* for the brief flight to Dallas, the last leg of a four-city, two-day presidential trip to Texas. The plane touched down at Love Field at 11:40 A.M., and after a brief airport ceremony, the presidential motorcade departed for a trip through downtown Dallas, its ultimate destination being the Trade Mart, where the president was scheduled to deliver a luncheon address. The motorcade consisted of police motorcycles and cars, a Lincoln convertible limousine bearing President and Mrs. Kennedy in the back seat, Texas Governor John B. Connally and his wife, Nellie, in folding jump seats in the middle, and two Secret Service agents, one driving, the other in the right front seat, a Secret Service vehicle, a convertible carrying Vice President Lyndon B. Johnson, his wife, Lady Bird, Texas Senator Ralph Yarborough, and two Secret Service agents, another Secret Service vehicle, more Dallas police motorcycles, and vehicles carrying politicians, presidential aides, and members of the press.[5]

Huge throngs turned out to greet John and Jacqueline Kennedy. As the big Lincoln moved slowly through the city's streets, the president appeared invigorated by the continuous applause and cheering. Twice, he ordered the vehicle stopped so he could get out and shake hands with the people. The motorcade finally ended its slow voyage through Dallas's downtown business district, and at 12:29 P.M., it turned right from Main Street onto Houston Street, at the eastern border of a wide-open area known as Dealey Plaza. After a one-block trek down Houston Street, the motorcade made a ponderous left-hand turn onto Elm Street. There the crowds had thinned considerably, and the presidential limousine had only a five-minute drive to the Trade Mart. It was 12:30 in the afternoon. At that time, Jack Ruby, a Dallas nightclub owner, remained in the offices of the Dallas *Morning News*, electing not to walk the four short blocks to Dealey Plaza to see the president whom some people would later claim he admired greatly.

While waiting for the motorcade, several people in Dealey Plaza noticed armed gunmen inside the Texas School Book Depository building at the corner of Houston and Old Elm Streets. Standing on Houston Street, about a half block away, Arnold Rowland saw a man holding a rifle in the southwest corner window of the building's sixth floor. Rowland called his wife's attention to the man, but when she looked at the window, she saw no one in any window on the sixth floor. About seven minutes before the motorcade arrived, Howard Brennan sat on a concrete ledge directly across the street from the Depository building. Brennan glanced up and noticed a man in the southeast corner window of the sixth floor. Brennan observed the man, who seemed to be standing, appear at and then leave the window a couple of times. Ruby Henderson and Carolyn Walther both observed two men, one of whom was armed with a rifle, standing in the sixth floor southeast corner window of the building. Together with several other inmates in the county jail on Houston Street, Johnny Powell also noticed two armed men at the window. However, an employee of the Depository, Bonnie Ray Williams, sat at a window on the sixth floor, only a few feet from the southeast corner, while eating a fried chicken lunch and saw and heard no one in the vicinity. Williams remained on the sixth floor until about 12:20 P.M., when he discarded the remains of his lunch and descended to the fifth floor to watch the motorcade with his friends and coworkers, James Jarman and Harold Norman.[6]

As the limousine traveled slowly down Elm Street, the sound of the cheering crowds was shattered by the report of a gun. President Kennedy responded to the shot, which struck him either in the throat or in the upper back, by wincing in pain, leaning forward and reaching his hands upward, as if to protect his face. Hearing the sound of that shot and recognizing it as the report of a rifle, Governor Connally, seated directly in front of Kennedy, turned to his right to see what had happened, but he saw nothing, so he decided to turn around to his left, but he only moved back to a straight ahead position. Then Connally, his movements having consumed about a second and a half, felt the searing pain of a shot that tore through his upper back, blasted his fifth rib, exited his chest, and then proceeded to penetrate through his wrist, shattering his radius. The impact of the blast caused Connally's right shoulder to slump sharply downward and to fill his cheek with air. About four seconds later, Howard Brennan looked up to the sixth floor of the Depository building, and the man he had seen prior to the arrival of the motorcade took aim, fired a shot, and paused for a second to make certain that he had hit his target. That shot struck Kennedy low in the back of his head. Almost immediately after, a second shot, which many spectators believed came from the right front, exploded against the president's right temple, driving him violently backward and to the left until he bounced off of the rear of the back seat and fell forward, mortally wounded. The explosion of blood and brain matter splattered Dallas police officer Bobby Hargis in the face, as he rode his motorcycle to Kennedy's left rear.[7]

Pandemonium ensued in Dealey Plaza. Stunned by the shock of seeing her husband's head blown apart almost in her lap, Jacqueline Kennedy crawled onto the trunk of the limousine. From the Secret Service car directly behind the presidential limousine, Agent Clint Hill ran and jumped onto the trunk of the Kennedy vehicle and assisted Mrs. Kennedy in returning to the back seat. Agent Hill saw the enormous damage to the president, with virtually the entire right half of the back of his head shattered. Standing on the curb only fifteen feet to the right front of the president at the time of the fatal shot, William and Gayle Newman fell to the ground and covered their children with their bodies. The Newmans had heard the sharp report and felt the shock wave of the fatal bullet as it coursed between them during its flight from a hilly embankment to their right rear that would come to be called the Grassy Knoll. From a railroad tower behind the knoll, Lee Bowers noticed a flash of light, and from the railroad overpass directly in front of the motorcade, S. M. Holland saw a puff of smoke emanating from the knoll. As his car passed the grassy knoll, Senator Yarborough smelled gunpowder.[8]

Fifteen-year-old Amos Lee Euins saw a man fire a shot from the sixth floor southeast corner window of the Depository building, while Robert H. Jackson, a press photographer riding in the rear of the motorcade, saw a rifle slowly withdrawn from that window after the last shot, as did television cameraman Malcolm O. Couch. Two employees of the Depository, Harold Norman and Bonnie Ray Williams, who watched the motorcade from the fifth floor southeast corner window, and who heard the sounds of rifle shells hitting the floor directly above them, remained at their window, staring at the commotion below, while their coworker, James Jarman, ran to the western end of the building to get a closer look at the crowds surging toward the Grassy Knoll. Hardly anyone standing in front of the Depository building reacted as if the shots had originated there, but almost instantaneously, dozens of spectators in the vicinity of the knoll ran up the grassy embankment because it appeared that shots had come from there or because they saw others running in that direction. One of the first of these individuals, Dallas police officer Joe Marshall Smith, scaled the wooden fence at the knoll's apex and saw a man getting into a car in a parking lot behind the knoll. Officer Smith told the man to stop, but he flashed Secret Service credentials, so Smith allowed him to drive away.[9]

As he escorted vehicles on Houston Street near the end of the motorcade, motorcycle policeman Marrion Baker heard the unmistakable sound of gunfire. Glancing upward, Baker observed a flock of pigeons fly from the roof of the Depository building. Certain that the shots came from the building, after the last shot was fired, Baker raced to the corner of Elm and Houston, jumped off his motorcycle, and ran toward the building entrance. As he ran up the front steps, Baker called for the manager, and the Depository's superintendent, Roy Truly, followed Baker into the building. Unable to operate the elevator, Baker ran up the stairs at the rear of the first floor. As he reached the second floor landing, he looked through a glass window panel on a door and saw a man standing inside a lunchroom. Pulling his gun out of his holster, Baker entered the lunchroom and pointed the gun at the man, who stood in front of a soft drink machine. Just then, Truly entered the room and identified the man as Lee Oswald, one of his employees. Both Baker and Truly noticed that Oswald behaved normally, neither out of breath nor agitated. Because Baker was certain that the shots he heard came from an upper floor or even the roof of the building, and because Oswald hardly behaved like a man who had fired shots less than ninety seconds previously, he replaced his gun in his holster, left the lunchroom, and resumed his ascent to the roof. Baker and Truly estimated that the lunchroom encounter with Oswald occurred no more than a minute and a half after the shooting. Less than one minute later, a Depository employee, Geraldine Reid, returned to her desk on the second floor from the stairs leading to the first floor entrance and noticed Oswald walking toward her "at a very slow pace." He carried a Coke in his hand, and his demeanor appeared perfectly normal, especially since he was headed toward the stairs that led to the building's front entrance at Old Elm and Houston.[10]

Eight minutes after the gunfire in Dealey Plaza, the motorcade arrived at the emergency room entrance to Parkland Hospital. After placing Governor Connally on a gurney, Secret Service agents, Dallas police, and nurses removed the moribund president from the limousine, placed him on a gurney, and wheeled him into Trauma Room One. Noticing a massive, gaping wound in the rear of President Kennedy's head, nurses Diana Bowron and Patricia Hutton knew instinctively that he stood little chance of survival. Doctors Paul Peters, Robert McClelland, James Carrico, Malcolm Perry, Charles Crenshaw, and other physicians also observed the huge wound in the back of the president's head, as well as the cerebral and cerebellar tissue oozing from the wound, and they silently confirmed the nurses' observation that Kennedy could not survive. Nevertheless, the Parkland medical team worked furiously in a vain attempt to resuscitate the dying president. Dr. Perry made a tracheotomy incision directly through a tiny bullet wound in Kennedy's neck just below the Adam's apple, a hole so tiny that Perry and the other medical personnel recognized it as a wound of entrance.[11]

After Dr. Perry finished the tracheotomy, he and other physicians and nurses performed other emergency resuscitative measures on the president, but they knew their efforts would be in vain. Dr. Kemp Clark, the head of neurosurgery at Parkland Hospital, saw the gaping wound at the rear of Kennedy's head, observed the cerebral and cerebellar tissue exuding from it, and, after learning that President Kennedy had no discernible heartbeat or blood pressure, officially pronounced him dead. Jacqueline Kennedy was informed of her husband's death, and she remained by his side in the emergency room until a Roman Catholic priest, Father Oscar Huber, arrived to perform the last rites of the church. After Father Huber did so, people left the room while two nurses and an orderly cleaned the body for placement in a coffin. They, too, noticed the large wound in the rear of the head, as well as a small bullet hole in Kennedy's back, several inches below his right shoulder. The driver of the ambulance that would transport the body back to *Air Force One* also observed the large wound in the rear of the head.[12]

About ten minutes after the assassination, a man boarded a Dallas bus on Elm Street about seven blocks from the Book Depository. A passenger on the bus, Mary Bledsoe, recognized the man as someone to whom she had rented a room in her house at the beginning of October

1963. Bledsoe claimed that the man, whom she later identified as Lee Harvey Oswald, looked like a "maniac," with a "distorted" face. As the bus headed in the direction of Dealey Plaza, it became ensnarled in the growing traffic congestion, so the man exited the bus, taking a transfer with him. The time was about 12:44 P.M. Four minutes later, a man approached a taxicab parked outside a Greyhound bus station located four blocks from where the passenger had exited the bus. As the man started to enter the cab, an elderly woman approached, and the man offered to let her have the cab, but she refused. The man then sat in the front seat next to the taxi driver, William Whaley, who would identify that passenger as Lee Harvey Oswald. Whaley drove him to around the 500 block of North Beckley Avenue, five blocks from Oswald's rooming house. The man left the taxi at about 12:57, leaving Whaley with a five-cent tip. At about 12:45, Dallas Deputy Sheriff Roger D. Craig stood on the median separating Elm and Main Streets. As he looked toward the grassy plain between the knoll and the Depository building, Craig saw a man run from the rear of the building, down the grassy incline, and get into a light-colored Nash station wagon driven by a dark-complexioned man. Later that afternoon, when he walked into the Homicide Bureau at Dallas police headquarters, Craig identified the man whom he witnessed run from the building as Lee Harvey Oswald.[13]

At Parkland Hospital, physicians examined Governor Connally in Trauma Room Two and found that he had suffered a serious sucking wound of the chest. The governor was taken immediately to the second-floor operating room, moved from his original stretcher, and placed on an operating table. An orderly put Connally's stretcher into a nearby elevator. In the operating room, Governor Connally was fortunate to have Dr. Robert R. Shaw as his principal surgeon. A board-certified and practicing thoracic surgeon, Dr. Shaw had served as the chief of thoracic surgery for the United States Army in France during World War II, and in that capacity, he had operated on more than a thousand gunshot and shrapnel wounds of the chest. Shaw observed a clean puncture wound of entry in Connally's back. The elongated 1.5-centimeter wound had an abrasion collar of bruising around it, a certain indicator of an entrance wound of a bullet that had not struck anything previously. Because the trajectory of the bullet through the chest lay in a leftward and downward direction, that bullet must have been fired from above, behind, and to the right of the governor. Dr. Shaw repaired the damage to the governor's chest, and after closing the incisions, he turned the surgery over to Dr. Charles Gregory, an orthopedic surgeon, who proceeded to repair the extensive damage to Connally's right wrist, damage that included a comminuted fracture of the radius. Dr. Gregory removed several tiny lead fragments from the wrist. Dr. Thomas Shires observed on an x-ray that Governor Connally had a bullet fragment two by three by four millimeters in dimension embedded in his left thigh, but Dr. Shires decided that he would do more damage to the governor's leg by removing the fragment than by leaving it alone, so he merely debrided the area surrounding the part of the thigh where the bullet or fragment had penetrated.[14]

During the surgery on Governor Connally, Darrell C. Tomlinson, Parkland Hospital's chief engineer, entered an elevator and noticed the empty gurney on which Governor Connally had originally been taken into the hospital. Tomlinson wheeled the gurney from the elevator and placed it in a corridor on the ground floor alongside another gurney. More than a half-hour later, Tomlinson returned to the ground floor and noticed that Connally's gurney remained where he had left it. The other gurney, however, had been moved so it blocked the passage through the corridor, so Tomlinson pushed it back against the wall. When he did, a bullet rolled out. Tomlinson's friend, Otis Elevator serviceman Nathan Pool, saw the incident of the stretcher bullet. Tomlinson immediately notified O. P. Wright, Parkland Hospital's chief of security, and Wright informed an FBI agent of the bullet. After the FBI agent expressed a total lack of interest, Wright told Secret Service agent Richard Johnsen, and Johnsen ordered Wright to retrieve the bullet from the stretcher. Wright went to the gurney, carefully picked up the bullet, which he and Pool recognized as a .30 caliber pointed-tip round of hunting ammunition. Wright took the bullet to Agent Johnsen, who put it in his pocket.[15]

Shortly after 1:00, as Earlene Roberts, the housekeeper at 1026 North Beckley Avenue, a rooming house in the Oak Cliff section of Dallas, watched the announcement of the president's death on television, one of the tenants, Lee Harvey Oswald, entered the house and went directly to his room. While Oswald was in his room, Roberts heard the "beep beep" sound of an automobile horn, and she peeked out of the front window through the Venetian blinds and saw a Dallas police vehicle parked directly outside. After waiting about a minute, Roberts again peeked through the Venetian blinds and noticed that the police car had left. One minute later, Oswald, wearing a lightweight jacket, descended the stairs and left the rooming house. Roberts again peeked through the blinds and observed Oswald standing by a bus stop, apparently waiting for a bus that would take him toward downtown Dallas. When she peeked through the curtains again, Oswald was gone.[16]

Dallas police officer J. D. Tippit rode alone in his patrol car as he slowly cruised the quiet, peaceful Oak Cliff region of the city. Together with other police officers, Tippit could not hear the chaos and confusion that accompanied the immediate aftermath of the assassination, for one of the motorcycle officers riding toward the rear of the motorcade had left his transmission button stuck in the depressed position, and this jammed police channel one. At 12:46, for no apparent reason, dispatcher Murray Jackson ordered Tippit and Officer Ronald C. Nelson to move into the central Oak Cliff area, but only Tippit obeyed. Nine minutes later, Jackson asked Tippit to give his location, and Tippit responded that he was at Lancaster and Eighth Streets. Dispatcher Jackson, apparently not trusting his friend Tippit's ability to ascertain his duties as a police officer, instructed him to "be at large for any emergency that comes in." Tippit then drove to the Gloco gas station, at the south end of the Houston Street viaduct, where he remained until about 1:10. Tippit then got in his patrol car and drove down Lancaster at a high rate of speed. At 1:11, Tippit entered the Top Ten Record Shop, located on Jefferson Boulevard, dialed a number on a telephone, and, after letting the phone ring seven or eight times, hung up and left. At 1:13 or 1:14 P.M., Tippit cruised east on Tenth Street, near the intersection of Patton Avenue, nearly three miles from his assigned patrol area.[17]

Tippit spotted a man walking east on the sidewalk, and he called him over to his patrol car. William Smith, James Burt, Jack Tatum, Helen Markham, and Domingo Benavides all saw the officer and the man engage in what appeared to be a friendly conversation. Suddenly Tippit opened the door and got out of the vehicle and began walking toward the left front fender. As he did, the man pulled a revolver from his belt and fired three or four shots at Officer Tippit directly over the hood of the patrol car. Tippit, mortally wounded, slumped to the street, and Tatum saw the gunman fire a shot into the fallen officer's head at close range. The gunman darted back to the intersection of Tenth and Patton, stopping on a lawn in front of a corner house to empty four cartridge cases and to reload with fresh ammunition. As the murderer raced onto Patton, cabdriver William Scoggins got a good view of him. Having witnessed the shooting, a terrified Helen Markham rushed to the aid of the fallen officer, where numerous other people quickly joined her. Afraid that the gunman would return, Domingo Benavides remained in his truck for a couple of minutes before he got out to assist. He fumbled with Tippit's police radio but did not know how to operate it. Another citizen, T. F. Bowley, drove up and got out of his truck. Glancing at his watch, Bowley noted the time as 1:10. Seeing that Tippit appeared "beyond help," Bowley took the police microphone from Benavides and called police headquarters. The call to the dispatcher came at 1:16.[18]

At around the same time that Officer Tippit was gunned down nearly four miles from Dealey Plaza, Dallas authorities finally began to focus on the sixth floor of the Texas School Book Depository building as one source of the shots. After squeezing through book cartons stacked around the window, Dallas city police and county sheriff's deputies discovered three expended cartridge cases lying on the floor near the sixth floor's southeast corner window. They also found lying nearby a large paper bag and the remnants of a fried chicken lunch: bones, wax paper, a sandwich bag, and an empty Dr. Pepper bottle. On the sixth floor's northwest side, diagonally opposite the southeast corner, they discovered a rifle stuffed down between several cartons of school textbooks. Shortly thereafter, Lieutenant J. C. Day of the Dallas police crime lab arrived to dust for prints, and he brought photographer Robert Studebaker to take photographs of the evidence. Studebaker, new on the job, failed to photograph the large paper bag, and Day failed to mark certain evidence, such as the precise location in which each cartridge case was originally sited. Day, however, did inscribe on the large paper bag, "found near sixth floor window. May have been used to carry gun." Day did not explain why he thought a gunman would carry his weapon in a paper bag. Police moved the cartons around the southeast corner window and produced four different photographic versions of how they were stacked when they originally discovered them. Outside the building, the police failed to seal off Dealey Plaza, the scene of the crime, and they allowed reporters inside the building before they had searched it thoroughly.[19]

In the Oak Cliff area, the man fleeing the scene of the shooting of Officer Tippit was seen by numerous people as he ran through a residential neighborhood with many commercial establishments. After shedding his windbreaker jacket, the man made his way to Jefferson Boulevard, one of the area's main thoroughfares, and he ducked into the lobby of a shoe store when he heard the sirens of police vehicles racing to the scene. A clerk at the store, Johnny Calvin Brewer, saw the man and followed him as he returned to the sidewalk. Brewer observed the man enter the nearby Texas Theater, and he informed the cashier, Julia Postal, that the man had entered the theater without paying. Postal called the police, and within minutes, a large number of police cars had surrounded the theater. Inside the theater, Brewer pointed out the man to Officer N. M. McDonald, who proceeded to the row where the man sat. McDonald approached the man and pulled out a gun. The man struggled with McDonald, pulling his own gun from his belt and aiming it at the officer. After a brief struggle, McDonald and several other policemen subdued the man and took him outside to a waiting car, where he was whisked to police headquarters. The man was Lee Harvey Oswald. As the police led Oswald to a waiting patrol car, a police officer shouted, "Kill the president, will you?"[20]

At Parkland Hospital, a serious dispute arose between President Kennedy's Secret Service entourage and officials of Dallas County. Under Texas law, all homicides fell under the jurisdiction of the county in which the crime occurred, and autopsies had to be performed on the bodies of all homicide victims. In Dallas County, the medical examiner, Dr. Earl Rose, had medicolegal jurisdiction over the presidential corpse, and Rose arrived at the hospital to claim the body. However, Roy Kellerman, the head of the White House Secret Service detail, insisted that they remove Kennedy's body from the hospital, transport it to Love Field, and fly it back to Washington. The reason lay in Lyndon Johnson's determination to remain in Dallas until Jacqueline Kennedy returned to *Air Force One*, and her refusal to leave the hospital without her husband's body. Refusing to obey the law, Kellerman demanded that the Secret Service be allowed to take the body with them, even though the agency had absolutely no jurisdiction over a presidential corpse. After a heated dispute, the Dallas authorities relented and allowed the Secret Service to take the corpse with them.[21]

At Dallas police headquarters, Oswald began an interminable series of interrogation sessions with various law enforcement personnel. Incredibly, no tape recordings or stenographic transcripts were made of the interrogation sessions, even though the Dallas police had the suspect in what was clearly the crime of the century in custody. According to various accounts by individuals present at the interrogation sessions, Oswald consistently maintained his innocence, repeatedly stating that he shot neither President Kennedy nor Officer Tippit. He denied owning a rifle and attributed his carrying a revolver in his belt as just a simple, innocent act. Captain Will Fritz, the legendary head of the Dallas police's homicide division, applied his renowned interrogation tactics, designed to break a suspect after prolonged questioning, but Oswald adamantly refused to confess. On the contrary, he asked for legal representation, and in brief remarks to the press that Friday night, stated that he was a "patsy," and that he had not shot anyone. In police lineups, Oswald shouted that the police were trying to railroad him by putting him in lineups with three men who did not resemble him, and who did not have cuts and bruises on their faces, as he did, after his scuffle with the police in the theater.[22]

Shortly after Jacqueline Kennedy boarded *Air Force One*, Judge Sara Hughes administered the oath of office to Lyndon Baines Johnson as the new president of the United States. As the presidential jet headed back to Washington, Johnson made numerous telephone calls, including one to J. Edgar Hoover, the longtime FBI director. Only two hours after the shooting, Hoover informed his old friend, Lyndon Johnson, that the suspect had been caught and was in custody. Furthermore, Hoover flatly asserted, he—Lee Harvey Oswald—was the only suspect in the assassination. After learning of his brother's death from Secret Service agent Clint Hill, attorney general Robert F. Kennedy overcame his grief and placed a telephone call to McGeorge Bundy, President Kennedy's national security advisor, to change the combinations on the slain president's files, to ensure that Johnson's people could not gain access to them. The files contained far too much damaging material on Jack Kennedy to risk having them fall into Johnson's hands. Robert Kennedy also telephoned Robert I. Bouck, the head of the Secret Service's Protective Research Division, and ordered him to dismantle the secretive tape recording system installed in the White House. Although Kennedy had absolutely no authority over the Secret Service, which reported to the Secretary of the Treasury, Bouck obeyed. Kennedy himself took possession of the tapes and would order trusted aides to erase any sections on the recordings that contained materials that might sully the slain president's reputation.[23]

When the presidential jet landed at Andrews Air Force Base outside Washington, D.C., President Kennedy's body was taken in a motorcade to the National Naval Medical Center in Bethesda, Maryland, for an autopsy. At the suggestion of Admiral George Burkley, one of Kennedy's personal physicians, Jacqueline Kennedy authorized the postmortem examination to take place at Bethesda because her husband had served in the navy during World War II. Captain John Stover, the commanding officer of the Bethesda Naval Medical School, ordered Lieutenant Commander James J. Humes, a pathologist who directed the facility's laboratories, to perform the autopsy. To assist him, Humes selected Lieutenant Commander J. Thornton Boswell, another hospital pathologist. Between them, Humes and Boswell had never performed autopsies on gunshot wound victims and had absolutely no training in forensic pathology. They would also face the fact that numerous army and navy brass who outranked them would witness the autopsy. As he made preparations for this critical event, Dr. Humes received a telephone call from Dr. Robert Livingstone, who commanded the Neuroscience Center at the National Institutes of Health, located directly across Virginia Avenue from the naval complex. A veteran of World War II who had operated on numerous gunshot wound victims, Dr. Livingstone had heard a press conference at which Dr. Malcolm Perry repeated three times that President Kennedy had been shot in the throat from in front. Dr. Livingstone emphasized to Dr. Humes the importance of dissecting this throat wound because that procedure would determine the origin of the shot, which appeared to be from in front of the president. Just as Dr. Livingstone began to elaborate, Dr. Humes cut off the conversation by stating that the FBI would not allow him to continue the discussion.[24]

Medical photographer John Stringer took numerous photographs of President Kennedy's corpse as it lay on the morgue table, both before and during the postmortem examination. Stringer's assistant, Floyd Riebe, also took many photos. Ordered by Dr. Humes to focus on certain wounds on the president's body, neither Stringer nor Riebe seemed able to capture the bullet wounds in a manner that would clearly reveal their nature. Some of their photographs would prove so out of focus as to be virtually useless, whereas others failed to orient the wounds with definite fixed points on the body. Nevertheless, the photographs starkly depicted the enormous damage inflicted on Kennedy's head, with a bullet hole so huge that many of the spectators gasped when they saw it. Both Stringer and Riebe would recall taking photographs of the interior of the president's chest, and Riebe vividly remembered taking many autopsy photographs with his 35-millimeter cameras.[25]

With the president's body lying on its back, Drs. Humes and Boswell could clearly see a large, gaping wound with irregular edges in the throat that they perceived as a tracheotomy incision, even though most tracheotomies were considerably smaller than the wide, gaping wound in Kennedy's throat. With no other damage to the front of the body below the neck, they turned to the examination of the head. Observing a huge 13-centimeter hole in the right front of the head, above and in front of the right ear with the bones beveled outward and extending all the way to the right rear, they concluded that it was a wound of exit. The wound in fact was so large that Dr. Humes easily removed the remaining part of the president's brain from the head through that hole without having to cut scalp or saw the skull bone. When they turned to the rear of the head, they found no entrance hole and seemed puzzled. After Humes and Boswell were joined by air force Colonel Pierre Finck, of the Armed Forces Institute of Pathology, they felt more confident about probing the scalp for signs of a bullet's entrance. But all they found was a small semicircular indentation low in the rear of the head. Later, authorities brought in several pieces of bone that they claimed were found at the assassination site in Dallas, and remarkably, one of the pieces filled in the semicircle so that it now became complete. The three pathologists then concluded that a bullet had struck the president low in the back of his head and made its exit from the right front. This clearly and obviously was the fatal shot.[26]

When the autopsy pathologists turned the president's body over, they were startled to discover a bullet wound of entrance high in his upper back, just to the right of the spinal column and about three inches below the shoulder. Ordered by one of the generals or admirals present at the postmortem examination not to dissect this back wound, Humes stuck his little finger into it and felt the end of the opening. Because there was no wound of exit for this bullet anywhere in the front of the president's body, and since x-rays revealed no bullet remaining in the body, the pathologists were puzzled as to the fate of the bullet that had entered Kennedy's back. Spending a considerable amount of time probing this wound, with little success, Drs. Humes, Boswell, and Finck grew increasingly frustrated at their inability to account for the bullet. Fortunately, someone from the FBI informed the pathologists that a bullet had been found on the president's stretcher. Dr. Humes then announced that the pattern was clear. A bullet had entered the president's back at a downward angle of forty-five to sixty degrees and had penetrated only a couple of inches. Then, during the external cardiac massage performed on Kennedy, the strap muscles in the back had relaxed, and the bullet fell out of the entrance wound in the back onto the stretcher. In their detailed report on the autopsy, which they attended, FBI agents William L. Siebert and Francis X. O'Neill duly recorded Dr. Humes's observations.[27]

The next morning, Saturday, November 23, Dr. Humes telephoned Dr. Malcolm Perry at Parkland Hospital in Dallas just to ensure that he had not omitted any details in his autopsy report. Undoubtedly Perry stunned Humes when he informed him about the tiny bullet wound in the front of President Kennedy's neck, for the autopsy pathologists had completely missed that wound. Faced with a dilemma of either acknowledging that the autopsy was badly flawed or rewriting the initial draft to reflect the new information about the throat wound, Humes decided on the latter. He took his notes made during the autopsy, as well as his initial draft that concluded that a bullet had entered Kennedy's back, but had not yet exited, to his home. On Sunday, November 24, learning that Lee Harvey Oswald had been murdered in

Dallas, thus obviating the necessity of a trial, Dr. Humes, almost certainly acting under the orders of his superior, Captain John H. Stover, and of Admiral George Burkley, burned the initial draft of the autopsy, as well as his personal notes made during the postmortem examination, and wrote another draft.[28]

The new, revised edition of the autopsy protocol that Dr. Humes drafted in his recreation room concluded that a bullet wound "presumably of entrance" was located in the president's back above the scapula (the shoulder blade). It also concluded that another wound "presumably of exit" was located in the throat just below the thyroid cartilage (the Adam's apple). This neat, simple revision enabled Humes to explain two bullet wounds in the president's body that he could not otherwise have accounted for. His original theory concocted during the autopsy that a bullet has penetrated only a couple of inches into the back and then worked its way back out during the external cardiac massage made no sense. The widely gaping wound in the front of the neck, some four to five centimeters long, also hardly looked liked the neat surgical slits of typical tracheotomies. By connecting the two wounds, with an entrance in the back and an exit in the throat, Dr. Humes, acting on the instructions of his superiors, provided a neat, simple explanation that rescued him and his colleagues, Drs. Boswell and Finck, from making the embarrassing admission that they had entirely overlooked the bullet hole in the throat and had failed to dissect the track of the bullet that had entered the president's back. This new edition would be labeled the official autopsy protocol, even though it contained words like *presumably*, lacked references to standard fixed points on the body, and entirely omitted the fact that John F. Kennedy had suffered from Addison's disease, graphically proven during the postmortem examination by the total atrophy of his adrenal glands.[29]

In Dallas, Jack Ruby, the owner of two striptease clubs, began to stalk Lee Harvey Oswald. Only an hour after the assassination, Ruby appeared at Parkland Hospital and spoke to an acquaintance, reporter Seth Kantor. Later, after Oswald's arrest, Ruby showed up for the first of several appearances at Dallas police headquarters. At a press conference early in the evening of November 22, Dallas district attorney Henry Wade had announced that Oswald had belonged to the

Free Cuba Committee, and Ruby, displaying an uncanny knowledge of Oswald's background, corrected Wade by stating aloud that it was the Fair Play for Cuba Committee. At Dallas police headquarters, Ruby, who knew hundreds of the members of the department, found little difficulty in having free access to many areas of the building. He even put on a press badge and stood among a crowd of reporters at Oswald's press conference that evening. On Saturday, Ruby again appeared at police headquarters a couple of times.[30]

On Sunday, November 24, Jack Ruby awoke in his apartment located only a few blocks from the scene of Officer Tippit's murder. According to his roommate, George Senator, Ruby made and received several telephone calls. The last call he received was from one of the strippers who worked for him. She told Ruby that she needed money, and Ruby promised to wire it to her in Fort Worth. He dressed, and as always, he took his favorite dog, Sheba, a dachshund, with him and drove off in his station wagon. Although at least two Western Union offices were located closer to his apartment, Ruby drove to the one only a half block from police headquarters. After wiring the money to the woman, Ruby walked the half block and somehow entered the basement parking garage, only a few minutes before Oswald was to be transferred from Dallas police headquarters to the more secure Dallas County Jail. As detectives led Oswald into the basement, Ruby suddenly darted from a crowd of police and reporters, pulled out his .32 caliber revolver, pointed it at Oswald's abdomen, and fired one well-aimed shot. The bullet penetrated several of the internal organs and punctured the descending aorta, causing massive internal hemorrhaging. As the police subdued Ruby and took him into custody, Oswald fell to the ground, mortally wounded. Seeing Oswald lapse into unconsciousness, a police officer told him that he was seriously injured and that he had one last chance to own up to killing the president, but in literally the last conscious action of his life, Lee Harvey Oswald shook his head when asked whether he had shot the president.[31]

Oswald was rushed to Parkland Hospital, where he died on the operating table as many of the same physicians who tried in vain to save John Kennedy's life now tried in vain to save Oswald's. During the surgery on Oswald, President Lyndon Johnson actually called the hospital and demanded to speak to one of the doctors present in the operating room. Dr. Charles Crenshaw took the call, and Johnson practically ordered Dr. Crenshaw to obtain a confession from Oswald, but Dr. Crenshaw informed the president that it was too late. After Oswald was pronounced dead, Dr. Earl Rose, the coroner, performed an autopsy, and the body was taken to a funeral home in Fort Worth. After the undertaker embalmed the body, late that night, a team of law enforcement officials entered the funeral home and fingerprinted Oswald's corpse. The undertaker spent a couple of hours cleaning the ink from his hands. The following day, Monday, November 25, Lee Harvey Oswald was buried in a Fort Worth cemetery.[32]

That same day, acting attorney general Nicholas deB. Katzenbach wrote a memorandum to presidential advisor Bill Moyers. Katzenbach proclaimed that "the world can scarcely see us in the image of the Dallas police." He insisted that the American people "must be convinced" that Oswald did indeed assassinate President Kennedy and that he "did not have confederates who are still at large." He further asserted that "the evidence was such" that Oswald "would have been convicted at trial." Coming from the man who acted as de facto head of the Justice Department while attorney general Robert Kennedy was busy with his brother's funeral, this precipitate conclusion by Katzenbach that Oswald had acted alone, made long before most of the evidence had been gathered, would characterize virtually the whole federal government's investigation into the assassination.[33]

J. Edgar Hoover pressured his friend, Lyndon Johnson, to allow the FBI to investigate the assassination and to submit a report of its findings to him. At first, the president appeared willing to "get by" with an FBI report, but, fearful of a full-fledged congressional investigation, he began leaning toward appointing a presidential commission comprising distinguished citizens. After several days of vacillating between the two options, Johnson settled on the latter and called on seven prominent members of the Washington establishment to sit on a panel, with Chief Justice Earl Warren as its chair. Initially, Warren refused Johnson's request, but after the president warned him of the possibility of a nuclear war if the truth was not disclosed, Warren relented and agreed to serve as the chair of the commission that would commonly bear his name. Of the other six members of the commission, Senator Richard Russell of Georgia proved the hardest for Johnson to persuade to serve. An avowed segregationist, Russell detested Warren for his key role in the court's 1954 school desegregation decision, but after several telephone calls from Johnson, Russell also agreed to serve.[34]

Secret Service agent Roy Kellerman, who turned them over to Robert Bouck, the head of the Secret Service's Protective Research Division, seized the negatives and film holders from the cameras used at the autopsy by John Stringer and Floyd Riebe. Bouck turned them over to Robert Fox, an agency photographer, and ordered Fox to have them developed. Fox took the negatives to the navy's photographic laboratory in Anacostia, Maryland, and watched as technician Saundra Spencer developed the photographs. As Spencer waited, the developed pictures rolled over drums during the drying process, and she noticed that the photographs depicted a tiny hole in the front of President Kennedy's throat and a much larger hole in the back of his head. Fox took the negatives and photographs back to Bouck, but Roy Kellerman told him to make a set for himself because "they will be history someday." In the meantime, White House photographer Robert Knudsen showed several autopsy photographs to some friends, who noticed that they depicted a hole the size of an orange in the back of Kennedy's head.[35]

Two days after the assassination, Drs. James J. Humes and J. Thornton Boswell conducted a supplemental autopsy on President Kennedy's brain. Humes took the badly damaged organ and sectioned it—that is, he sliced it into thin parts so he and Boswell could examine the interior for signs of a bullet track. John Stringer took a number of photographs of the brain before, during, and after the sectioning. Several days later, Humes and Boswell, now joined by Dr. Pierre A. Finck, conducted another supplemental autopsy on another brain. This one had nowhere near the damage as did the previous brain. The three pathologists did not section the organ. Instead, they merely examined it, and someone took photographs of it. These photographs, together with the virtually intact brain housed in a stainless steel container, would be turned over to Robert Bouck, who placed them in his safe alongside numerous other items from the autopsy.[36]

Furious at President Johnson's refusal to allow the FBI the exclusive right to investigate the assassination, J. Edgar Hoover decided to place the Warren Commission in an impossible position by ordering the bureau to issue the results of its investigation before the commission had even hired its staff. The FBI report was issued on December 9, 1963, only two and a half weeks after the assassination. That report unequivocally declared that Lee Harvey Oswald was solely responsible for the assassination and that no conspiracy existed. The FBI found that the first shot struck President Kennedy in the back, the second shot struck Governor Connally in the back, and the third, and fatal, shot struck President Kennedy in the back of the head. Hoover personally leaked this FBI report to friendly reporters, ensuring that it would receive widespread publicity and placing great pressure on the Warren Commission to reach the same conclusion. At the very first executive session of the commission, one of its members, Representative T. Hale Boggs of Louisiana, expressed his indignation at the FBI's preemption of the commission's mandate: "They have tried the case and reached a verdict."[37]

Constrained by the FBI's report, and under pressure by Chief Justice Warren to conduct a hasty investigation because Warren did not want to cancel his vacation scheduled for August 1964, the Warren Commission conducted a perfunctory inquiry into the assassination. Junior counsel Arlen Specter devised the single bullet theory to explain the discrepancies between the FBI's finding that Kennedy and Connally were struck by separate bullets and the impossibility of Oswald or anyone else having the ability to fire the Mannlicher-Carcano rifle twice within the elapsed time of the shooting. His request that a panel of independent experts examine the autopsy x-rays and photographs was rejected by Robert Kennedy, who seemed to possess a veto power over certain actions of the commission. Specter relied on the findings of the autopsy pathologists to conclude that Kennedy had been struck only twice, with both shots coming from above and behind him. Junior counsel David Belin led the team that investigated the Tippit killing and concluded that Oswald had acted alone. Other junior counsels investigated Jack Ruby's background and determined that Ruby killed Oswald in an impulsive act of fury, and that no one had ordered him to commit that crime. Commission chairman Warren refused Ruby's request to allow him to testify in Washington under federal protective custody, rather than in Dallas, where he feared for his life and that of his siblings.[38]

By the late spring of 1964, the Warren Commission staff was ready to write the initial drafts of their chapters. These drafts underwent review by members of the commission. In one instance, Congressman Gerald Ford elevated the draft's location of one of the president's wounds from the shoulder to the neck to align the wound more precisely with the trajectory of the single bullet theory. In another instance, commission member John McCloy insisted that the staff had neither proved that only three shots were fired nor that all the shots had come from the rear, but no changes were made. In a telephone conversation with his protégé, Lyndon Johnson, Senator Richard Russell flatly stated that he did not believe the single bullet theory. Johnson replied that he did not believe it either. Despite these differences, the Warren Commission publicly displayed unity when its members paraded into the White House in late September 1964 and presented President Johnson with a copy of their report. Both the members of the commission and the president confidently believed that the American people would accept their conclusions that Oswald and Ruby had acted alone, and that there existed no evidence of a conspiracy.[39]

Conflict: The Evidence

Anyone who has watched crime shows on television knows that a fundamental principle of law enforcement maintains that the integrity of the scene of the crime must be preserved as thoroughly as possible. The yellow tape that police departments use to surround the scenes of crimes stands as a stark, visible reminder of this principle. Only authorized law enforcement investigators are allowed to cross the tape, and they themselves must follow certain routine procedures. The experience of Detective Mark Furman and some of his colleagues in the Los Angeles police department in their handling of some of the evidence in the infamous O. J. Simpson case illustrates the importance of proper technique. Numerous authorities, including the well-known forensic scientist, Dr. Henry Lee, have written and spoken on the necessity of protecting the integrity of the scenes of crimes, especially homicides. To summarize a highly complex subject, the following steps have to be taken to ensure that any evidence relating to the commission of a crime be handled as carefully as possible both to assist authorities in proper maintenance of that evidence and to provide the necessary constitutional protection to individuals accused of committing crimes.

First, only properly trained representatives of law enforcement agencies should be allowed to enter the scene of the crime and to handle evidence. Ordinarily, that means that only members of a police department's crime scene unit have the authority to encroach into the physical setting of a crime. Police photographers are instructed to photograph all evidence in place before it is removed from the scene, thus providing a visual record of the original physical setting at the time of the discovery of the crime. Only after the photographers have finished are such other specialists as fingerprint personnel and coroner's office representatives allowed to come into physical contact with evidence. Second, any evidence discovered must be photographed in place, then carefully placed in sealed containers and marked with the initials of the officers who discovered it, thus ensuring the preservation of a chain of evidence. Third, assuming that the police arrive at the scene of a crime within a reasonable time after it has been committed, no person is allowed to leave the general vicinity without first being questioned by a police officer to ensure that he or she may not be a possible suspect or possess information to provide regarding the commission of the crime.[1]

In the case of a homicide, it is especially important that a proper autopsy be performed on the body of the victim. The victim's clothes are carefully examined to determine such matters as bullet holes of entrance and exit, as well as the pattern of bloodstains on the garments. In the morgue, the victim's body is stripped of all clothing, weighed and measured, and placed on the autopsy table. The coroner or medical examiner, preferably someone certified in forensic pathology, carefully inspects every aspect of the body's exterior surface, noting both normal and abnormal features. Every bullet hole or knife slash or other sign of trauma is carefully recorded, including its precise location in relation to fixed points on the body. A photographer takes numerous photographs, focusing on those parts of the body that display indications of violence. Incisions are made, with the pathologist meticulously cutting through the path of bullets, the scalpel guided by metal probes to ensure that it follows the bullet track. Internal organs, such as the heart, liver, adrenal glands, kidneys, and brain, are removed, weighed, and pathologically examined to ensure that an accurate accounting is compiled. At the direction of the pathologist, the photographer continues to take numerous photographs of the body's interior, as well as of those organs that reflect trauma. The reason for this meticulous care is simple. The evidence gathered from the crime scene and from the postmortem examination of the body constitutes legal evidence ultimately to be used in a court of law. If any aspect of that evidence is tainted or has not been thoroughly documented—from its discovery at the scene of the crime to the courtroom—it will be disallowed as evidence in court.[2]

Incredibly, in the assassination of the president of the United States, the wounding of the governor of Texas, and the murder of a Dallas police officer, none of these measures, so fundamental to accurate police work, was taken. On the contrary, the Dallas police, the Dallas County sheriff's office, the FBI, and the Secret Service ignored virtually every rule of crime scene investigation. Even though numerous law enforcement officers were present, they neglected to seal off the scene of the crime, Dealey Plaza, and they allowed spectators, reporters, and curiosity seekers to roam all over the area, possibly destroying critical evidence. Both the police and sheriff's deputies let people come and go at will, and of the more than seven hundred persons present in Dealey Plaza at the time of the assassination, only a third were questioned. Most simply left, never to be heard from again. Even inmates in the Dallas County jail, who viewed the motorcade from an upper floor of the facility and who literally constituted a captive audience, were not questioned. According to the official account, even the alleged assassin, Lee Harvey Oswald, simply walked out of the front door of the Texas School Book Depository building and walked east down Elm Street without being stopped. The police neglected to divert traffic, and automobiles, buses, and trucks proceeded on Elm, Main, and Commerce Streets as if nothing had happened. Fifteen minutes after the shooting, according to the official account, Oswald caught a taxi that proceeded back through the area. So lax was the attempt to comb Dealey Plaza for evidence that the day after the assassination, Billy Harper, a young man visiting the scene, found a piece of President Kennedy's skull lying in the grass in the median between Elm and Main Streets. Spectators took photographs and movies during the shooting, but few were questioned. Abraham Zapruder, the Dallas clothing manufacturer who took the most famous film of the assassination, simply left Dealey Plaza, Bell and Howell movie camera in hand, without being stopped. This negligent handling of the scene of the crime by the authorities contributed to the successful escape of the gunmen, as well as the possible destruction of critical evidence.[3]

Nor did the authorities bother to conduct a serious search of either the Grassy Knoll or the Depository building, not even of the sixth floor, where attention focused as one possible origin of the gunfire less than an hour after the shooting. An oversized paper bag, supposedly used as the container for the fatal weapon, was not photographed in place, and of the first six law enforcement officers to arrive at the southeast corner window, only three even recalled seeing the bag in that location. Three expended cartridge cases, found on the floor near the southeast corner window, were placed in envelopes without distinguishing which of them was found where. One original Dallas police evidence sheet actually lists two cartridge cases, although the official version maintains that three were found on the floor. Nineteen book cartons were located within a six-foot radius of that window. Three prints of Lee Harvey Oswald, who worked in the building, were found on those cartons; twenty-four prints of Dallas police were found on the same cartons, another indicator of the gross mishandling of evidence by the authorities. Several book cartons directly on the windowsill or adjacent to it formed a so-called sniper's nest, from which an assassin allegedly fired shots. The Dallas police rearranged the cartons in various configurations without identifying which came first. We have, as Harold Weisberg observed, four "official yet contradictory versions" of the cartons in the window, so we do not know how they were actually arranged at the time of the assassination. A rifle was found carefully hidden inside a stack of cartons in the northwest corner of the sixth floor. The discovery of the sniper's nest and the rifle in diagonally opposite parts of the sixth floor should have signaled the Dallas police to conduct a thorough search of that entire floor, yet no such search took place. Oswald's blue jacket and his clipboard were both discovered in the northwest area of the sixth floor, only a few feet from the place where police found the rifle, by Depository employees several weeks after the assassination. No other floor was searched, not even the second-floor lunchroom, where the suspect, Lee Harvey Oswald, was seen by a police officer and by the building superintendent less than two minutes after the shooting. Nor did the police make any effort to ascertain whether Oswald's prints lay on any of the surfaces in that room.[4]

When Lieutenant J. C. Day, the head of the Dallas police crime unit, arrived on the sixth floor, he inspected the rifle, although he failed to smell it to determine whether it emitted the odor of gunpowder recently having been ignited, and he dusted its exterior surface for prints. Finding only smudges, he disassembled the rifle and dusted the interior of the weapon. Discovering the clear impression of a palmprint on the metal barrel, where it had been covered by the wooden stock, Day failed to order any photographs taken of this print, even though it obviously constituted vital evidence. He also exercised such diligence in lifting the print from the rifle with Scotch tape that no trace of either the print or the lifting of the print was found at the FBI crime lab, which had never before in tens of thousands of cases encountered an object that did not contain traces of a print's having been lifted from it. Day discovered an unfired cartridge in the rifle's firing chamber, yet failed either to have it photographed or dusted for prints. After inspecting and dusting the rifle, Day walked over to the southeast corner window and seeing the large, three-foot-long paper bag in the corner, wrote on it: "Found next to sixth floor window. May have been used to carry weapon." Why Lieutenant Day thought that an assassin would transport the weapon to be used for such an important task as killing the president of the United States in a paper bag remains unknown. Why he failed to have this important piece of evidence photographed in place remains equally unknown, but that failure would have rendered the bag inadmissible in a court of law.[5]

At Parkland Hospital, where the president and governor were rushed after the shooting, little effort was made to preserve the integrity of the evidence. A nurse handed President Kennedy's clothes to Secret Service agent William Greer, who promptly crumpled them in a ball and carried them to the limousine, where he placed them in the trunk. By the time the clothes arrived back in Washington, it was too late for any serious, objective examination of them to occur. The bullet holes in the back of Kennedy's shirt and suit jacket, both nearly six inches below the tops of the collars, appeared to be entrance holes, but because of the lackadaisical manner in which they were handled, they proved virtually useless as evidence. For example, the direction of the fibers in their original condition could not be determined because of Greer's sloppy and careless manner of handling the garments. Additionally, slits in the collar near where the tie was knotted had fibers that appeared to penetrate both inward and outward because Greer neglected to handle the shirt with care. Again, no photographs were taken of the garments until they reached the FBI crime lab, far too late to depict them in their original condition. Therefore, any conclusions that various individuals have made about the bullet holes and the slits in Kennedy's clothing obviously have no evidentiary value. Furthermore, those conclusions exhibit decided bias. For example, in a report to the Warren Commission, FBI Director J. Edgar Hoover described the slits in the shirt collar as "holes" and stated that a bullet exiting the president's throat made them. This conclusion reflected Hoover's bias toward the lone assassin thesis, for the slits meant nothing. For some unknown reason, Texas Congressman Henry Gonzalez took charge of Governor Connally's clothes. To guarantee that no serious deductions could be extracted from the governor's clothes, Gonzalez turned them over to the Connally family, which eventually had them dry cleaned before turning them over to the FBI crime lab, obviously obliterating any trace of evidence that the governor's clothing may have originally contained.[6]

The Magic Bullet

One of the most critical pieces of evidence in the entire Kennedy assassination case, the bullet known as Bullet 399 because it was labeled as Warren Commission Exhibit 399, also found its evidentiary value destroyed by haphazard, careless, and neglectful handling. This was the bullet fired from Oswald's rifle that the commission claimed entered the back of President Kennedy's neck, exited from the front of his throat, then entered Governor Connally's back, passed through his chest, exiting just below his right nipple, then entered the underside of his right wrist and exited from the top of it, and finally lodged in his left thigh. This bullet, sarcastically called the "magic bullet" by conspiracy theorists, clearly constituted a critical piece of evidence in the case. Yet the story of its discovery is so laden with inconsistencies, improbabilities, and impossibilities that it could not have been introduced as a genuine piece of evidence in a court of law.

After being examined in Trauma Room Two, Governor Connally was transported to a second-floor operating room, still lying supine on the original hospital gurney that he was placed on when he was removed from the limousine. Hospital attendants removed Connally from that gurney and placed him on an operating table. One attendant wheeled the original gurney into an elevator. Darrell Tomlinson, a senior hospital engineer, got on the elevator and wheeled the Connally gurney into a corridor on the ground floor and placed it next to another gurney that had nothing to do with the assassination. The first gurney blocked the door to a men's restroom. About forty-five minutes later, Tomlinson, accompanied by his friend, Nathan Pool, an employee of Otis Elevator Company, returned to the ground-floor corridor and noticed that the original gurney, not Connally's, was blocking the corridor because someone had used the men's room and had failed to return the gurney to its original position. When Tomlinson pushed that gurney back against the wall, he and Pool noticed that a bullet, which had apparently been lodged under the mat, rolled out.[7]

Aware that the president and governor had been shot, Tomlinson immediately called the hospital's security director, O. P. Wright, who came to the ground-floor corridor. Both Wright and Pool looked at the bullet on the stretcher and saw a pointed-tip missile that appeared to be a .30-caliber round of ammunition. Having previously worked in law enforcement and having completed the FBI's firearms and ballistics course, Wright walked down the corridor and informed an FBI agent about the stretcher bullet, but the agent seemed uninterested. Wright then informed Secret Service agent Richard Johnsen about the bullet, but Johnsen stated that he could not leave his post—he guarded the area near Trauma Room One, where President Kennedy's body lay—and ordered Wright to bring him the bullet. Wright carefully retrieved the bullet from the gurney and brought it to Johnsen, who proceeded to put it in his pocket without marking it in any way, placing it in a plastic container, or even wrapping it in his handkerchief. Shortly thereafter, Johnsen left with the Kennedy entourage to the airport. Late that night, after he arrived in Washington, Johnsen drove to Secret Service headquarters and turned the stretcher bullet over to James Rowley, the director of the Secret Service. Rowley telephoned the FBI, which sent a courier to Rowley's office to pick up the bullet. The courier took it to FBI headquarters and gave it to Robert Frazier, the head of the FBI's ballistics lab.[8]

This account clearly establishes that the chain of evidence connecting the bullet discovered on the stretcher at Parkland Hospital with the bullet claimed by the FBI and Warren Commission to be that projectile, Bullet 399, contains numerous missing links. No photographs were taken of the bullet while it lay on the stretcher. Wright, Johnsen, and

Rowley did not mark the bullet with their initials. Of the three people who saw the bullet on the stretcher—Tomlinson, Pool, and Wright—Tomlinson did not recall its exact appearance, but Pool and Wright adamantly insisted that Bullet 399 was not the bullet they saw. However, in his interview with a staff member of the House Select Committee on Assassinations, Pool distinctly recalled its having a pointed tip, quite unlike the rounded-tip Bullet 399. O. P. Wright not only had worked in law enforcement, he also had sold ammunition in a sporting goods store and therefore could claim a certain degree of authority on the subject. Wright insisted that the stretcher bullet was a pointed-tip .30-caliber round of ammunition, similar to a .30-.30 or a 30.06 hunting round, and when shown a photograph of Bullet 399, emphatically declared that it could not have been the stretcher bullet. Instructively, Secret Service agent Richard Johnsen and Secret Service Director James Rowley, both of whom handled and observed the stretcher bullet, refused to identify Bullet 399 as the one they turned over to the FBI. In short, there is not a single witness who can place Warren Commission Exhibit 399, a round-tip, copper-jacketed bullet fired from the rifle of Lee Harvey Oswald, on the hospital gurney from which it was allegedly retrieved, thereby destroying its evidentiary value. The absence of photographic evidence forces us to rely on eyewitness testimony, and that testimony disproves the Warren Commission's central contention that Bullet 399 came from Governor Connally's stretcher.[9]

Nevertheless, Warren Commission junior counsel Arlen Specter concluded that the bullet came from Governor Connally's stretcher. In his questioning of Darrell Tomlinson, Specter convinced the hospital engineer to admit the possibility that he found the bullet on Connally's stretcher, even though Tomlinson originally believed that he had discovered it on the other gurney, one that had no connection to the assassination. In sharp prosecutorial tones, Specter interrogated Tomlinson almost as if he were a hostile witness, because Tomlinson's original scenario had the bullet discovered on a gurney that had nothing to do with either President Kennedy or Governor Connally. This, of course, would have inevitably raised the possibility of the bullet's having been planted, thereby demonstrating the existence of a conspiracy. To avert this unpleasant possibility, Specter simply ignored

Tomlinson's clear, convincing original account and badgered him into conceding the remote possibility of being mistaken. It should be noted that since his hostile interrogation by Specter, Tomlinson has never wavered in his original statement that he found the bullet on the other stretcher—that is, not Connally's—and he repeated his original story for a television program in 1988 and reconstructed it for the television show. The videotape clearly shows Tomlinson retrieving the missile from the stretcher that had nothing to do with the assassination.[10]

Because the FBI produced a bullet fired from Oswald's rifle, and because a bullet had been found on a stretcher, the Warren Commission conveniently combined the two into one scenario utterly unsupported by the evidence. The commission's reconstruction of this event would actually entail the following fantastic scenario: the bullet that lodged in Governor Connally's thigh nearly to the femur somehow worked its way back up through his thigh, ascended through the bullet holes in his undershorts and trousers, rolled down from the trousers, and worked its way back down under the mat on the gurney. Prominent forensic pathologist William Eckert told me that this could not possibly have happened in real life. Bullets simply do not mysteriously ascend back through entrance wounds and through holes in clothing. In a courtroom, a defense attorney would immediately have objected to the introduction of this missile as evidence, for the chain of possession had been broken numerous times. In addition, Johnsen's placing the bullet that Wright handed him in his pocket clearly contaminated it. Never even considered by the Warren Commission, the possibility of a plant to implicate Oswald looms as plausible an explanation for the appearance of Bullet 399, as does the official account.

Medical Evidence

Harold Weisberg observed that President Kennedy's accused assassin, Lee Harvey Oswald, received an autopsy worthy of the president of the United States, while President Kennedy received an autopsy more suitable to that of a Bowery bum. Weisberg went on to point out that no one has ever questioned the results of the wounds inflicted on Oswald's body by the shot from Jack Ruby's gun, but there exist nothing but questions about the nature of the wounds on Kennedy. It seems almost incomprehensible that four decades after the assassination, we remain no closer to a complete understanding of the president's wounds than in 1963, yet it is the truth. Allegations of missing or altered autopsy photographs and x-rays, the destruction of critical medical evidence, including tissue slides, organs, and documents, and even the substitution of one brain for another may no longer be ascribed to paranoid conspiracy theorists. On the contrary, the release of long-suppressed documents by the Assassination Records Review Board (ARRB), including the declassification of voluminous materials of the House Select Committee on Assassinations (HSCA), as well as the ARRB's own groundbreaking depositions of key autopsy witnesses, clearly demonstrate a systematic campaign of deceit, deception, and cover-up in the medical evidence in the assassination.[11]

The story begins at Dallas's Parkland Hospital, when the Secret Service illegally snatched the president's corpse from the legal custody of the Texas authorities, placed it aboard *Air Force One*, and flew it to Andrews Air Force Base, whence it was transported to the National Naval Medical Center in Bethesda, Maryland, for an autopsy. In 1963 the murder of John Kennedy fell under Texas law, because it occurred in Dallas. Legally, the president's body should have remained in Dallas, where the autopsy would have been performed by the Dallas county medical examiner, Dr. Earl Rose, a qualified, competent forensic pathologist, but the Secret Service refused to obey the law—and indeed violated its own regulations. Nothing in federal law gave that agency jurisdiction over the corpse of a president, yet it claimed such jurisdiction. In interviews with me, Roy Kellerman, the head of the Secret Service's White House detail during the Dallas motorcade, and Robert I. Bouck, the head of the Secret Service's Protective Research Division, admitted that the agency possessed no legal authority to remove President Kennedy's body from Dallas, yet did so anyway. They both claimed that they considered it essential for the new president, Lyndon Johnson, to fly back to Washington immediately, but Johnson refused to leave Dallas without Mrs. Kennedy. She refused to leave the hospital without her husband's body. Therefore, they claimed, the urgency of protecting the new president took precedence over the technical legal question of where President Kennedy's body would be autopsied. Because *Air Force Two* remained on the tarmac at Love Field, the solution appeared simple—fly Johnson back to Washington on *Air Force One*, await the results of the autopsy, then fly Jacqueline Kennedy and her husband's body back on the other plane. The Warren Commission, the HSCA, and the ARRB did not bother to explore this puzzling behavior by the Secret Service.[12]

Fortunately, more than a dozen and a half experienced, trained physicians and nurses observed President Kennedy's body at Parkland Hospital, and their observations, verbally uttered at the time, handwritten in contemporaneous medical reports, and testified to under oath before the Warren Commission, provide unanimous, convincing descriptions of certain wounds inflicted on the president's body as they appeared less than fifteen minutes after he was shot. Of those who saw the president's throat before Dr. Malcolm Perry performed a tracheotomy, all described a tiny, three- to five-millimeter hole in the middle of the throat just below the thyroid cartilage (the Adam's apple). This tiny hole clearly had the characteristics of an entrance wound. Only two hours after President Kennedy died, Dr. Perry, for example, told a press conference that this wound was "an entrance wound." Responding to a specific question from a reporter who asked, "Doctor, describe the entrance wound. You think from the front in the throat?," Perry stated, "The wound appeared to be an entrance wound in the front of the throat; yes, that is correct." In a handwritten medical note that he penned on the day of the assassination, Dr. James Carrico called the throat wound a "small penetrating wound of anterior neck in the lower 1/3." Nurses Pat Hutton and Doris Nelson also recalled the throat wound as a tiny, neat, round hole clearly resembling a wound of entrance.[13]

Obviously, if a bullet entered the front of Kennedy's throat, and if he faced forward, as films and photographs depicted, then the assassin who fired that shot must have been situated in front of the president. Because the president and governor each had bullet wounds of entrance in their backs, the assassin or assassins who fired those shots must have been located behind them. The implication is clear: gunmen situated both in front of and behind the limousine fired shots, and this constituted prima facie evidence of a conspiracy. Because the government needed, as assistant attorney general Nicholas deB. Katzenbach wrote to Bill Moyers, one of President Lyndon Johnson's advisors, only two days after the assassination, "something issued so we can convince the public that Oswald is the assassin," the Warren Commission never seriously entertained the possibility of a conspiracy. Indeed, before the commission undertook any investigation, its outline of its work contained the major heading: "Identity of the Assassin," in the singular. From the onset of its inquiry, therefore, the Warren Commission steadfastly insisted that only one assassin committed the crime. In his excellent work, *Breach of Trust*, Gerald McKnight documents the commission's deliberate distortion of the medical evidence to promulgate the lone assassin theory.[14]

It became necessary, then, to convince the Parkland medical personnel that the tiny round hole they observed in the front of President Kennedy's throat was actually a wound of exit, thereby eliminating the assassin from in front. Before their testimony before the Warren Commission, Secret Service agent Elmer Moore visited several Dallas physicians, spending considerable time with Dr. Malcolm Perry, and as Moore later told a researcher, "badgered" them into conceding that the wound in Kennedy's throat was conceivably one of exit. Indeed, after being shown the autopsy protocol and after receiving briefings from the Secret Service, Perry, Carrico, and several other Dallas physicians told the commission that the wound in the throat could have been either one of entrance or of exit, although several Parkland doctors and nurses continued to insist that the wound could have been only one of entrance.[15]

The autopsy failed to resolve this issue, because none of the three autopsy pathologists—nor, indeed, any of the more than almost a dozen other doctors present at the autopsy—had sufficient experience in forensic pathology to try to reconstruct the original margins of the throat wound by placing the skin back together. Dr. Perry's tracheotomy incision, which he made through the bullet hole in the throat, merely extended the outer margins of the wound, rather than obliterating it. As Dr. Milton Helpern, the chief medical examiner of New York City, observed, a qualified forensic pathologist would have sewn the neck wound back together, thus restoring the bullet hole as it originally appeared in Kennedy's throat. The autopsy photographs of the throat clearly reveal the upper and lower margins of the wound, and it would have taken only a few stitches to reconstruct the wound. No such reconstruction occurred, leaving us with the official conclusion that the tiny hole originally observed in the president's throat was one of exit.[16]

This conclusion defies all known experiences of medical personnel treating gunshot wounds, as well as law enforcement officers and military veterans who had observed gunshot wounds. For example, in his career, Dr. Helpern, who performed or supervised autopsies on more than sixty thousand gunshot wound victims, stated that he had never seen even one case in which an exit wound appeared as tiny as that observed by the Dallas physicians and nurses in Kennedy's throat. Another experienced, highly respected forensic pathologist, Dr. William Eckert, confirmed Dr. Helpern's observation and vehemently disagreed with the HSCA's Forensic Pathology Panel's conclusion that the reason for the extremely small exit wound in the front of Kennedy's throat lay in the fact that his collar was buttoned and necktie knot pulled taut, thus stretching the skin in the throat and allowing a tiny puncture wound of exit. Dr. Eckert stated that in his extensive experience, precisely the opposite occurred—the exit wound in taut skin invariably proved larger than in loose skin. Dr. Robert Shaw, who served as chief of the U.S. Army's thoracic surgery unit in France during World War II, and who operated on nearly one thousand soldiers shot in the back and chest, also stated that he had never seen a bullet exit wound so tiny. Drs. Robert Livingstone and Claude Craighead, surgeons who treated numerous gunshot wounds during World War II; Orien Anthon, a medic who observed and assisted in treating hundreds of entrance and exit wounds during World War II; and Dr. Edward Brown, who served as a medic during the Korean War, all had the same experience—wounds of exit made by military-style, fully jacketed ammunition similar to that fired from Oswald's rifle, invariably proved significantly larger than their corresponding entrance wounds. The Warren Commission's own tests, performed by the army, with Oswald's rifle, revealed that bullets fired from that weapon invariably made exit wounds two to three times the diameter of entrance wounds. Dr. Joseph Dolce, the world-renowned wounds ballistics expert who supervised the tests with Oswald's rifle, the only such tests ever performed with the alleged murder weapon, verified this result. "Without exception," Dolce stated, "the wounds of exit measured at least twice as large as the wounds of entrance." When told the dimensions of the bullet hole in Kennedy's throat, Dr. Dolce exclaimed that it had to have been one of entrance, that a wound of exit could not possibly have been smaller than the diameter of the bullet that presumably inflicted it. It is little wonder that the commission denied Dr. Dolce, the longtime chief wounds ballistics consultant for the U.S. Army, the opportunity to testify before it.[17]

The other wound that the doctors and nurses at Parkland Hospital observed on President Kennedy was a large, gaping hole in the right rear of his head. No fewer than nineteen doctors and nurses made this observation. Dr. Marion Jenkins wrote that there existed a "great laceration on the right side of the head (temporal and occipital) [the areas above the ear and in the lower back of the head], causing a great defect . . . even to the extent that the cerebellum [that part of the brain that is located in the lower rear] protruded from the head." Dr. Charles Baxter noted that the "right temporal and occipital bones were missing." Dr. James Carrico described the head wound as a "defect in the posterior skull, the occipital region." Dr. Malcolm Perry noted a "large wound of the right posterior cranium." Dr. Charles Crenshaw saw that the "right occipital parietal [the skull bone just above the occipital bone] portion of his brain appeared to be gone." Dr. Kemp Clark, the neurosurgeon who pronounced the president dead, saw a defect in the right occipital portion of the skull. Dr. Ronald Jones stated under oath that Kennedy had a "large wound in the right posterior side of his head." Dr. Paul Peters noticed a "large defect in the occiput."[18]

By far the most detailed description of the president's head wound came from Dr. Robert McClelland, a surgeon present in the emergency room:

> I could very closely examine the head wound, and I noted that the right posterior portion of the skull had been extremely blasted. It had been shattered, apparently, by the force of the shot so that the parietal bone was protruded up through the scalp and seemed to be fractured almost along its posterior half, as well as some of the occipital bone being fractured in its lateral half, and this sprung open the bones in such a way that you could actually look down into the

skull cavity itself, and see that probably a third or so, at least, of the brain tissue, posterior cerebral tissue and some of the cerebellar tissue had been blasted out.

On numerous occasions since his Warren commission testimony, Dr. McClelland has repeated his firm conviction that the large hole that he closely observed in the back of Kennedy's head was an exit wound from a bullet fired from the front.[19]

These descriptions of President Kennedy's head wound, made contemporaneously or several months later under oath by the Dallas physicians who observed the wound in Trauma Room One at Parkland Hospital, clearly describe an exit wound in the rear of the head. Because the president faced forward when he was struck, the existence of an exit wound in the back of his head meant only one thing: the assassin who fired that shot must have fired from in front. Again, because both Kennedy and Connally had wounds of entrance in their backs, wounds inflicted by assassins located behind them, the existence of at least one assassin in front proved a conspiracy. The convincing evidence of the unanimous observations of the Dallas medical personnel that the president had a wound of entrance in the front of his throat and a wound of exit in the back of his head appears persuasive. Yet the autopsy findings, buttressed by the autopsy photographs and x-rays, contradict these observations and depict these Dallas medical personnel as grossly incompetent observers of something as fundamental and intrinsically simple as looking at a wound and seeing whether it is one of entrance or of exit. To accept the validity of the official contention that only one shot struck President Kennedy in the head, and it made just a small fifteen-by-seven-millimeter (0.6 by 0.36 inches) hole in the rear of his head, one must reject the contemporary medical observations of nearly two dozen medical personnel and believe that those persons were so incompetent that they imagined a large exit wound in the right rear of Kennedy's head where none existed.

In courts of law, evidence obtained from autopsies carries great weight, for it consists of carefully ascertained medical conclusions based on a thorough postmortem examination of the body, supported by photographs, x-rays, histological examination of tissue samples, and other scientifically determined materials. The autopsy protocol typically results from a rigorous adherence to the detailed guidelines of the Armed Forces Institute of Pathology. The autopsy on President Kennedy was ostensibly supported by the observations of more than two dozen witnesses who watched as Drs. Humes, Boswell, and Finck performed the postmortem exam. That autopsy concluded that Kennedy suffered four bullet wounds: one, "presumably of entrance," located high in his upper back; a second, "presumably of exit," located in the front of his throat; a third, of entrance, located "slightly above" the external occipital protuberance, the bony knob at the base of the skull; and a fourth, of exit, located on the right side of the head, primarily in the parietal bone, but also extending "somewhat" into the temporal and occipital bones. In other words, President Kennedy was shot twice from above and behind and had neither an entrance wound in his throat nor an exit wound in the back of his head.[20]

These findings clearly contradict those of the Dallas physicians and nurses of an entrance wound in the front of the throat and an exit wound in the back of the head. But the HSCA concluded, "In disagreement with the observations of the Parkland doctors are the 26 people present at the autopsy. All of those interviewed who attended the autopsy corroborated the general location of the wounds as depicted in the photographs; none had differing accounts. . . . It appears more probable that the observations of the Parkland doctors are incorrect." Because the HSCA chose to suppress the records of its interviews with these persons present at the autopsy, it appeared that this statement provided strong support for the autopsy conclusions. But the release of the interviews by the ARRB, as well as interviews with some of the Bethesda witnesses by such researchers as David Lifton and Harrison Livingstone, as well as me, in addition to the extensive research into this topic by Dr. Gary Aguilar, demonstrate that the HSCA grossly distorted the actual observations of these people.[21]

Under the terms of the President John F. Kennedy Assassination Records Collection Act, the ARRB had a mandate to uncover and release all records held in federal agencies that pertained to the assassination. Those records included the files of the HSCA, and when the ARRB released that committee's transcripts or summaries of interviews with some of the witnesses present at the Bethesda autopsy, it became immediately apparent that the author of the HSCA summary statement had deliberately distorted the truth by claiming that the Bethesda witnesses corroborated the original autopsy report. In reality, the records reveal that the Bethesda witnesses actually corroborated the observations of the Parkland medical personnel by depicting the president's head wound as a massive exit wound in the rear. For example, Drs. Robert Karnei, John Ebersole, David Osborne, and Calvin Galloway all remarked that there existed a large defect in the rear of President Kennedy's head. Medical technicians James Jenkins, Paul O'Connor, Jan Gail Rudnicki, and Jerroll Custer also confirmed the existence of an exit wound in the rear of the head.[22]

I have also spoken with two physicians present at the autopsy who have rarely been interviewed by others about the wounds on the president. Dr. Robert Canada, the commanding officer of the medical hospital at Bethesda, told me in an interview that he observed a "very large, 3 to 5 cm [1.2 to 2 inches] wound in the right rear of the president's head, in the lower right occipital region, 2.5 cm [1 inch] below the external occipital protuberance and 3.5 cm [1.4 inches] to the right of the midline of the skull." Dr. Canada went on to describe it as "clearly an exit wound," because the occipital bone was "avulsed" (exploded) outward. When informed that the official autopsy protocol mentioned only a small entrance wound in the rear of the head, Dr. Canada responded that that document had to have been rewritten to conform to the lone assassin theory. Canada stated that he heard through the grapevine that Captain John Stover, the commanding officer of the National Naval Medical School, ordered all naval personnel present at the autopsy to maintain silence on penalty of court-martial; and in fact, documentary evidence confirms that Stover did do so. In addition, Stover, undoubtedly acting on orders from his superiors, demanded that the original autopsy protocol be rewritten to conform to the lone assassin thesis. Dr. Canada insisted that the contents of this interview be kept secret until at least a quarter century after his death. Because that time period has elapsed, I present its essential points for the first time. The other physician I discussed the case with, in a brief telephone conversation, was Dr. George Burkley, one of President Kennedy's personal physicians, and the only physician present at both Parkland and Bethesda. Burkley admitted that Kennedy had a large wound that had "all the appearances of an exit wound" in the back of his head. When informed that if this were true, then the assassin who fired that shot must have been located in front of the president, Burkley stated that he always believed in a conspiracy, a remark that he had previously made to another assassin researcher, Henry Hurt. However, he quickly terminated the conversation without providing any details.[23]

Other witnesses to the autopsy expressed similar views. Secret Service agents William Greer and Roy Kellerman both recalled a large wound in the back of the head. FBI agents James Sibert and Francis O'Neill observed a gaping hole in the back of the head. When shown the autopsy photographs in 1996, O'Neill proclaimed that they had been "doctored." General Godfrey McHugh, a presidential aide, and undertaker Tom Robinson, who helped reconstruct the head, both remembered seeing a hole "the size of an orange" in the rear of the head. Even two of the autopsy pathologists, Drs. James Humes and J. Thornton Boswell, described both orally and in writing substantial damage to the back of the head, although both insisted that Kennedy had only a wound of entrance in that area. Of the people present at the autopsy, only Dr. Pierre Finck has consistently and unequivocally maintained that the only visible damage to the back of the president's head was a small wound of entrance in the occipital region.[24]

The extant autopsy photographs contradict the virtually unanimous opinion of the persons at both Parkland and Bethesda—and indeed of the autopsy protocol about the wound in the rear of President Kennedy's head. The photographs depict the back of the head intact except for a red spot near the cowlick, close to the top of the back of the skull. A number of medical examinations of the photographs, x-rays, and other evidence have concluded that this red spot was an entrance wound, located ten centimeters (four inches) above the external occipital protuberance. This location, upheld by such bodies as the medical panel appointed by attorney general Ramsey Clark in 1967, the medical panel appointed by the Rockefeller Commission in 1976, and the Forensic Pathology Panel appointed by the HSCA in 1977, placed the wound of entrance nearly four inches above that recorded in the autopsy protocol. Independent examinations of the autopsy materials by such physicians as urologist John Lattimer, forensic pathologist James Weston, and surgeon Robert Artwohl have also confirmed the much higher location of the entrance wound in the back of the head. The autopsy, of course, located this wound low in the back of the head, nearly four inches below that evident in the autopsy photographs. Forensic pathologist William Eckert stated that this glaring discrepancy alone destroyed any serious evidentiary value that the autopsy photographs and x-rays may have provided.[25]

Thus, the evidence of the wounds inflicted on President Kennedy remains the subject of fierce contention between the defenders and the critics of the lone assassin theory. Instead of resolving the differences, the autopsy materials have contributed to the confusion and contradiction. Part of the problem lies in the manner in which these materials were handled. During the autopsy, photographers John Stringer and Floyd Riebe took numerous color transparencies and 35-millimeter black-and-white photographs of the president's body. Under orders from Robert I. Bouck, Secret Service agent Roy Kellerman confiscated all film from Stringer and Riebe. When asked why he ordered Kellerman to confiscate the autopsy photographs, Bouck responded that Robert Kennedy wanted the materials in secure hands where they would not be released to the public. When I asked Bouck what authority Robert Kennedy possessed over the Secret Service, Bouck stated that he was the president's brother and therefore held the proper authority. Bouck lied. The Secret Service actually reported to the Secretary of the Treasury, and Robert Kennedy had absolutely no authority over it. Moreover, because John Kennedy was dead and therefore no longer president, his brother could claim no proper authority. Bouck also claimed possession of the autopsy x-rays, as well as tissue slides, the president's brain, and various other items related to the autopsy, even though these materials, constituting legal evidence, should have been turned over to the Texas authorities. A couple of days after the assassination, Bouck ordered James Fox, a Secret Service photographer, to have the negatives developed, although Fox recalled that Roy Kellerman gave him the order. In any event, rather than developing the photographs at the Secret Service laboratory, Fox took them to the Naval Photographic Center in Anacostia, Maryland, where navy technicians developed them. According to David Lifton, Fox claimed that Roy Kellerman told him to make a set of the autopsy photographs for himself because "they'll be history someday." Fox did so, and in 1982, he sold his set to Lifton. These Fox photographs have been circulated and published in many works.[26]

The story gets more complicated. Robert Knudsen, a White House photographer, claimed that he took the autopsy photographs and that they depicted a large hole in the back of Kennedy's head. The HSCA stated that Knudsen, whom it identified as Jacqueline Kennedy's personal photographer, accompanied Fox to the Naval Photographic Center. Knudsen showed his set of photos to a friend, Joseph O'Donnell, who told the ARRB that they depicted an "orange-sized" hole in the rear of Kennedy's head. Somewhat later, Knudsen showed O'Donnell a second set of autopsy photographs that depicted the back of the head as intact. Saundra Spencer, a technician at the Naval Photographic Center, testified under oath to the ARRB that she developed autopsy photographs from color negatives given to her by James Fox that showed a large hole in the back of Kennedy's head, as well as a small hole in the front of his throat. When shown the official autopsy photographs at the National Archives, Spencer stated that she did not develop those. Possessing an extant sheet of photographic paper from the same time in 1963, Spencer demonstrated that the official autopsy photographs could not have been the ones she developed. Furthermore, she developed color negatives, but the official set consists of color transparencies and black-and-white negatives.[27]

Certain lone assassin theorists have suggested that Spencer's recollections deserve little credence because she was nothing but a navy photographic technician. However, one of the many documents released by the ARRB lends credibility to her story. An official Secret Service account of the autopsy photographs signed by Robert Bouck, Edith Duncan, Bouck's secretary, Secret Service Inspector Thomas Kelly, and James K. Fox, states that Bouck gave the photographic negatives to Fox on November 27 and that Fox took them to the Naval Photographic Center for processing. The document also claims that Lieutenant Vincent Madonia, Saundra Spencer's superior, did the actual processing. Most notably, the document states unequivocally that in addition to black-and-white negatives that were developed, color positives were also developed. The current collection of autopsy photographs contains only black-and-white prints and color transparencies. Because Spencer specifically claimed that she processed color prints, and because Lieutenant Madonia himself denied that he developed any autopsy photographs, the evidence tends to support Spencer. Furthermore, the color positives specifically mentioned in the document have disappeared from the official inventory of the autopsy materials, further complicating the story.[28]

It should be noted that Douglas Horne, a senior analyst for Military Records for the ARRB, personally took the autopsy photographs to the Kodak laboratories in Rochester, New York, for authentication, and Kodak experts found no evidence of forgery, alteration, or other methods of falsifying the images. Nevertheless, grave doubts remain about their evidentiary value. Horne also discovered suppressed HSCA documents that consisted of communications between HSCA staff and the Department of Defense. In essence, the HSCA requested the camera used to take the autopsy photographs, but the HSCA's panel of photographic experts determined that the camera sent to them by the Department of Defense as the "only [camera] in use at the National Naval Medical Center in 1963" could not have taken the autopsy photographs. The Defense Department statement was demonstrably false, because photographer Floyd Riebe testified that at the autopsy, he took numerous 35-millimeter photographs, as well as nearly one hundred pictures with a large-format "press pack" camera that produced four-by-five-inch developed pictures. None of these photographs remains in the official collection. Nevertheless, the camera, or at least the lens, produced by the Defense Department could not have been the one used to take autopsy photographs. To complicate matters even further, in sworn testimony before the ARRB staff, photographer John Stringer stated that he photographed the supplemental autopsy of President Kennedy's brain and used unnumbered black-and-white Kodak pan portrait film. The current collection, which Stringer testified he did not photograph, consists of black-and-white numbered Ansco film. The color transparencies of the brain also did not match Stringer's use of Kodak Ektachrome film.[29]

In summary, the autopsy photographs currently classified as the only official photographs taken of President Kennedy's postmortem examination lack all of the rigid criteria by which evidence is measured. Not a single witness to either the medical treatment of the president at Parkland Hospital in Dallas or at the autopsy has ever authenticated all of the photographs as consistent with what he or she observed. The glaring contrast between the picture of Kennedy's head depicted in the photographs and the unanimous descriptions of his wounds by more than thirty trained medical personnel, the absolute inability of anyone to orient one of the photographs with a clear reference point on the head, the refusal of the actual photographers to authenticate the extant collection, and the disgraceful, outrageous, and illegal handling of the photographs by Robert Bouck, James Fox, and Roy Kellerman clearly place their evidentiary value in serious dispute. Even the HSCA's Forensic Pathology Panel, which strongly supported the lone gunman from the rear theory, labeled the autopsy photographs as lacking the necessary identification measures to have them introduced as evidence in court. The strange recollections of Robert Knudsen, Saundra Spencer, Joe O'Donnell, and others clearly raise the possibility that at least one other set of autopsy photographs existed—a set that demonstrated the existence of an assassin firing from in front, and that in all probability was destroyed. Aggravating the situation is a discovery made by historian Robert Dallek, who was given unprecedented access to John Kennedy's medical records. Accompanied by a physician, Dallek examined the records. He discovered a large set of x-rays that demonstrated that Kennedy's bones had suffered serious deterioration from osteoporosis, undoubtedly caused by his steady consumption of enormous quantities of steroids. Yet the autopsy x-rays reveal no such bone deterioration. Dallek also discovered that Robert Kennedy ordered Dr. Burkley to destroy various autopsy records because they revealed the existence of Addison's disease (atrophy of the adrenal glands) and other illnesses that President Kennedy suffered.[30]

In addition to the utter lack of consistency with the documentary record about the autopsy photographs and x-rays, an undetermined amount of other autopsy material has disappeared from the official repository. President Kennedy's brain, removed from his head during the autopsy and never dissected, was placed in a stainless steel container, where it lay in Bouck's office in the Executive Office Building until April 26, 1965, when, acting under illegal instructions from Robert Kennedy, Bouck transferred the autopsy materials to President Kennedy's secretary, Evelyn Lincoln, who had an office at the National Archives. About a month later, Robert Kennedy instructed Lincoln to transfer the materials to his secretary, Angie Novello. On October 29, 1966, the materials were turned over to the permanent custody of the National Archives. The official inventory recorded several critical items that had disappeared: President Kennedy's brain; autopsy photographs of the interior of his chest; and a number of histological slides made of tissue around the margins of the wounds in the president's head, chest, and back. Several researchers, notably Gus Russo, citing photographs of the reburial showing a box supposedly containing the brain at the feet of Cardinal Cushing, have contended that Robert Kennedy had the brain buried when President Kennedy's body was placed in its permanent grave site in 1967. No independent evidence has surfaced either to confirm or refute this claim. Nevertheless, the fact that the brain, photographs, and tissue slides are missing from the evidence provides evidence of the lack of a concrete chain of evidence regarding the medical materials.[31]

Other Evidence

Among the main items of evidence in the Kennedy assassination case are several bullet fragments, two supposedly removed from President Kennedy's head during the autopsy, and two discovered on the front seat of the presidential limousine at the Secret Service garage in Washington. Both fragments removed during the autopsy came from the front of the head, directly behind the forehead. These were so tiny that they could not be identified as having come from a particular weapon, or even having the characteristics of a distinctive caliber weapon. In short, their evidentiary value remains nonexistent. Curiously, as Dr. David Mantik, a radiation oncologist who has examined the autopsy x-rays more thoroughly than anyone else, has pointed out, these two forehead fragments that Dr. Humes allegedly removed from Kennedy's head were much smaller than the large 6.5-millimeter fragment embedded between the inner and outer tables of the back of the head, as clearly viewed on the x-rays. Mantik contends that Humes would surely have removed the much larger rear fragment than the smaller frontal ones had the rear fragment actually existed at the time of the autopsy. In reality, Mantik believes, the rear fragment was deliberately added to the x-rays of Kennedy's head after the autopsy to give the appearance of a rear-entering shot.[32]

Examinations of the x-rays by the Ramsey Clark Panel of medical experts, the Rockefeller Commission Panel of experts, and the HSCA's Forensic Pathology Panel all concluded that the 6.5-millimeter metal bullet fragment embedded in the back of the skull was sheared off from the Mannlicher-Carcano bullet as it drove into the president's head at the level of the cowlick, thus providing further evidence of a rear-entering shot. Yet the two bullet fragments allegedly found on the front seat of the limousine consist of the nose of the bullet and the copper jacket surrounding its exterior, including the base of the missile. Therefore, the only part of the bullet that could have sheared off and remained embedded in the rear of the skull was the lead core, a physical impossibility. Forensic pathologist William Eckert told me that no bullet could possibly have deposited its interior at the point of impact while depositing its exterior at the point of egress. Sidney Johnston, who conducted extensive ballistics tests on Mannlicher-Carcano rifles using the same lot of ammunition as Oswald is alleged to have used, also confirmed the physical impossibility of a Carcano bullet shearing in that manner. Johnston, who conducted his ballistics tests for the United States Special Forces, was adamant in his insistence that if a 6.5-millimeter fragment of lead was indeed embedded in the rear of Kennedy's skull, it could not possibly have come from the same bullet that deposited the two fragments on the front seat of the limousine. Then whence came this mysterious 6.5-millimeter fragment as seen on the x-rays? It must have been, as Dr. Mantik contended, deliberately inserted on a skull x-ray to give the impression of a rear-entering shot.[33]

From the time the presidential limousine arrived at the emergency room entrance to Parkland Hospital, at 12:38 P.M., until its departure an hour and a half later, numerous individuals had ready access to the vehicle, including a large crowd of spectators at the emergency entrance to the hospital. Shortly after 2:00 P.M. on Friday, November 22, 1963, Secret Service agent George Hickey drove the presidential limousine from Parkland Hospital to a Dallas airport and placed it aboard an air force cargo plane, which flew it to Andrews Air Force Base. Upon its arrival at Andrews, Secret Service agent Samuel Kinney drove the vehicle to the White House garage, arriving there at about 9:00. Two agents, Deputy Secret Service Chief Paul Paterni and assistant special agent Floyd Boring, who was in charge of the White House detail, then examined the limousine. Paterni discovered a large bullet fragment lying on the front seat approximately midway between the right and left seats. Thomas Mills, a hospital corpsman, who, oddly enough, was asked by Paterni and Boring to assist them in their search of the limousine, found another large fragment on the front seat. These fragments would later be matched to Oswald's Mannlicher-Carcano rifle. However, neither fragment was photographed in place. Although photographs exist of the blood-splattered seats of the limousine, it is curious that none depicts the fragments. At the time, Lee Harvey Oswald was alive and, insofar as was known, would stand trial in Texas for the murder of President Kennedy. Therefore, the limousine constituted criminal evidence, and if bullet fragments indeed lay on the front seat, as the government would later claim, then one wonders why the Secret Service would not have carefully photographed them in place. It is also questionable that the Secret Service would examine the vehicle in the first place because that agency possessed no legal investigative authority. Yet a team of FBI investigators, which did possess that authority, was not allowed to examine the limousine until shortly after 1:00 A.M. on November 23. Once again, it is impossible to create an unbroken chain of evidence regarding the limousine fragments because of the suspicious manner in which they were allegedly found.[34]

Late in the afternoon of Saturday, November 23, 1963, William A. Harper, a college student, was taking photographs in Dealey Plaza when he discovered a large fragment of bone lying in the median between Elm and Main Streets, about thirty feet behind and to the left of President Kennedy's location at the instant of the fatal head shot. Harper took the fragment to his uncle, Dr. Jack Harper, who turned it over to Dr. A. B. Cairns, the chief pathologist at Dallas's Methodist Hospital. Drs. Harper, Cairns, and Gerhard Noteboom examined the bone fragment and positively identified it as occipital bone. The doctors photographed the bone fragment, and then shipped it to Dr. George Burkley, who turned it over to the FBI. Previously, Dr. Harper had spoken with FBI special agent George Anderton, who notified the Secret Service. Robert I. Bouck instructed Anderton to send the fragment to the White House and to maintain strict silence about its discovery.[35]

When I asked Bouck what authority he possessed over the FBI, he appeared astounded at the effrontery of such a question, replying that the Secret Service had every right to investigate the assassination of a president. It is most interesting that Dr. Burkley would turn the Harper fragment over to the FBI, yet refuse to turn over autopsy photographs and x-rays, tissue slides, and even Kennedy's brain. Somehow the FBI "lost" the Harper fragment, and the only evidence we have of its existence lies in photographs taken of it at Methodist Hospital in Dallas. These photographs depict a trapezoidal shaped piece of bone approximately 7 by 5.5 centimeters (2.75 by 2.2 inches). On the basis of their examination of the photographs, forensic anthropologist Lawrence Angel and neuroanatomist Joseph Riley have identified the Harper fragment as a piece of parietal bone, while radiation oncologist David Mantik has identified it as upper occipital bone. Because the bone itself has disappeared, the best indication of its actual origin must come from the three physicians, Drs. Harper, Cairns, and Noteboom, who examined the actual fragment and positively identified it as occipital bone (from the lower back of the skull).[36]

The significance of this identification of the Harper fragment as coming from the lower rear of President Kennedy's head is that it challenges the authenticity of the autopsy photographs and x-rays. Both the photographs and the x-rays depict an intact occipital region, while the Harper fragment provides strong evidence that a sizable chunk of occipital bone was blown nearly thirty feet behind and to the left of the president. This strongly supports the claim of those who believe that Kennedy suffered an exit wound in the rear of his head from a bullet that entered in the front. It also confirms the contemporaneous accounts of the Parkland physicians who saw an exit wound in the rear of Kennedy's head. Dr. Malcolm Perry described the wound in the rear of the head as an "exit" wound. Drs. Ronald Jones, Robert McClelland, Paul Peters, and Kemp Clark, as well as many other Dallas physicians, observed the large exit hole in the back of the head, thus contradicting the hypothesis of the lone assassin from the rear.[37]

In the case of the murder of Officer J. D. Tippit, the handling of the evidence proved equally lacking in care. Within minutes after Tippit was shot, an ambulance arrived and took his body to nearby Methodist Hospital, where he was pronounced dead on arrival. Less than two minutes after the ambulance left the scene, Dallas police arrived. Like their counterparts in Dealey Plaza, they made no effort to seal off the scene of the crime, which was the area around Tippit's patrol car near the intersection of East Tenth Street and Patton Avenue. On the contrary, the police allowed witnesses, spectators, and reporters to swarm all over the area, and even to put their hands—and, in the case of one witness, her shoes—on Tippit's car. Dale Myers's book, *With Malice*, contains many photographs depicting the utter lack of concern by Dallas police officers with protecting the scene of the crime, even though one of their fellow officers had been killed. Some photographs show spectators roaming all over the scene of the crime. This lack of attention to fundamental police procedure obviously contaminated whatever evidence might be found in the vicinity.[38]

Bystanders, not the police, found four expended cartridge cases near the scene of the Tippit killing. Only two were marked by police officers with their initials in a manner that would have allowed for their admission into court as evidence. Four bullets were removed from Tippit's body during his autopsy, and all were so badly mangled that it was impossible to ballistically match them to a particular weapon. Three of the four were placed in a file cabinet at police headquarters, where they remained for three months. Of the four cartridge cases, three were Winchester-Western and one a Remington Peters. Of the bullets, two were Winchesters and two were Remingtons. The discrepancy has never been resolved. In a court of law, a competent defense attorney for Oswald could easily have persuaded a judge to throw out virtually all of the prosecutorial evidence.[39]

This brief survey of only a small portion of the questionable evidence in the Kennedy assassination should suffice to persuade those who readily cite such "evidence" to hesitate. Secrecy, deception, dissembling, and suppression characterized the official investigations, not to mention careless, haphazard handling of evidence. The failure of the authorities to seal off the scene of the crime, to photograph vital evidence in place, to provide an unbroken chain of possession of the evidence, and their ability to "lose" or "misplace" such crucial evidence as the president's brain and the Harper fragment, necessarily leave numerous questions unanswered. It should be emphasized that the assassination was a crime under Texas state law. To ensure the accuracy of the above remarks, I discussed the evidence at length with two acknowledged authorities on both Texas and United States law, former U.S. Supreme Court Justice Abe Fortas and former Watergate special prosecutor and assistant Texas attorney general Leon Jaworski. After reviewing the evidence and its handling by the authorities, both Fortas and Jaworski unhesitatingly declared that virtually all of the evidence gathered by the authorities would eventually have been disallowed because of the shamefully incompetent and sinister manner in which it was handled.[40]

Conflict: The Case for the Lone Assassin

Although a considerable number of studies of the assassination have concluded that it resulted from the act of one man, the large majority has concluded the opposite—that it originated in a conspiracy. This dichotomy was reflected in the conclusions of two of the two official United States government investigations, those of the Warren Commission and of the House of Representative's Select Committee on Assassinations. The Warren Commission, of course, staunchly maintained that Lee Harvey Oswald fired all the shots in the assassination, that he alone murdered Officer J. D. Tippit, and that Jack Ruby also acted alone in murdering Oswald. Furthermore, the commission flatly stated that it found no evidence of a conspiracy, "foreign or domestic." The House Select Committee on Assassinations, on the other hand, found that the assassination "probably" resulted from a conspiracy, that Oswald had at least one accomplice in Dealey Plaza, and that the most likely suspects as the masterminds behind Kennedy's murder included either individuals connected with the organized crime syndicates of Carlos Marcello in Louisiana or of Santos Trafficante in Florida, or persons involved with anti-Castro activities in the United States.[1]

The Lone Assassin Theory

The first approach, that Lee Harvey Oswald and Jack Ruby acted alone, requires detailed elaboration. Its simplistic solution to an extraordinarily complex issue clearly appeals to some people. Buttressed by strong support among the political establishment and among the leading organs of the press and media, the lone assassin proponents focus their argument on three central themes. First, the most credible evidence—scientific and medical reports, ballistics, photographs—establishes that Oswald fired all the shots from the sixth-floor southeast corner window of the Texas School Book Depository building, the sole source of the gunfire. It also establishes that Oswald murdered Officer Tippit, and that Jack Ruby murdered Oswald, in both instances acting alone. Second, the men who composed the Warren Commission were all decent and honorable men, with long, distinguished careers of public service who would never have lent their names and reputations to such a blatant distortion of the truth as their critics allege. Third, those who espouse conspiracy theories have engaged in such outrageous misrepresentations, have perpetuated such fraudulent hypotheses upon their gullible followers, have employed such reprehensible tactics as character assassination, personal harassment, innuendo, mudslinging, and similar actions, that their theory of an assassination conspiracy must be wrong.[2]

Most advocates of the lone assassin theory base their argument on the foundation of what they perceive to be the most credible, reliable evidence in the assassination. Although they generally acknowledge that the Warren Commission erred in certain of its approaches to the evidence, they contend that the great weight of that evidence convincingly substantiates the commission's fundamental conclusions. The first of those conclusions, that all the shots came from the sixth-floor southeast corner window of the Texas School Book Depository building, is supported by numerous pieces of physical and eye- and earwitness evidence. Two people, Howard Brennan and Amos Lee Euins, saw a man fire a shot from that window. Significantly, no one saw shots fired from any other location in Dealey Plaza. It is also indisputable that a large percentage of those individuals who heard the sound of gunfire reported that all or some of the shots came from the Depository building. Witnesses also saw either a rifle barrel or a cylindrical object protruding from the window immediately after the shooting. Three employees of the depository, Harold Norman, James Jarman, and Bonnie Ray Williams, watched the motorcade from the fifth-floor southeast corner window, directly beneath the so-called sniper's nest, and all three testified that they heard either a shot from directly above them or the sound of cartridge cases hitting the floor above them. Two of the men, together with Howard Brennan and Amos Lee Euins, can be seen in television footage of the scene describing what they saw to the police and pointing up toward the sixth-floor window less than fifteen minutes after the assassination.[3]

The scene of the crime contained an abundance of evidence clearly pointing to the sixth-floor southeast corner window as the source of the shots. In the southeast corner of the sixth floor of the Texas School Book Depository building, book cartons arranged in a sniper's nest configuration, stacked near and on the windowsill allowed the gunman to rest his weapon and steady his aim as he fired the fatal volley. It also provided him with protection from the spectators on the street below, for the bottom of the window was open only fifteen inches from the floor. Therefore, all he needed to do was to remain kneeling, concealed from observation while he took aim. Three expended cartridge cases lay on the floor next to the southeast corner window. Significantly, no other ammunition of any kind was found anywhere else in Dealey Plaza. A paper bag, constructed of wrapping paper and tape from the Depository's shipping department, was discovered next to the window, and it, too, provided evidence of that southeast corner area being the location of the shooter. Dallas police Lieutenant J. C. Day, the head of the crime lab, immediately recognized the bag as a possible container for the assassin to have carried his weapon into the building. Near the northwest corner of the sixth floor, a 6.5-millimeter Mannlicher-Carcano rifle rested hidden inside a stack of book cartons, discarded there by the assassin as he fled down the adjacent stairs. Again, no other weapon was found anywhere else in the plaza. Indeed, even though some witnesses believed that they heard shots fired from other locations, not a single iota of physical evidence was found at any of these sites, in stark contrast to the plethora of evidence found on the sixth floor. It is instructive that spectators ran immediately to the Grassy Knoll, the source of the alleged head shot, yet they found no one there and uncovered absolutely no evidence of shots having been fired from there.[4]

Other evidence also proved compatible with that found on the sixth floor. At Parkland Hospital, the bullet that Darrel Tomlinson found on Governor Connally's stretcher contained numerous ballistic identifiers, such as lands and grooves, that positively identified it as having been fired from the rifle found on the sixth floor to the exclusion of all other weapons. In addition, Secret Service agents found two sizable bullet fragments on the front seat of the presidential limousine, one, the nose, or front end, of a Mannlicher-Carcano bullet, and the other, the base, or rear end, of a Mannlicher-Carcano bullet. Both fragments, composed primarily of the copper jacketing, also were ballistically proven to have been fired from the Depository rifle to the exclusion of all other weapons. The FBI firearms experts also positively identified the three expended cartridge cases found at the southeast corner of the sixth floor as having been fired from that weapon. Critics of the Warren Commission have never provided a plausible alternative explanation of this evidence, other than engaging in utterly unsubstantiated speculation about unnamed conspirators planting these items at the scene of the crime.[5]

The Single Bullet Theory: The Lone Assassin Perspective

Nothing in the entire Kennedy assassination saga has proved as controversial as the Warren Commission's single bullet theory. The brainchild of one of the commission's junior counsels, Arlen Specter, the theory maintains that a bullet fired from the southeast corner window of the sixth floor of the Depository building struck President Kennedy high on his upper back, or even in his lower neck, penetrated through his neck and exited from his throat just below the Adam's apple, causing a nonlethal wound. That same bullet, the theory contends, entered Governor Connally's back between his right armpit and his right shoulder blade, entering his thoracic cavity, slapping against his fifth rib, shattering it, and exiting just below his right nipple. The bullet then proceeded to strike the governor's right wrist, breaking the radius in two, before it exited the wrist and entered the left thigh, where it caused a superficial wound. Although it is impossible to pinpoint the precise instant of this shot, both defenders and critics of the theory agree that Kennedy evidenced an obvious reaction to having been struck as the limousine emerged from behind the Stemmons Freeway sign, or no later than Zapruder film frame Z225, while Connally appears to react no later than frame Z238.[6]

In its original reconstruction of the assassination, the FBI concluded that the first shot struck President Kennedy, and that the second shot hit Governor Connally. However, when Arlen Specter began to investigate the medical and ballistics evidence for the Warren Commission, he discovered several inconsistencies between the actual evidence and the FBI's claim that the two men were hit by separate shots. First, the FBI ignored the obvious question. If the first shot entered Kennedy's back and exited from his throat but did not strike the governor, where did it go? No damage was found anywhere in the limousine, except for a crack on the inside surface of the windshield caused by a fragment from the head shot. Specter's examination of the evidence led him to conclude, therefore, that the only place the bullet could have gone was into Governor Connally. To test this hypothesis, Specter recreated the assassination, paying particular attention to the relative positions of the president and governor in the limousine, to ascertain whether they were aligned in the proper trajectory for a shot fired from the sixth-floor window to have struck both men. He concluded that the trajectory of a bullet fired from the window would have gone through both men.[7]

Because the medical evidence proved beyond dispute that a bullet, fired from the rear, entered Kennedy's upper back and did not lodge anywhere in his body, it must have exited from the front. Because the only opening made by a bullet in the president's body below the head lay in the front of his neck, just below the Adam's apple, that must have been the wound of exit. Critics of the single bullet theory ignore this incontrovertible fact. The trajectory of that bullet was downward relative to Kennedy's position in the limousine, because Elm Street itself had a three-degree downward inclination at the instant of the shot. Because Kennedy sat in a normal upright position, or even leaned forward slightly, the bullet, fired from an elevated position, must have exited his throat at a downward angle. Because Kennedy's seat was positioned higher than Connally's, because of the alignments of their seats in the limousine, that placed the president above the governor. Therefore, a bullet exiting from the front of Kennedy's throat at a downward angle could have struck Connally in the upper back. Using FBI agents as stand-ins for Kennedy and Connally, and after allowing for a downward street grade of nearly four degrees, Specter measured the angle of the impact on Kennedy's back as approximately seventeen degrees, forty-three minutes, an angle perfectly compatible with the shot having been fired from the sixth-floor window.[8]

Arlen Specter anticipated other possible objections to the single bullet theory. At a press conference held the afternoon of the assassination, Dr. Malcolm Perry, who cut the tracheotomy incision through the small bullet hole in Kennedy's throat, described that wound as one of entrance on three separate occasions. Obviously, if a bullet entered Kennedy's throat, it must have been fired from in front, and the single bullet theory, as well as the lone assassin thesis, would have crumbled. In his interrogation of Dr. Perry before the Warren Commission, Specter convinced Perry, as well as several other Parkland physicians, to admit that the wound in the president's throat could have been either one of entrance or of exit. Wounds ballistics experts as well as the autopsy pathologists also testified that the throat wound was one of exit. Subsequent examinations of the autopsy photographs and x-rays by various medical specialists have produced an overwhelming majority in favor of the bullet's having exited the president's throat. For example, the Forensic Pathology Panel of the House Select Committee on Assassinations, concluded, by an eight-to-one majority, that a bullet entered Kennedy's back, exited from his throat, and entered Connally's back. Experiments performed by Dr. John Lattimer, who used a Mannlicher-Carcano rifle and the exact type of ammunition used by the assassin, revealed that bullets fired through simulated human tissue produced wounds strikingly similar to those inflicted on Kennedy's back and throat.[9]

The reason for Specter's determination to prove the single bullet theory lay in a timing problem. Test firings of the Depository rifle by FBI experts revealed that the fastest possible time for someone to fire two separate shots from that rifle, even without aiming, was 2.25 seconds. However, a careful analysis of the Zapruder film revealed that Kennedy and Connally showed reactions to having been struck no more than 1.6 seconds apart. The FBI computed the average speed of a film taken by Abraham Zapruder's camera as 18.3 frames per second. Therefore, by analyzing the film frame by frame, it became possible to calculate the timing of the shots. Concluding that Kennedy was struck no earlier than frame Z210 and Connally no later than frame Z238, the commission determined that the men show reactions to having been wounded within twenty-eight Zapruder film frames, or 1.6 seconds of each other. Because that time is less than the minimum amount of time for anyone to fire two separate shots from the Mannlicher-Carcano rifle, even without aiming, only two conclusions are possible: two separate gunmen fired two separate shots; or one shot struck both men, and Governor Connally evinces a delayed reaction to his wounds. Specter decided that only the latter alternative fit the known facts.[10]

Nothing about the single bullet theory has provoked as much argument as has that over the condition of the bullet that inflicted the damage on the president and governor. The bullet that Tomlinson found on Governor Connally's stretcher at Parkland Hospital was in nearly pristine condition. Other than a slight flattening near its base and a tiny bit of lead protruding from the base, the bullet was in perfect condition. Even under microscopic examination, the lands and grooves embedded on the bullet's copper jacket as it spiraled through the rifle barrel remained intact, with not the slightest degree of deformation or damage. Aware of the potential criticism of such a bullet inflicting seven different wounds and breaking two bones, Specter showed Bullet 399 to each of the Parkland physicians who operated on Governor Connally, and each responded that it could have caused his wounds. In addition, Specter asked Dr. Alfred Olivier, the head of the wounds ballistics team that test-fired the Depository rifle through goats' chests and cadavers' wrists, if it could have caused all the wounds, and Dr. Olivier replied in the affirmative. Furthermore, spectrographic examination and neutron activation analysis of the bullet, as well as of fragments removed from Connally's wrist, performed for the FBI, revealed that they were identical in chemical composition.[11]

In the years since the Warren Commission investigation, critics have pounced on the condition of Bullet 399 as proof that a massive cover-up took place, arguing that no piece of ammunition could have possibly inflicted such damage and remained in nearly pristine condition. Yet defenders of the single bullet theory have strong rebuttals to this contention. First, they claim that the bullet passed through Kennedy's neck without striking bone and therefore suffered no damage. When it coursed through Connally's chest, it merely slapped against his rib, breaking it but not smashing directly into it, and Dr. Robert

Shaw, who operated on Connally's chest wound, admitted that Bullet 399 could have inflicted the damage to his rib. The slap against the rib caused the flattening of the bullet near the base, for it entered Connally's back nose end first as it tumbled after exiting Kennedy's throat. After exiting Connally's chest, the bullet, now slowed considerably from its initial muzzle velocity of almost 2,100 feet per second, struck the wrist nose end first, breaking the radius, and causing the slight deformation and loss of fragment in the base itself. By the time the bullet reached Connally's wrist, it retained sufficient velocity to break the radius, but insufficient velocity to flatten itself. Experiments with the Depository rifle proved this theory. Shots fired directly through cadavers' wrists caused far more damage to the radius than Connally had suffered because they had not been slowed by having penetrated other objects first. An experiment performed by Dr. Martin Fackler, a leading wounds ballistics expert, for the American Bar Association in 1992 further confirmed this theory. Dr. Fackler fired a Mannlicher-Carcano bullet of the same manufacture as that of Bullet 399, at a muzzle velocity of 1,100 feet per second, which he had estimated as the velocity of the bullet when it struck Connally's wrist. The bullet broke the radius of a cadaver, inflicting more damage than Connally's radius suffered, but it emerged in even more pristine condition than Bullet 399, thereby demonstrating that a Mannlicher-Carcano bullet could indeed remain intact while breaking bone. No Warren Commission critic has convincingly refuted Fackler's confirmation of the validity of the single bullet theory.[12]

During its investigation, the House Select Committee on Assassinations hired Dr. Vincent Guinn, a leading authority, to conduct new neutron activation analysis (NAA) tests on Bullet 399, as well as two fragments removed from Governor Connally's wrist. Dr. Guinn bombarded the objects first with neutrons, then with gamma rays. Then he measured the half-life of the decay of certain elements, such as antimony, silver, and copper, that the objects contained. Dr. Guinn also performed NAA on a batch of Mannlicher-Carcano bullets from the exact same batch as the assassination ammunition that he obtained to ensure accuracy of data. His conclusion was that Bullet 399, the stretcher bullet, and the fragments removed from Connally's wrist were identical in chemical composition. Therefore, Dr. Guinn concluded that in all probability the fragments had come from Bullet 399. Recent analyses of Dr. Guinn's data by Dr. Kenneth Rahn, who has performed numerous NAA experiments, lent further credence to Guinn's conclusion that there exists evidence of only one bullet causing the wounds to Governor Connally.[13]

The House Select Committee on Assassinations also hired experts to determine whether Kennedy and Connally were properly aligned to be wounded by one bullet. The experts concluded that they were indeed properly aligned. More sophisticated computer-assisted reconstructions of the men in the limousine by the PBS television program *Nova* by assassination researcher Dale Meyers, by noted forensic pathologist Dr. Vincent DiMaio, and by ABC News, have also concluded that the two men were aligned to receive a single bullet through their bodies. Very careful photographic analysis of the Zapruder film by Dr. Michael West revealed that in frame Z223, the lapel on Governor Connally's suit coat suddenly flaps outward—a flap that came from the bullet as it exited the chest near the lapel. Such eminent forensic pathologists as Drs. Russell Fisher, Werner Spitz, Thomas Weston, Michael Baden, and Charles Petty have examined the original autopsy x-rays and photographs of President Kennedy, as well as x-rays of Governor Connally, together with the relevant medical reports, and have concluded that the single bullet theory was indeed compatible with the medical evidence. In summary, the evidence proves the single bullet theory beyond the slightest shadow of a doubt.[14]

The Fatal Shot: The Lone Assassin Perspective

Almost as controversial as the single bullet theory is the contention by lone assassin theorists that President Kennedy was killed by a shot fired from the sixth-floor southeast corner window of the Texas School Book Depository. The bullet, they claim, entered the back of the president's head, drove through his brain, and exploded outward from the right front and top of the head. The explosion of blood, brain tissue, and skull bone from the front drove Kennedy violently backward, slamming him against the rear seat of the limousine. This, the only shot that struck him in the head, was fired from above, behind, and to his right. No evidence—medical, ballistics, audiovisual, or otherwise—provides even the slightest degree of proof that any shots fired from elsewhere hit the president.[15]

At the autopsy, the three pathologists, Drs. James J. Humes, J. Thornton Boswell, and Pierre A. Finck, made a serious mistake; they located the wound of entrance in the back of President Kennedy's head much too low. Perhaps the intense pressure they faced, performing the postmortem examination before an audience of high-ranking military and naval brass, facing questions from FBI and Secret Service agents, listening to Admiral George Burkley, the president's personal physician, relay orders to them from the Kennedy family, anxiously waiting upstairs for the autopsy to end—perhaps all of these factors caused the doctors to make such a fundamental error. In any event, they located the wound of entrance in the rear of the head as "slightly above the external occipital protuberance," the bony knob low in the back of the head. In reality, the autopsy photographs and x-rays clearly depict the entrance wound as high on the top of the head, in the area of the cowlick. This discrepancy of four inches between the pathologists' location and the actual location of the rear wound has provided fodder for innumerable accusations by conspiracy theorists of tampering with the photographs and covering up the real site of the entrance wound in the head—the front.[16]

Even as late as 1996, in sworn depositions before the chief counsel for the Assassination Records Review Board, Drs. Humes, Boswell, and Finck maintained that the bullet entered low on the president's head, regardless of what the autopsy photographs revealed. Virtually all subsequent reviews of the medical evidence by experts, even by those who do not support the lone assassin thesis, have agreed that the entrance wound was indeed located high on the rear of the head. The autopsy photographs clearly depict an elongated wound, approximately nine by fifteen millimeters in its horizontal and vertical diameters, located ten centimeters, or four inches, above the external occipital protuberance. In short, there does exist a major disagreement between the recollection of the autopsy pathologists and what the evidence reveals. Significantly, however, these medical examinations have reaffirmed the fundamental conclusion reached at Bethesda on the night of the assassination that one bullet, and only one bullet, fired from the rear, entered Kennedy's head. For example, in a peer-reviewed article in a forensic science journal, Dr. Cyril Wecht, a longtime vocal critic of the lone assassin theory, admitted that the medical evidence provides no support for those who claim that the president was struck by a shot fired from the front.[17]

At the autopsy, after reflecting the hair and the scalp, the pathologists discovered a semicircle in the rear of President Kennedy's head. Later, pieces of bone were brought into the morgue, and the pathologists were able to fit one of those pieces into the missing half of the circle, thus recreating the actual hole of entrance in the rear. The small size of the wound, the lack of major damage to the skull and tissue around it, and the fact that the bone was beveled inward all defined the wound as one of entrance. As they examined the rest of the head, Drs. Humes, Boswell, and Finck observed the increasing amount of destruction caused by the bullet as it expanded and fragmented during its flight through the president's brain. By the time it exploded from the right front and top of the head, the bullet had disintegrated into numerous small fragments while shattering the skull and inflicting massive, fatal damage to the right side of the brain. They discovered that the margins of the massive wound of exit revealed bones that were beveled outward, positive indicators of a wound of exit.[18]

Regardless of the location of the entrance wound in the rear of the head, the autopsy photographs and x-rays depict only one bullet, fired from above, behind, and to the right of the president, that struck him in the head and killed him. The x-rays show a hole in the back of the head, slightly above a 6.5-millimeters metallic object embedded in the outer table of the skull. This object was obviously sheared off the bullet as it entered the head. The x-rays also show a trail of metallic fragments running from the wound of entrance in the rear to the wound of exit in front. The x-rays also show the huge fractures of the skull and the large amount of skull missing from the top and right front of the head. The photographs confirm this. They depict the undamaged back of the head, intact except for the small wound of entrance. By contrast, they depict the huge, gaping exit hole in the top and right front of President Kennedy's head, with a large flap of skull hanging over the right ear, and a big mass of brain tissue oozing from the top of the head. The only argument that conspiracy theorists offer to refute the photographs and x-rays is that they are forgeries.[19]

Conspiracy theorists maintain that the Zapruder film shows Kennedy's head thrust violently backward and leftward at the instant of the fatal shot, a certain indicator that the shot came from the right front—that is, from the Grassy Knoll. The evidence, however, does not support that contention. First, a careful examination of the relevant Zapruder film frames reveals that the president's head actually drives forward for one-eighteenth of a second before it moves backward. Second, one possible explanation for the backward thrust of the head from a rear-entering shot is that proposed by the majority of forensic pathologists who have scrutinized the medical evidence: a neuromuscular reaction. This theory claims that the destruction of the cerebral cortex, severe damage to the medulla oblongata, and widespread injury to other critical parts of the brain caused a violent neuromuscular reaction that propelled the head backward. The second theory is that proposed by Nobel prize-winning physicist Luis Alvarez, the "jet effect." In experiments performed by firing bullets into melons wrapped in bandages, Alvarez noted that the melons fell from the pedestals on which they were situated in the direction of the gun because the kinetic energy of the pulp forced from the rear of the melons as the bullet exited from them created a reverse propulsion similar to that of a jet plane's thrust from its engines. In a similar manner, the violent explosion of skull, blood, and brain tissue from the exit wound in the right front of Kennedy's head created this jet effect, which propelled him backward. Finally, lone assassin theorists argue that persons shot in the head do not always fall in the same direction as the bullet. For example, Senator Robert F. Kennedy was killed by a bullet fired from the rear, entering just behind the mastoid bone, located behind the ear. He was also struck by two other bullets that entered from the rear. Yet Senator Kennedy fell flat on his back, and not on his face, as conspiracy theorists would have us believe. It is also instructive that Governor Connally, who everyone agrees was shot in the back from behind, did not fall forward.[20]

The House Select Committee on Assassinations hired many experts, nearly all of whom concluded that President Kennedy was struck by only two bullets, both fired from above, behind, and to his right. An exhaustive trajectory analysis by Thomas Canning concluded that the wounds on both Kennedy and Connally were compatible with their having been struck by bullets fired from the sixth floor of the Texas School Book Depository. Wounds ballistics experiments by Larry Sturdivan confirmed the Warren Commission's conclusion that all the shots that struck were fired from the Mannlicher-Carcano rifle found on the sixth floor of that building. Later experiments for television programs and by private researchers reached the same conclusions. Firearms experts have carefully examined the rifle, Bullet 399, and the fragments from Connally's wrist and from Kennedy's head and have agreed that they were fired from the Depository rifle. Finally, Dr. Robert Grossman, an internationally respected neurosurgeon, was present in Trauma Room One, observed Kennedy's head wounds very closely, and saw nothing that contradicted the Warren Commission's assertion that the president was struck in the head by one bullet fired from the rear.[21]

The Identity of the Assassin: The Lone Assassin Perspective

The evidence not only proves that all the shots came from the sixth-floor southeast corner window of the Book Depository, it also proves that Lee Harvey Oswald fired those shots. A native of New Orleans who spent most of his childhood and adolescence in that city and in the Dallas–Fort Worth metropolitan area, Lee Oswald was, by all accounts, a loner, someone who kept to himself and made few friends. At the age of seventeen, in 1956, he joined the marines and spent nearly three years in that organization. When he left the marines in 1959, Oswald almost immediately left for the USSR, where he lived for the next two and a half years. Returning to the United States in 1962 with a Russian wife, Marina, and a daughter, June, Oswald lived in the Dallas–Fort Worth area until April 1963, when he moved to New Orleans. In September of that year, the Oswalds separated; Marina went to live with her friend, Ruth Paine, in Irving, Texas, a Dallas suburb, and Lee left for Dallas via Mexico City. In mid-October, Lee got a job as an order filler at the Depository, where he worked until the day of the assassination. Although not conclusive, the Warren Commission's case against Oswald was powerful and persuasive, with additional evidence against him added by later investigations.[22]

The commission's case against Lee Harvey Oswald began with the assertion that Oswald owned and possessed the rifle from which the shots were fired. In March 1963, Oswald ordered by mail a Mannlicher-Carcano rifle from Klein's Sporting Goods of Chicago. Klein's shipped a Mannlicher-Carcano rifle, manufactured in Italy in 1940, bearing the serial number C2766, to a person named A. Hidell at a post office box in Dallas. The Questioned Documents Division of the FBI examined several documents relating to these events: a completed coupon for the rifle; a money order made out to Klein's Sporting Goods; and a slip completed for the rental of the post office box. It determined that all these documents bore Oswald's handwriting, a finding fully endorsed by a panel of handwriting examiners hired by the House Select Committee on Assassinations. The serial number, of course, matched that of the rifle found on the sixth floor an hour after the assassination. "A. Hidell" was one of several aliases Oswald used. According to officials present at the interrogation sessions, Oswald denied owning a rifle, but the evidence clearly connected the Depository weapon to him.[23]

After finding the rifle carefully hidden inside a stack of book cartons, the Dallas police examined it. Lieutenant J. C. Day dusted it for fingerprints and found no identifiable prints on the weapon's exterior surface. However, when Day disassembled the rifle, he discovered a palm print on the underside of the barrel about three inches behind the front end of the wooden stock. In other words, the palm print was made when the rifle was disassembled. Lieutenant Day lifted the print from the rifle barrel with cellophane tape. It was positively identified as the right palm print of Lee Harvey Oswald by the Dallas police department, and a week after the assassination, when the lifted print was turned over to the FBI, this finding was affirmed by the FBI's leading fingerprint expert, Sebastian Latona. Furthermore, the cellophane tape containing the palm print also contained the impressions of markings from Oswald's rifle, a fact conveniently omitted by many conspiracy theorists. Nearly thirty years later, photographs made of the rifle after it had been dusted for prints revealed several partial prints on the exterior surface—prints that certain experts have identified as those of Oswald. The print evidence, therefore, proves that Oswald handled the assassination weapon.[24]

The FBI also discovered a tuft of several fibers in a crevice between the end of the rifle's wooden stock and the metal butt plate. The fibers, cotton with brown, yellow, and orange shades, had the same color pattern, fabric, and twist as the shirt Oswald wore when he was arrested. In addition, a blanket that Lee and Marina Oswald owned left similar fibers on a paper bag that Oswald used to carry the rifle into the Depository building the morning of the assassination. As the Warren Commission admitted, fiber evidence is not conclusive, as is fingerprint identification, because many different fabrics could have left identical fibers on the rifle. Yet it is instructive that the only fibers found on the rifle matched those of the shirt Oswald wore that day. Indeed, the only prints or other physical evidence found on the rifle came from Lee Harvey Oswald or from objects that he owned and handled.[25]

The Warren Commission also published several photographs of Oswald standing in the backyard of his Dallas apartment. He holds a rifle in one hand and has a revolver in a holster on his hip. Marina Oswald took the photographs in April 1963 with their camera. Oswald himself claimed that the photographs were fakes, that someone had superimposed his face on someone else's body, and over the years, many conspiracy theorists have maintained that the backyard photographs are forgeries. Yet again, the evidence belies this claim. The House Select Committee on Assassinations hired a panel of photographic experts to examine the photographs, the negatives, and the original camera for any evidence of forgery. They found none and felt comfortable in their unanimous conclusion that the photographs were authentic. In addition, the panel of experts found that the rifle in the photographs matched the Depository rifle in all observable characteristics. Although photographs of Oswald with a rifle taken in April 1963 do not prove that he possessed that same rifle seven months later, they do lend credence to the commission's claim that he owned and possessed the rifle.[26]

The person who lived with Lee Harvey Oswald and saw more of him than anyone else was, of course, his wife Marina. In one of the most dramatic moments of the Warren Commission's hearings, Marina Oswald identified the weapon found on the sixth floor of the Texas School

Book Depository as the "fateful rifle of Lee Oswald." Not only had Marina photographed Lee with the rifle in Dallas in April 1963, she also heard him practicing opening and closing the bolt action of the rifle as he sat on the screen porch of their New Orleans apartment during the spring and summer of 1963. When Marina left New Orleans to live with her friend Ruth Paine in Irving in late September of that year, the rifle was wrapped in a blanket and placed in Paine's station wagon. When Ruth Paine arrived back in Irving, she unloaded the station wagon because Marina was eight months pregnant. She put the blanket in the garage. About a week later, Marina went into the garage and thought she saw the rifle's wooden stock in the blanket. Both Ruth Paine and her husband Michael saw the blanket in the garage. Michael Paine actually picked it up and moved it. In testimony before the commission, the Paines stated that the Depository rifle wrapped in the blanket was the same approximate weight and shape as the blanket in their garage. In sum, the evidence clearly demonstrates that Lee Harvey Oswald owned and possessed the rifle from which the shots were fired.[27]

The Warren Commission also asserted that Oswald carried the rifle into the Depository building on the morning of the assassination. The day before, Thursday, November 21, Oswald asked his coworker at the Depository, Buell Wesley Frazier, if he could ride with Frazier to his house. Surprised that Oswald asked for a ride during the week instead of on weekends, as he had done before, Frazier asked him why, and Oswald responded that he needed to get some curtain rods. Frazier lived with his sister, Linnie Mae Randall, in Irving about a half block from the home of Ruth Paine, where Marina Oswald stayed. Oswald rode home with Frazier that evening, and, as usual, said little during the ride to Irving.[28]

That Thursday evening, Lee Oswald behaved in a normal manner. He played with two-year-old June on the front lawn of the Paine home, ate supper, and watched television. Between eight and nine o'clock, Ruth Paine and Marina Oswald bathed the children and got them ready for bed. After nine, Ruth went to the garage and noticed that the light was on. Certain that she had not left it on, she assumed that Lee had gone to the garage for something and forgot to turn the light off when he was finished. The one-hour time span gave Oswald plenty of time to remove the rifle from the blanket in which it was wrapped, disassemble it, and put it in the paper bag he had brought home with him. Lee and Marina went to bed around ten o'clock, and he slept soundly. The following morning, Friday, November 22, the alarm clock rang at seven o'clock. Marina heard it and awakened Lee, who had overslept. As Marina went back to sleep, Lee quickly dressed and left the house. When Marina awakened, she noticed that Lee had left $170 on the dresser together with his wedding ring, which he had always worn before.[29]

Linnie Mae Randall stood in her kitchen and looked out of the window. She noticed Lee Oswald walking toward her carport. He carried a package in a heavy brown bag. He gripped the top of the bag in his fingers, and the bottom almost touched the ground as he walked. A couple of minutes later, Buell Frazier walked into the carport, and as he got into the driver's seat of his car, he noticed a brown paper bag about two feet long lying on the back seat. Oswald responded "curtain rods" when Frazier asked him what was in the bag. After parking in the Depository parking lot about two blocks north of the building, Frazier decided to remain there and idle the engine of his car to ensure that it would start that afternoon. Oswald took the package from the back seat and walked toward the building, the first time he had not entered work with Frazier when they rode together. As Oswald walked in front of him, Frazier noticed that he held one end of the package cupped in his right hand, with the other end tucked under his armpit.[30]

The evidence clearly pointed to this paper bag as the container for the rifle. The bag was manufactured from heavy brown wrapping paper and tape from the Depository's shipping department. It contained two of Oswald's prints, a right palm print located on the bottom of the bag, and a left index fingerprint found on the side of the bag near the bottom. Oswald's prints meant that he had handled the bag. This bag was found near the sixth-floor window from which the shots were fired. Although its length, thirty-eight inches, was longer than the bag Randle and Frazier recalled seeing Oswald carry, they could have been mistaken. The bag also contained fibers that matched those of the blanket in which the rifle had been wrapped. Conspiracy theorists claim that none of the evidence proved that Oswald carried the rifle into the Depository building in that paper bag the morning of the assassination, but they fail to mention that Oswald had ample opportunity to sneak the rifle into the building at some other time, hide it wrapped inside the paper bag, then retrieve it for his deadly mission. Because Oswald's room already had curtain rods, the excuse that he gave Frazier for riding home with him that Thursday lacked credibility.[31]

Other evidence pointing to Oswald as the assassin included the fact that the last Depository employee to see him before the assassination saw him on the building's sixth floor. Charles Givens, one of a crew of floor layers working on the southwest corner of the sixth floor, went downstairs with his friends to eat lunch. Forgetting his cigarettes, Givens rode the freight elevator back up to the sixth floor, and he saw Oswald walking toward the elevator from the direction of the southeast corner. No other Depository employee is known to have seen Oswald until after the shooting. Oswald's actions, therefore, are consistent with his having been on the sixth floor at the time of the assassination.[32]

Unlike the scenario mapped out by conspiracy theorists of gunmen in several different locations, only one location, that of the sixth-floor southeast corner window of the Texas School Book Depository, could claim eyewitness identification. Several witnesses saw a gunman in the window before the assassination, and two witnesses, Amos Lee Euins and Howard L. Brennan, saw him fire shots. Euins's description of the assassin was too vague to fit a particular individual, but Brennan's description, which he gave to police officers minutes after the shooting, was quite specific. The man who committed this heinous act was white, about five feet, ten inches tall, weighed one hundred sixty pounds, was slender and about thirty years old, and wore light-colored clothing. This was the description broadcast over police channels several times, the first transmission coming at 12:45. In films taken by local television stations, Brennan, a steamfitter wearing his metal hard hat, can be seen talking to a police officer and pointing upward toward the sixth floor of the Depository building less than twenty minutes after the gunfire.[33]

Of even greater significance is the fact that Brennan identified the man he observed shoot the president as Lee Harvey Oswald. Brennan claimed that he arrived at the corner of Elm and Houston Streets about seven minutes before the motorcade arrived. While sitting on a concrete ledge directly opposite the Depository building, Brennan glanced upward and noticed a man looking out of the sixth-floor southeast corner window. On several occasions, the man disappeared, then returned to the window. Brennan was certain that the window was the sixth-floor southeast corner window because he also observed three African American men looking out of the fifth-floor window directly below. Photographs taken seconds after the shooting confirm Brennan's observation. Shortly after the motorcade turned onto Elm Street, Brennan heard the sound of what sounded like a motorcycle backfire or of a firecracker being thrown from the Depository building. He looked upward and saw to his horror the man he had observed previously take careful aim into the telescopic sight of a rifle, squeeze the trigger, and stand there for a moment "as if to assure hisself that he hit his mark."[34]

After Lee Oswald was arrested, Brennan was brought to police headquarters to view a lineup. Seeing Oswald in the lineup, Brennan knew that he was the same man he had seen shoot the president, but, afraid that the assassination might be a "communist conspiracy," he failed to identify Oswald to protect himself and his family. In testimony before the Warren Commission, Brennan stated flatly that the man he saw aim and fire was Lee Harvey Oswald, a position he would maintain until his death three decades later. Warren Commission critics pointed to inconsistencies in Brennan's account: (1) the gunman could not have been standing when he fired; (2) Brennan was not wearing his glasses at the time; (3) Brennan did not pick Oswald out of the police lineup; and (4) Brennan heard only two shots, when at least three were fired. Warren Commission defenders respond by claiming: (1) from Brennan's perspective six floors below the window, it appeared that the man was standing, and the famous photograph taken by Tom Dillard of the fifth and sixth floors of the Depository building only a few seconds after the shooting depicts two black men looking out the fifth-floor window. These men appear to be standing, but in reality, they were kneeling. (2) Brennan wore glasses only for close-up reading. His distance vision was perfect. Therefore, his identification of Oswald as the gunman must be given great credence. (3) Brennan was understandably afraid the night of the assassination, although he recognized Oswald the instant he saw him in the lineup. (4) Many witnesses heard either more or fewer than three shots, and Brennan's account focused not on the number of shots he heard, but on the identity of the person who fired them.[35]

Although Howard Brennan was the only witness to identify Lee Harvey Oswald as the assassin, many other witnesses confirmed his account of the shots being fired from the sixth-floor window. Again, Amos Lee Euins saw a man fire shots from that same window. The three men in the fifth-floor window directly below the Oswald window, James Jarman, Harold Norman, and Bonnie Ray Williams, heard shots coming from above them, as well as the sound of empty cartridge cases hitting the floor. Several people riding in the motorcade behind the presidential limousine heard the shots, looked at the upper floors of the Depository building, and saw either a rifle or a cylindrical object that appeared similar to a rifle barrel slowly being withdrawn from the window. Several police officers riding in the motorcade heard shots fired from an upper floor of the Depository. Numerous spectators heard shots fired from the Depository building.[36]

Oswald's actions in the building after the assassination are consistent with his having been present on the sixth floor at the time of the shooting. Riding his motorcycle near the rear of the motorcade on Houston Street, Officer Marrion Baker heard shots, looked upward toward the Depository building, and saw a flock of pigeons fly upward from the roof. Certain that the shots came from the building, Baker raced his motorcycle to the corner of Elm and Houston, jumped off, and ran up the stairs leading to the front entrance of the Depository. Roy Truly, the superintendent of the Texas School Book Depository, accompanied Baker as he ran into the building. Unable to work the elevator, Baker raced up the stairs, heading to the roof, but as he reached the second-floor landing, he saw a man go into a lunchroom, so he followed him. As Officer Baker entered the lunchroom, he saw the man standing in front of a Coke machine. Baker drew his revolver from his holster and approached the man. As he did, Roy Truly identified the man as one of his employees, so Baker put his revolver back and resumed his ascent to the building's roof. About half a minute later, Geraldine Reid, who worked in the Depository, ran to her desk in the middle of the second floor and saw Lee Oswald walking "at a very slow pace" and drinking a Coke. Both Baker and Truly reconstructed their movements for the Warren Commission, and a Secret Service agent reconstructed Oswald's movements. The reconstruction found that Oswald could have reached the second-floor lunchroom well ahead of Baker.[37]

The Tippit Killing: The Lone Assassin Perspective

Lone assassin theorists argue that Lee Harvey Oswald's cold-blooded murder of Dallas police officer J. D. Tippit approximately forty-five minutes after the Kennedy assassination provides powerful evidence of his complicity in the president's murder. Because Tippit was slain nearly four miles from Dealey Plaza, it is necessary to trace Oswald's movements from the time that Geraldine Reid saw him on the second floor of the Depository to the scene of the Tippit killing. Because Reid saw Oswald walking in the direction of the stairs leading down to the front entrance of the building, the Warren Commission concluded that he left the building through that entrance about 12:33 p.m. The very fact of Oswald's departing the Depository building only three minutes after the assassination provides further evidence of his suspicious behavior.[38]

Oswald then walked seven blocks down Elm Street, where he caught a bus. The bus, which traveled on the Lakewood-Marsalis route, would have let Oswald off just a few blocks from the rooming house where he lived. The evidence of Oswald's having caught the bus consists first of a transfer found in his shirt pocket after his arrest. Marked Nov. 22, 1963, with P.M. punched out, the transfer was traced to a bus driven by Cecil J. McWatters, who picked Oswald from a lineup as the man who had boarded his bus at about 12:40 P.M., some seven blocks east of the intersection of Elm and Houston. Many conspiracy theorists deliberately overlook the compelling evidence of the transfer as proof that Oswald had indeed caught a bus. Several months later, when he testified before the Warren Commission, McWatters retracted his identification of Oswald, claiming that the man who really caught his bus was a teenager named Milton Jones. The other evidence of Oswald's bus ride came in the testimony of another passenger on the bus, Mary Bledsoe, who had rented a room to Oswald in October 1963. Bledsoe testified that she saw Oswald board the bus, noticed that he looked "like a maniac," and that he had a hole in the right elbow of his shirt. Because Bledsoe knew Oswald, and because the shirt he wore did indeed have a hole in the right elbow, the commission placed great credence in her account.[39]

Because the bus slowed considerably as a result of traffic congestion near Dealey Plaza, Oswald left the vehicle at 12:44 and walked four blocks to a Greyhound bus station. He got into a taxi driven by William Whaley, who saw Oswald's picture in the newspaper the day after the assassination and recognized him as the passenger who had boarded his taxi. Taken to police headquarters, Whaley picked Oswald from a lineup. Whaley stated that Oswald sat in the front seat next to him and said nothing during the drive. He left Oswald off at the 500 or 700 block of North Beckley Avenue, a few blocks from Oswald's rooming house. Whaley remembered Oswald well because the fare was ninety-five cents, and Oswald gave him a dollar and told him to keep the change. Whaley retraced the taxi ride from the bus station to North Beckley Avenue, and the ride took six minutes. Because Oswald entered the cab about 12:48, he left it about 12:54. Because his rooming house was only a few blocks away, he arrived there about 1:00.[40]

Earline Roberts, the housekeeper at 1026 North Beckley, watched television and heard the announcement of the president's assassination at about 1:00 P.M. Shortly after that, she saw Lee Oswald enter the rooming house. She told him that the president had been shot, and he mumbled something and went to his room. Shortly after Oswald entered his room, Roberts heard the "beep beep" sound of an automobile horn outside. Peeking through the curtains, she saw a Dallas police car numbered 107 or 207 parked outside. About a minute later, she peeked through the curtains again, and the police car had left. Shortly after, Oswald, wearing a jacket, left the rooming house. About a minute later, or around 1:05 P.M., Roberts again peeked through the curtains and saw Oswald standing at a bus stop in front of the rooming house. Shortly after, she again looked out and saw no one.[41]

The next time Oswald was seen, he walked east on Tenth Street toward Patton Avenue. Helen Markham, a waitress, stood on the corner and saw a police car approach Oswald from the rear. The officer driving the car motioned Oswald over, and Oswald leaned over and talked to him through the right front window. The policeman, J. D. Tippit, had almost certainly heard the description of the man wanted for shooting the president broadcast over police channels one and two. The description, of a white man, thirty years old, five feet, ten inches tall, one hundred sixty-five pounds, fit Oswald almost perfectly. Just before this encounter, Oswald walked erratically to and fro, and one witness had even seen him "relieve himself" in some bushes in broad daylight. Tippit may have noticed the erratic demeanor and called Oswald to his car to question him. After a brief conversation, Tippit got out of the car, and as he approached the left front fender, Oswald pulled a revolver from his belt, pointed it at Tippit, and fired three or four shots, striking Tippit and causing him to fall to the ground. Oswald then walked over to the wounded Tippit and fired a shot point-blank into his head, as if to administer a coup de grâce.[42]

As he fled back toward Patton Avenue, Oswald stopped on the front lawn of a corner house, opened the chamber of his revolver, emptied four expended cartridge cases and threw them on the grass, and reloaded the weapon with fresh rounds. Observed by numerous witnesses, Oswald fled through the residential neighborhood, hiding in several places. He discarded his jacket and eventually wound up on Jefferson Avenue, the principal thoroughfare in the Oak Cliff section of Dallas. Once there, Oswald ducked into the lobby of a shoe store because police cars were racing down Jefferson toward the scene of the Tippit killing five blocks away. After the cars passed, Oswald walked back onto the sidewalk. Suspicious, Johnny Brewer, a clerk in the shoe store, followed Oswald and saw him sneak into the Texas Theater without paying. Brewer informed Julia Postal, the theater cashier, and she called the police. Within minutes, police had the theater surrounded, and Officer Nick M. McDonald arrested Oswald.[43]

The evidence against Lee Harvey Oswald in the murder of Officer J. D. Tippit is overwhelming. Several witnesses, including Helen Markham and Domingo Benavides, who sat in his truck only fifteen feet from the murder scene, saw Oswald shoot Tippit. One witness, Jack Tatum, saw Oswald fire the fatal shot into Tippit's head. More than a dozen witnesses, including Barbara and Virginia Davis, who ran onto their front porch just in time to see Oswald eject the empty cartridge cases from his revolver onto their lawn; William Scoggins, who sat in his taxi just around the corner; and Warren Reynolds, who worked a block from the murder scene, saw Oswald flee the scene of the crime. When arrested, Oswald carried a fully loaded Smith and Wesson .38-caliber revolver, and he had a pocketful of Winchester–Western and Remington .38-caliber bullets. Oswald resisted arrest and tried to fire his gun at Officer McDonald, who needed assistance in subduing Oswald.[44]

Most significantly, the cartridge cases found at the scene of the crime were fired from Lee Harvey Oswald's revolver, to the exclusion of all other weapons. Initially, the bullets removed from Tippit's body appeared too mutilated to be ballistically matched to Oswald's revolver. However, Courtland Cunningham, an Illinois state police firearms expert, matched one of the bullets removed from Tippit's body with a bullet test-fired from Oswald's revolver. If innocent, as his defenders claim, why would Oswald have acted so guiltily as to murder a police officer who merely wanted to ask him some questions? Why did he flee the scene of the crime? Why did he have a revolver with him? Why did he resist arrest? Indeed, these and a myriad of other questions relating to Oswald's actions after the assassination point to his guilt and in the opinion of the famed Texas legal authority, Leon Jaworski, would have provided an abundance of proof for a prosecutor to persuade a jury that Oswald did indeed kill Tippit. Jaworski went on to proclaim that "even the least competent prosecutor in the state of Texas" could easily have won not only a conviction, but a decision to employ the death penalty in the Tippit case.[45]

Lee Harvey Oswald: The Lone Assassin Perspective

The assassin, Lee Harvey Oswald, was a misfit, unable or unwilling to accommodate himself to the society in which he lived. Born in New Orleans in October 1939, Oswald found himself shuffled between living with his mother, Marguerite, spending time in orphanages, and living with relatives during the first five years of his life. In 1945, Marguerite moved to Fort Worth, and Lee, together with his older brother Robert and his stepbrother John Pic, moved to many different houses in the Dallas–Fort Worth metropolitan area during the next seven years.

Unlike John Pic and Robert, Lee failed to make friends and appeared both confused and angry at the constant moving. Although of above-average intelligence, he made mediocre grades in school and seemed to continuously get into fights with his mother. Marguerite's third marriage failed, and because Lee's father had died a couple of months before he was born, he was raised without the fatherly influence he seemed to need.[46]

In 1952 Marguerite moved to New York City, and the thirteen-year-old Lee Oswald found himself in a strange environment, mocked by his classmates for his Texas accent and clothing, and doing poorly in school. He skipped school so often that a truant officer took him to the local home for juvenile delinquents. There Lee stayed for six weeks and undertook a battery of psychological and intelligence tests. The psychiatrist, Dr. Renatus Hartogs, as well as social workers concluded that Lee suffered from various psychiatric disorders caused primarily by the absence of a father figure in his home and by his domineering mother. Dr. Hartogs found Lee capable of committing acts of violence, and after interviewing Marguerite, he concluded that she needed to spend more time with her son.[47]

When Lee was fifteen, Marguerite moved back to New Orleans. Lee attended junior high and high school, again making grades considerably below his potential. He had very few friends and became known as a loner, a characteristic he would retain the rest of his short life. Lee worked at various jobs and by all accounts performed his duties adequately. He also first became acquainted with Marxism. Perhaps because he was bored in school, perhaps because of the publicity that the term *communism* received during the height of MacCarthyism, Lee checked out several books on the subject from the public library. He also joined the Civil Air Patrol, an organization of teenage boys that trained in a military-style environment.[48]

When Lee Oswald reached the age of seventeen in October 1956, he joined the United States Marine Corps, following in Robert's footsteps. After passing the rigorous marine basic training in boot camp, Lee took various intelligence tests and made high scores. Therefore, he was assigned to a special radar unit, and after receiving instruction at Keesler Air Force Base in Biloxi, Mississippi, the unit was assigned to overseas duty. Oswald served in various posts in the Pacific, including

Guadalcanal and Okinawa, but his most controversial was duty at the Atsugi Air Force Base in Japan. There Oswald's radar unit was assigned to a top-secret U-2 spy plane sector of the base. To serve there, Oswald had special security clearance.[49]

In the marines, Oswald studied Russian, achieving a sound knowledge of the language. As in school, he made few friends and was known as a loner. While in Japan, he frequented a brothel operated by a woman known to be a Russian spy, although whether Oswald came into contact with Soviet agents remains unknown. On one occasion, he got into a fight with a sergeant and wound up in the brig. On another, he allegedly shot himself in the arm to avoid being shipped out to Guadalcanal, but his injury, only a flesh wound, did not prove serious enough to prevent his being shipped out with his unit. He also twice took marksmanship tests with an M-1 rifle, the first time scoring at the sharpshooter level, the second time just barely making the marksman level, the lowest ranking (the military does not have a category known as "poor shot").[50]

In August 1959, Oswald, claiming that his mother needed him to care for her after she injured herself at work, received a hardship discharge from the marines. He returned to Fort Worth and spent a week with Marguerite and Robert, but then departed for New Orleans. There he boarded a freighter bound for Europe. Ultimately, he wound up in Helsinki, Finland, and from there, he traveled to the Soviet Union. In Moscow, Oswald applied for permanent residency in the USSR and informed the American Embassy of his intention to defect. In October 1959, while staying in a Moscow hotel, despondent over hearing that the Soviet government would not welcome him into its country, Lee Harvey Oswald tried to commit suicide by slashing his wrist. Taken to a Moscow hospital, Oswald was successfully treated for his superficial wounds, and he soon learned that he would be allowed to remain in the USSR. Given a well-paying job in the city of Minsk, about two hundred miles west of Moscow, Oswald lived comfortably. He had his own apartment and was allowed much greater freedom of movement than the average Soviet citizen.[51]

At a dance in Minsk, Lee met Marina Prusakova, the niece of a KGB official, with whom she lived. After a brief romance, Lee and Marina were married in 1961 and soon had a baby daughter June. In 1962, disillusioned by the reality of communism, as opposed to the theory about which he had read, Oswald applied for permission to return to the United States. In June of that year, he, Marina, and the baby left the Soviet Union and journeyed to Fort Worth. There Oswald got a job in a company specializing in photographic interpretations of topographic maps and similar materials. Oswald quit this job, and he and Marina lived off his unemployment checks. While they were living in Dallas in March 1963, Oswald ordered a Mannlicher-Carcano rifle from Klein's Sporting Goods of Chicago. In April, Marina took several photographs of Lee standing in their backyard, as he held the rifle in one hand and a brochure of socialist literature in the other. One night, Lee took the rifle to the home of retired army major general Edwin A. Walker, and as Walker sat in the living room, Lee, hidden behind a bush on a grassy knoll in Walker's front yard, fired one shot that barely missed Walker.[52]

In April 1963, Oswald moved to New Orleans, where he rented an apartment in the uptown section of the city. After getting a job at the Reily Coffee Company, he brought Marina, now pregnant with their second child, to New Orleans. For the next five months, Lee and Marina experienced increasing marital difficulties, partially caused by his failure to keep a steady job and partially by his frequent abuse of her. Although Lee took Marina on various outings and introduced her to members of his family in New Orleans, they failed to resolve their differences. Ultimately, they decided to separate, and in September, Marina went to live with her friend Ruth Paine, who had a house in Irving, a Dallas suburb.[53]

During the spring and summer of 1963, Oswald spent a great deal of time in New Orleans's central business district, especially the area near Lafayette Square, about five blocks from the main thoroughfare, Canal Street. Accompanied by several Hispanics, Oswald visited the office of attorney Dean Andrews to see if Andrews could file the legal papers necessary for Oswald's discharge from the marines to be changed back to honorable. He quit his job and lived off unemployment funds. In August he visited the store operated by Carlos Bringuier, a leading member of a vehemently anti-Castro organization. Oswald told Bringuier that he was an ex-marine, an excellent shot, and would like to participate in anti-Castro activities. A few days later, Bringuier was walking on Canal Street when he saw Oswald handing out pro-Castro literature. Enraged, Bringuier attacked Oswald, and Oswald wound up getting arrested for disturbing the peace. After being interviewed by the FBI while in jail, Oswald was released when an acquaintance of his uncle, Dutz Murrett, a bookie who worked for Carlos Marcello, posted his bail.[54]

In New Orleans, Oswald came into contact with numerous members of the city's large Cuban exile community. According to author and researcher Gus Russo, Oswald almost certainly learned from some of these Cubans that the Kennedy administration had plans to eliminate Fidel Castro through either assassination or another military invasion of Cuba. Russo maintains that Oswald, who had publicly proclaimed his support for Castro in a radio interview and by handing out pro-Castro literature, became irate at the Kennedy administration and probably made up his mind to eliminate the president. Whether Russo's scenario is realistic cannot be ascertained by the known facts, but it is certain that on September 25, 1963, Lee Harvey Oswald left New Orleans for Houston.[55]

In Houston, Oswald boarded a bus that took him to Mexico City, where he spent a week. In the Mexican capital, Oswald visited both the Cuban and Russian embassies. His intention was to obtain a visa to travel to Havana and thence to Moscow. He met with several officials of the Soviet embassy, including members of the KGB. He also met with several Cuban officials. According to one account, someone in the Cuban embassy gave Oswald a large sum of money to assassinate President Kennedy. After a week, Oswald boarded a bus out of Mexico City and ended up in Dallas, where he rented a room.[56]

Arriving in Dallas in the first week of October 1963, Lee Harvey Oswald would remain there until his death seven weeks later. He often visited Marina and June at the Irving home of Ruth Paine and appeared to make an effort to reconcile with her. When Ruth Paine learned from her neighbor, Linnie Mae Randall, that job vacancies existed at the Texas School Book Depository, where her brother Buell Frazier worked, Paine told Lee Oswald about the opening, and he applied for it. When he got the job as an order filler, by all accounts he proved to be a loyal and industrious employee. When Marina gave birth to their second daughter, Rachel, in the third week of October, Lee visited her and paid a good deal of attention to two-year-old June. Despite Lee's efforts to reconcile, Marina still maintained her distance from him because she wanted and needed the assurance of a stable relationship.[57]

Lone assassin theorists argue that when he heard the news that President Kennedy was coming to Dallas on November 22 and that his motorcade would pass directly in front of the building where he worked, Lee Harvey Oswald grasped the opportunity to make a name for himself. A social outcast, a misfit in society, Oswald, in his twisted mind, viewed assassinating Kennedy as a means both of attaining the recognition he had heretofore not received and as a means of exacting revenge against the society that had shunned him. When Dallas County Deputy Sheriff Roger Craig saw Oswald in the office of Captain Will Fritz, the head of the homicide bureau of the Dallas police, the afternoon of the assassination, Craig identified Oswald as the man he saw run from the Depository building shortly after the assassination. Hearing Craig's identification, Oswald rose dramatically from his chair and stated that "everybody will know who I am now!" At last, people would take notice when they heard the name of Lee Harvey Oswald.[58]

Another possible motive for Oswald's murder of Kennedy was his strong pro-Marxist and pro-Castro political viewpoint. In New Orleans, Oswald had come into contact with numerous anti-Castro Cubans and heard from them that the Kennedy administration had planned to launch another invasion of Cuba and to have Fidel Castro assassinated. Infuriated at this brazen attempt by the Kennedy administration to overthrow the Marxist paradise that Castro had established in Cuba, Oswald decided to thwart that attempt by killing Kennedy first. In Mexico City, during his meetings with Cuban officials, Oswald may very well have received money, or at least strong encouragement, to assassinate Kennedy. His earlier unsuccessful attempt to assassinate General Walker provided concrete evidence of his disposition to take human life. A recent documentary, aired on German television, showed interviews with former Cuban and Soviet intelligence agents to demonstrate that Cuba hired Oswald to kill Kennedy in retaliation for the United States' attempts on the life of Fidel Castro.[59]

Summary

To anyone with an open mind, lone assassin theorists maintain that the evidence is clear, convincing, and incontrovertible. Lee Harvey Oswald murdered President Kennedy and Officer Tippit and wounded Governor Connally. The exhaustive investigations of the Warren Commission, the House Select Committee on Assassinations, the FBI, the Rockefeller Commission, the Dallas police, the state of Texas, and the Justice Department all concluded that Oswald fired the shots that killed Kennedy and wounded Connally. Although some lone assassin theorists contend that Oswald acted on his own initiative, others argue that he may have conspired with someone or some institution. In any event, the only conclusion that a reasonable person can reach after objectively examining the evidence is that Lee Harvey Oswald fired all of the shots that struck the president and the governor.

4

Conflict: The Case for Conspiracy

A poll taken by the Zogby organization in the summer of 2001 revealed that 68 percent of Americans believe that the assassination of President Kennedy resulted from a conspiracy. The reason is simple. Americans do not trust their government to tell the truth about most issues, and the widespread and systematic cover-up of critical evidence by various government agencies has persuaded most people to doubt the official explanation of Kennedy's murder. In addition, the vast majority of studies of the assassination, popularized and scholarly, in both fiction and nonfiction books, articles, documentaries, and movies have sharply criticized the official version that Oswald acted alone. The proponents of an assassination conspiracy argue that the physical and scientific evidence demonstrates that more than one gunmen fired shots at President Kennedy and Governor Connally. They contend also that if Lee Harvey Oswald acted alone, with no conspiratorial involvement by any other individual or organization, then why did the government go to such lengths to suppress the truth by classifying millions of documents and destroying thousands of others?[1]

Conspiracies in History

Many leading members of the political, journalistic, and academic establishments have labeled those who believe that John Kennedy was assassinated as the result of a conspiracy "buffs," "kooks," "nuts," and "conspirati." By grouping all conspiracy theorists together, they have combined responsible researchers with sensation seekers, refusing to acknowledge that history comes replete with countless examples of conspiracies that no one would seriously deny. For example, many of the same people who look with scorn on those who believe in a Kennedy assassination conspiracy are among the most vociferous champions of the conspiracy theory in Watergate, involving Richard Nixon, H. R. Haldeman, John Ehrlichman, John Dean, John Mitchell, Jeb Stuart Magruder, James McCord, and a host of others. Yet in the Kennedy assassination, they seem to ignore the existence of historical forces and insist that this seminal event in recent American history, "the seven seconds that broke the back of the American century," as Don DeLillo called the assassination in *Libra*, occurred in the most simplistic manner possible, as the act of a lone gunman.[2]

In fact, some of the most important events in history resulted from conspiracies. For example, the most famous crime, and arguably one of the most critical events in nineteenth-century American history, the assassination of Abraham Lincoln, was caused by a plot involving nearly a dozen individuals, even though only one man, John Wilkes Booth, pulled the trigger. Similarly, the event that touched off the outbreak of World War I, the assassination of Archduke Franz Ferdinand, resulted from a conspiracy of Serbian nationalists, with the assassin, Gavrilo Princip, being a member of such a group. In 1950, two Puerto Rican nationalists, Grisselia Torreselo and Oscar Collazo, attempted to assassinate President Harry Truman, a crime indisputably the result of a conspiracy. Two events that changed the course of American history, the Japanese attack on Pearl Harbor on December 7, 1941, and the terrorist attacks on the World Trade Center and on the Pentagon on September 11, 2001, also resulted from conspiracies. Watergate, the event that led to the resignation of President Richard Nixon, came about from a conspiracy involving the president, many members of his administration, and several influential officials of his 1972 reelection committee. The worst mass murder committed by American citizens, the bombing of the Alfred P. Murrah Federal Building in Oklahoma City in 1995, an event that claimed the lives of 169 persons, resulted from a conspiracy between Timothy McVeigh and Terry Nichols, and possibly others. The assassination of Julius Caesar in 44 B.C. resulted from a conspiracy of senators anxious to rid the Roman Republic of a dictator. During the sixteenth and seventeenth centuries, several assassination plots against Queen Elizabeth I and King James I by Roman

Catholic fanatics were thwarted by British intelligence. A brief list of victims of other assassination conspiracies in history will illustrate their commonality: Czar Alexander II; Mohandas Ghandi; Anwar Sadat; Rafael Trujillo; Leon Trotsky; Pancho Villa. The list could be expanded to include those who survived assassination plots against their lives: Adolf Hitler; Fidel Castro; Pope John Paul II; and Charles DeGaulle.[3]

These examples should serve to rebut those commentators who associate anyone trying to connect the notion of a conspiracy in the Kennedy assassination with the lunatic fringe, with those who view conspiracies lurking everywhere. Some authors, such as Daniel Patrick Moynihan, Patrick O'Donnell, and Timothy Melley, argue that belief in a Kennedy assassination conspiracy clearly places its adherents into what Richard Hofstadter called the "paranoid style in American politics." In his letter to the *Washington Post* criticizing Oliver Stone's movie, *JFK*, Moynihan, summarizing Hofstadter, actually discussed those Americans in the 1790s who believed in a plot by the Bavarian Illuminati, and by implication, included them in the same "crackpot" category as Kennedy assassination conspiracy theorists. This guilt by association, needless to say, hardly contributes to an understanding of that monumental event in recent American history. Indeed, it merely serves to emphasize the tendency of lone assassin theorists to engage in guilt by association.[4]

To be sure, a number of Kennedy assassination conspiracy theories clearly fall into the categories of bizarre, absurd, and ludicrous. Perhaps the most bizarre I have encountered came in June 1995. After I testified before the Assassination Records Review Board (ARRB) about the necessity for releasing all assassination-related records still being suppressed, I was interviewed on a New Orleans television station. A couple of days later, I received a letter from a woman convinced that the Antichrist, in the person of television star and host Robert Stack, masterminded the murder of President Kennedy. Another conspiracy theory, both absurd and ludicrous, I first encountered during a question-and-answer session after my lecture on the Kennedy assassination at Louisiana Tech University in 1993. An elderly gentleman in the audience proclaimed that the assassination conspiracy began in December 1913. Puzzled, I asked him to elaborate, because John F. Kennedy was not even born until 1917. He stated that in that month, President Woodrow Wilson signed the legislation establishing the Federal Reserve System, and he explained that President Franklin Roosevelt's abolishing the gold standard in 1933 was part of this ongoing conspiracy by the world's moneylenders, most of them Jewish, to dominate the human race. He then asserted that when President Kennedy decided to return to the gold standard, the moneylenders had him assassinated. Since that initial encounter, I have uncovered several other Federal Reserve System conspiracy theories, many with their own Web sites. I have received communications tracing the Kennedy assassination to the same sinister forces that emblazoned a pyramid with an eye on the back of the one-dollar bill. The recent book *Rule by Secrecy*, by Kennedy assassination conspiracy theorist Jim Marrs, offers an elaborate amplification of the Federal Reserve theory. Marrs argues that secret societies, such as the Illuminati, the Knights Templar, the Freemasons, the Council on Foreign Relations, the Trilateral Commission, the CIA, the Vatican, and international Jewry have conspired to rule the world for millennia. They had Kennedy assassinated because he threatened to end American involvement in Vietnam, the war they created.[5]

Other ludicrous conspiracy theories include those naming as the mastermind behind the assassination: Aristotle Onassis—to get Jackie away from Jack; Martha Mitchell—for some unfathomable reason; Secret Service agent George Hickey, riding in the car behind Kennedy's—whose finger accidentally squeezed the trigger of his weapon; Richard Nixon—to exact revenge against Kennedy for the 1960 election; the same sinister forces that compelled President Harry Truman to fire General Douglas MacArthur; the KGB—which murdered the real Oswald and replaced him with a clone programmed to kill Kennedy; and cliques of black militants, white racists, homosexuals, Texas oil millionaires, Texas drug lords, Enron executives (even though the company did not even exist in 1963), and sundry other nefarious groups. The list could be extended almost endlessly, but the point is clear. In the Kennedy assassination, there exists a wide variety of ridiculous conspiracy theories. Nevertheless, the evidence of a conspiracy is substantial, and it is to that evidence that we now turn our attention.[6]

The Single Bullet Theory: The Conspiracy Perspective

Virtually every serious Kennedy assassination researcher believes that the Warren Commission's single bullet theory is essential to its conclusion that only one man fired shots at President Kennedy and Governor Connally. The awkwardness of the Mannlicher-Carcano's bolt action mechanism, which forced FBI experts to fire two shots in a minimum of 2.25 seconds, even without aiming, coupled with the average time of 18.3 film frames per second as measured on Abraham Zapruder's camera, constitute a timing constraint that compels the conclusion either that Kennedy and Connally were struck by the same bullet, or that two separate gunmen fired two separate shots at the two men. Although a handful of researchers contend that the first shot struck Kennedy at frame Z162 or Z189, thereby allowing sufficient time for Oswald to fire a separate shot with the Carcano and strike Connally at frame Z237, the vast majority of assassination scholars maintain one of two scenarios. First, both Kennedy and Connally were struck by the same bullet at frame Z223 or Z224, evidenced by the quick flip of the lapel on Connally's suit jacket as the bullet passed through his chest. Second, the first bullet struck Kennedy somewhere between frames Z210 and Z224, and the second bullet struck Connally between frames Z236 and Z238, evidenced by the visual signs on the film of Connally reacting to being struck.[7]

The evidence clearly establishes, however, that Kennedy and Connally were struck by separate bullets. The location of the bullet wound in Kennedy's back has given rise to considerable controversy. Originally, the Warren Commission staff draft of the relevant section of the Warren Report stated that "a bullet had entered his back at a point slightly above the shoulder and to the right of the spine." The problem lay in the course of the bullet through Kennedy's body. If a bullet fired from the sixth-floor window of the Depository building nearly sixty feet higher than the limousine entered the president's back, with the president sitting in an upright position, it could hardly have exited from his throat at a point just above the Adam's apple, then abruptly change course and drive downward into Governor Connally's back. Therefore, Warren Commissioner Gerald Ford deliberately changed the draft to read: "A bullet had entered the base of the back of his neck slightly to the right of the spine." Suppressed for more than three decades, Ford's deliberate distortion was released to the public only through the actions of the ARRB. When this alteration first surfaced in 1997, Ford explained that he made the change for the sake of "clarity." In reality, Ford had elevated the location of the wound from its true location in the back to the neck to ensure that the single bullet theory would remain inviolate. The actual evidence demonstrates the accuracy of the initial draft. Bullet holes in Kennedy's shirt and suit jacket, situated almost six inches below the top of the collar, place the wound squarely in the back. Because JFK sat upright at the time, and because photographs and films show that neither the shirt nor the suit jacket rode up over his collar, the location of the bullet holes in the garments prove that the shot struck him in the back. Kennedy's death certificate places the wound at the level of the third thoracic vertebra. Autopsy photographs of the back place the wound in the back two to three inches below the base of the neck.[8]

At the autopsy, Dr. Humes did not dissect the wound in Kennedy's back, even though dissection was the only certain method of tracking the missile's path through the body. In an impassioned interview with *JAMA*, the journal of the American Medical Association, Humes declared that it would have been "criminal" to dissect the back/neck wound. In fact, Humes opened the entire abdominal cavity, removed the heart, liver, spleen, and other internal organs, and removed the brain from the head. A small dissection of a one-quarter-inch track through the upper thoracic region would hardly have maimed the body any further. The truth, testified to under oath at the Clay Shaw trial by autopsy pathologist Pierre A. Finck, was that the pathologists were ordered by one of the admirals or generals present not to dissect the back/neck wound. The reason for the order remains unknown, but if, as lone assassin theorists claim, a back-to-front bullet track through the president's neck existed, then dissection would have provided additional weight to the single bullet theory. The failure to dissect the track of the bullet through Kennedy's body fuels more suspicion of a cover-up to conceal evidence of multiple gunmen. Dr. Robert Canada stated that "the bullet entered the back at T3 [the third thoracic vertebra], lodged in the chest near the stomach, and did not exit." This assertion, made by the head of the naval medical hospital, who was present throughout the postmortem examination, strongly supports the claim that the bullet struck Kennedy in the back.[9]

In his testimony before the Warren Commission, Dr. Humes insisted that the autopsy pathologists had uncovered a bullet path through Kennedy's body, from the hole of entrance in the upper back to the hole of exit in the front of the throat. In reality, they discovered no such path. At the autopsy, they observed a large, gaping, irregular horizontal gash in the president's throat, which they mistakenly believed was a tracheotomy incision. Because they lacked experience in forensic pathology, they completely missed a tiny bullet wound in the front of the throat, obscured, although not obliterated, by the tracheotomy. This tiny hole, described by the physicians and nurses at Dallas's Parkland Hospital as three by five millimeters or four by six millimeters (one-eighth to one-quarter inch) in diameter, had all the appearances of an entrance wound. Indeed, the Dallas medical team almost unanimously called it an entrance wound in their initial, contemporaneous oral and written records. Yet if a bullet struck the president from in front as he faced forward, the gunman who fired that shot must have been situated in front, while the gunman who fired the shot that struck him in the back must have been situated behind him. This would have constituted irrefutable evidence of a conspiracy. Yet the autopsy report said nothing about this entrance wound in the throat. Dr. Canada said that "we were aware from telephone calls to Dallas and from news reports that the president had an entrance wound in the throat, but we could not write that in the official protocol because it would have proven the existence of a gunman firing from the front."[10]

All three pathologists tried to find the track of the bullet that struck the president in the back. In addition to metal probes, they actually stuck their fingers into that wound, to no avail. The insertion of their fingers into the wound clearly and convincingly demonstrates their gross incompetence to perform the postmortem examination of the century. All they felt was the end of the opening about one to two inches into the body. The confusion was best summarized in the Warren Commission testimony of Secret Service agent Roy Kellerman, who recalled asking Dr. Pierre Finck during the autopsy where the bullet had gone. Finck responded, "There are no lanes for an outlet of this entry in this man's shoulder." FBI agents James Sibert and Francis O'Neill also summarized the confusion in their report on the autopsy. After noting that Dr. Humes had probed the wound with his finger and had the audacity, based solely on sticking his finger into the hole, to estimate the angle of the bullet path as downward between 45 and 60 degrees, Sibert and O'Neill stated that "inasmuch as . . . no complete bullet could be located in the back or any other area of the body," Humes, Boswell, and Finck found themselves "at a loss to explain why they could find no bullets." Shortly after, Humes was informed that a bullet had been found on a stretcher at Parkland Hospital. He then concluded that the bullet that entered Kennedy's back "had worked its way out of the body during external cardiac massage," falling onto his stretcher. This is what Humes wrote in his original autopsy report and what everyone present at the autopsy believed. Press accounts based on sources present at the autopsy reported that a bullet had lodged in the president's back or shoulder and had not exited. In short, there was no exit wound in the throat.[11]

On Sunday, November 24, Dr. Humes learned that Jack Ruby had shot and killed Lee Harvey Oswald, thus negating the necessity of a trial. Therefore, undoubtedly acting on instructions from superiors, Humes burned the original autopsy protocol, together with notes he made at the autopsy, in his fireplace, then wrote an entirely new report. The date of the new report cannot be ascertained because the official autopsy protocol is undated. It appears from contemporaneous accounts that the autopsy report published in the Warren Report was probably written several months after the assassination to conform to the single bullet theory. As many researchers, including Sylvia Meagher, have noted, press accounts based on information from sources at the autopsy continued to mention that a bullet had entered the president's back and had penetrated only an inch or two without exiting long after the autopsy had ended. For example, as late as January 26, 1964, more than two months after the autopsy, the *New York Times* stated that a bullet had entered the upper back and lodged in the right shoulder. Therefore, it appears that the revised autopsy report was written around February to conform to the single-bullet theory.[12]

No such confusion existed about Governor Connally's wounds because the Parkland medical reports were quite clear. In addition, the physicians who operated on Connally gave convincing testimony both times they testified before the Warren Commission. A bullet struck Connally in the upper right side of his back midway between the right shoulder blade and the right armpit. It traveled downward through his chest at an angle of approximately twenty-five degrees and exited from the chest just below the right nipple. Because it penetrated into the back at a sharp downward angle, the bullet left a vertically elongated wound of entrance, 1.5 centimeters (0.6 inches) in diameter. According to Dr. Robert Shaw, the thoracic surgeon who operated on the governor's back/chest wound, the bullet that caused the wound had not previously struck any other objects and left a normal wound of entrance with an abrasion collar of bruising around the edges. In several interviews, Dr. Shaw emphatically asserted that the bullet that entered Governor Connally's back had not previously gone through President Kennedy's neck. It should be noted that Dr. Shaw was a board-certified thoracic surgeon who had served as the chief of the U.S. Army's thoracic surgery unit in France during World War II, during which service he had operated on more than a thousand gunshot and shrapnel wounds of the chest. In addition, Dr. Shaw had treated hundreds of gunshot wounds of the chest during his service at Parkland Hospital. Dr. Shaw also definitively refuted the claims of lone assassin theorists that the bullet that entered Connally's back left a 3.0-centimeter (1.2 inch) elongated hole because it had tumbled after leaving Kennedy's neck and struck Connally's back with its full length. Shaw emphatically rejected that assertion, stating that the original entry wound in Connally's shoulder was 1.5 centimeters long. He extended it to 3.0 centimeters only after debriding the wound.[13]

Long after the autopsy had ended, government officials believed that Kennedy and Connally were struck by separate bullets. The official FBI report on the assassination, released to the public on December 5, 1963, concluded that the first shot struck the president, and that the second shot struck the governor. In a meeting of the Warren Commission on January 27, 1964, more than two months after the assassination, chief counsel J. Lee Rankin told the commission members that "there is a great range of material in regard to the wounds, the autopsy and this point of exit or entrance in the front of the neck, and all that has to be developed much more than we have at the present time." On

April 30, 1964, more than five months after the assassination, junior counsel Arlen Specter wrote to J. Lee Rankin that "the Commission should determine with certainty that the shots came from the rear" and that "the Commission should determine with certainty that the shots came from above." Defenders of the Warren Commission commonly gloss over this compelling documentary proof that the autopsy completely failed to resolve any of the mysteries surrounding the controversy about the wounds on President Kennedy.[14]

The condition of Bullet 399 also belies the single bullet theory. This bullet, which, according to the official version, penetrated through Kennedy's neck, exited from his throat, then proceeded to enter Connally's back, shattering his fifth rib, penetrating his wrist, breaking the radius, then entering his left thigh, emerged slightly flattened along its side with a tiny bit of lead protruding from the base. The markings on its exterior surface, the lands and grooves etched on the copper jacket as it coursed through the barrel of Oswald's rifle, are completely intact. In interviews with me, countless military veterans, law enforcement officers, hunters, and physicians have vehemently denied that a bullet could cause this much damage and emerge in nearly pristine condition. The world-renowned wounds ballistics authority, Dr. Joseph Dolce, who observed the tests performed with Oswald's rifle on human cadavers and animal carcasses, has stated that Bullet 399 could not possibly have caused the damage that lone assassin theorists claim it caused. Dolce refuted a principal argument of the lone assassin defenders that by the time the bullet struck Connally's rib and wrist bone, it had lost a considerable amount of its initial velocity, thereby allowing it to inflict the damage without suffering any mutilation. Dolce specifically stated that in the tests with Oswald's rifle at Aberdeen Proving Grounds, which he supervised, shots were fired at both high and low velocities, and "in every instance," the bullets that broke bones wound up badly flattened and misshapen. It should be noted that these tests were the only ones ever performed with Oswald's rifle. Dolce stated that even if the bullet had gone through Kennedy's neck first, it could not possibly have lost as much velocity as lone assassin theorists claim. "That bullet [Bullet 399] positively did not cause Governor Connally's wounds," he exclaimed. Dr. Robert Shaw agreed. Shaw emphatically stated that in his extensive career as a surgeon, including his wartime experience, he "never saw a bullet cause as much damage as this one and remain in pristine condition."[15]

The Head Shot: The Conspiracy Perspective

The most graphic and unforgettable scene in the Zapruder film comes at frame Z313, when the right front side of John Kennedy's head explodes in a burst of red and orange. In the ensuing eight frames, or slightly less than a half second in time, the president flies violently backward and leftward until he slams against the back of the rear seat of the limousine. To almost everyone who views the film, it appears obvious that Kennedy was struck by a shot fired from the front, the impact of which caused him to fly backward. This backward movement has posed formidable problems for defenders of the Warren Commission's lone gunman thesis because they became obligated to explain how a shot fired from behind could cause Kennedy to fall backward. The commission resolved the problem by ignoring the backward motion, but other lone assassin theorists have used such explanations as the jet effect or a neuromuscular reaction.

Persons who have witnessed other people shot in the head have unanimously agreed that the Zapruder film depicts a shot fired from the front of Kennedy. Henry Morris, the former superintendent of the New Orleans police department, twice wounded in the line of duty and a war veteran, stated emphatically that "there's no way that shot [frame Z313] could have come from behind." Dr. William Eckert, a prominent forensic pathologist, said the same. Sidney Johnston, who served in combat in Vietnam and who tested many weapons for the Special Forces, said that the backward and leftward motion of Kennedy's head "proved that the shot came from the right front, i.e., the Grassy Knoll." Actual cases of gunshot wounds to the head confirm these observations. After a .30-caliber bullet exploded against his right jaw, Dr. Martin Luther King fell flat on his back. This bullet disintegrated as it drove through King's neck and inflicted far more damage to the central nervous system than did the bullet that struck Kennedy in the head, yet the shot did not cause a neuromuscular reaction. The famous Eddie Adams photographs of a Viet Cong prisoner shot in the head by South Vietnamese brigadier general Nguyen Ngoc Loan show the prisoner falling in the same direction that the bullet traveled. The film of the same execution depicts it even more graphically. Loan's pistol aims at the prisoner's right temple, Loan squeezes the trigger, and as the bullet exits from the left temple, he falls dead to his left. Videos of a police shootout with two bank robbers in North Hollywood, California, in 1997 clearly depict one of the robbers falling in the same direction as the bullet that struck him in the head.[16]

Both police officers riding motorcycles to the left rear of the president, the rear of the back seat, and Kennedy's shirt and suit jacket were splattered with blood and brain tissue. Graphic photographs of the president's clothing reveal the far greater extent of blood on the rear than on the front of the garments. The piece of Kennedy's skull that Billy Harper found approximately thirty feet to the left rear of the limousine also provides a grisly piece of evidence of a front-entering, rear-exiting shot. Some conspiracy theorists claim that because the Zapruder film depicts no damage to the back of Kennedy's head, no bullet exited there. However, this argument is refuted by the fact that the film depicts no damage to the throat or the upper back/shoulder area, and no one disputes that JFK was hit in those areas. David Mantik and Charles Wilber, two medical authorities who support the conspiracy theory, assert that Kennedy's backward head movement was too great for it to have been caused by a 6.5-millimeter bullet fired from a rifle with a muzzle velocity of about 2,000 feet per second. In reality, Kennedy was probably struck in the right temple area by a bullet of larger caliber and fired from a much more powerful weapon than the Mannlicher-Carcano. The increase in muzzle velocity—anywhere from 3,000 to 4,000 feet per second—would have increased the kinetic energy and the resulting impact by geometrically higher levels, explaining the rapid backward head movement.[17]

Every physician and nurse at Parkland Hospital who examined the president's head wounds described a large wound in the right rear of the head. In other words, they described a bullet wound of exit in the back of the head, which meant that the bullet came from in front of Kennedy because he faced forward. In their original descriptions of the wound in Kennedy's head, Drs. Malcolm Perry, James Carrico, Robert McClelland, Paul Peters, Ronald Jones, and others clearly described a large wound of exit in the occipital region. In addition, they observed both cerebral and cerebellar tissue oozing from the wound. Nurses Patricia Hutton, Diana Bowron, Audrey Bell, and other medical personnel also gave a similar description of an exit wound in the back of the head. Virtually everyone present at the autopsy saw the same thing. Drs. Robert Canada and Calvin Galloway, and medical technicians James Jenkins, Paul O'Connor, and Jan Rudnicki gave the same account: President Kennedy had a large exit wound in the back of his head. These accounts by trained medical observers provide powerful evidence of a front-entering shot that exploded out the back of the president's head.[18]

Oswald's Guilt: The Conspiracy Perspective

Conspiracy theorists insist that there exist serious questions about whether Lee Harvey Oswald fired any shots in the assassination. The Warren Commission's assertion that the rifle found on the sixth floor of the Depository building was owned by and in the possession of Oswald simply does not accord with the known facts. FBI-questioned documents examiners claimed that Oswald purchased the 6.5-millimeter Mannlicher-Carcano rifle via mail order from Klein's Sporting Goods of Chicago in March 1963. Various documents, such as the application for the Dallas post office box where the rifle was shipped, the money order used to pay for the rifle, and the order blank from the *American Rifleman* magazine supposedly reflected Oswald's handwriting. Neither the FBI nor the Warren Commission explored the possibility of forgery. The forging of the autobiography of Howard Hughes by Clifford Irving, the Hitler diaries hoax, and the countless forgeries made by Mark Hoffman, all of them positively authenticated by prominent questioned documents and handwriting experts and all committed after the Kennedy assassination, attest to the uncertainty of this "science." The photographs of Oswald standing in the backyard of his Dallas apartment, depicting him holding the rifle, even if genuine, prove only that he possessed a rifle in April, seven months before the assassination. The assertion that Oswald possessed the rifle is refuted by the evidence of the Warren Commission itself. The commission claims that the rifle was stored in a blanket in Ruth Paine's garage until Oswald retrieved it the night before the assassination. Therefore, he did not possess the rifle until eighteen hours before he allegedly fired it.[19]

The argument that Oswald carried the rifle into the Depository building the morning of the assassination bears no relation to the facts. Only two people, Buell Wesley Frazier and his sister, Linnie Mae Randall, saw Oswald with a package the morning of November 22, and both testified that they saw him carry a package that could not possibly have contained the rifle. Gus Russo speculates that Oswald may have hidden the rifle in the building at a previous time, but he provides no evidence on how he carried it all the way from Irving to downtown Dallas without being seen. Another argument—that Oswald was present at the sixth-floor southeast corner window of the Depository building at the time of the assassination—has only one piece of corroboration: the flimsy, speculative, and contradictory testimony of Howard Brennan. Brennan claimed that he saw Oswald appear at the window, then withdraw from it, several times in the seven minutes prior to the gunfire. He also testified that he saw Oswald fire the last shot. No other witness saw Oswald anywhere at the time of the assassination. As critics have often pointed out, Brennan failed to pick Oswald from a police lineup the evening of the assassination as the man he saw fire the shot. Two weeks later, he changed his mind and told the FBI that Oswald was indeed the man he saw. Three weeks after that, he changed his mind and withdrew his identification of Oswald. Two months later, he again said that the man was Oswald. Although even the Warren Commission admitted that anyone firing from the half-open window must have been either sitting or kneeling, Brennan claims that he saw Oswald performing duck walks in the moments before the motorcade's arrival. In a court of law, as Brennan himself admitted, a competent defense attorney would have demolished his testimony. The existence of three of Lee Harvey Oswald's prints on two of the nineteen book cartons within a six-foot radius of the southeast corner window provides another reason for the Warren Commission's claim that he was present "at the window from which the shots were fired." The fact that Oswald worked in the Depository building and specifically needed to go to the sixth floor to pick up book cartons did not deter the commission from attaching "probative value" to this finding of his prints.

Only one of the three prints was fresher than twenty-four hours old, and the fact that nineteen prints of Dallas law enforcement officers were recovered from the same boxes renders any inference to this case impossible.[20]

At a maximum time of ninety seconds after the assassination, two persons, a Dallas police officer, Marrion Baker, and the superintendent of the Depository building, Roy Truly, saw Lee Harvey Oswald in a second-floor lunchroom standing in front of a soft drink machine. If Oswald fired the shots, then he would have had to slowly withdraw the rifle from the window, wipe his prints off its outer surface, squeeze between six-foot-tall stacks of fifty-five-pound book cartons, walk along the corridor across to the northwest corner, squeeze between another equally tall and heavy stack of boxes, carefully lay the rifle on the floor, slide out from the boxes, return them to their original position, walk down four flights of stairs, enter the second-floor lunchroom, and walk over to the soft drink machine—all within a space of less than one and a half minutes. He also had to accomplish this feat without exhibiting signs of breathlessness, agitation, apprehension, or any other physical or psychological emotion. Both Baker and Truly testified that when they confronted Oswald in the lunchroom, he was not out of breath, did not appear startled or afraid, and in fact, seemed perfectly normal and composed. Both men reconstructed their movements, and the longest time it took them to reach the second-floor lunchroom was one minute, thirty seconds.[21]

Oswald's "escape" from the Depository consisted of walking "at a very slow pace" toward the stairs leading to the front entrance on Old Elm Street because these were his pace and direction when Geraldine Reid saw him near her second-floor desk two minutes after the assassination. The official account then has him departing from the front entrance, stopping to chivalrously give directions to a pay phone to a reporter, then walking seven blocks down Elm Street to catch a bus headed right back toward Dealey Plaza. As Mark Lane observed, it may or may not be apocryphal that a murderer returns to the scene of the crime, but usually the interval is longer than ten minutes. The only witness to place Oswald on the bus, Mary Bledsoe, proved so hostile and belligerent toward Oswald that she could hardly be deemed credible. Bledsoe, who still owed Oswald two dollars' back rent on a room that she had rented him, stated that Oswald looked "so distorted in his face," quite the opposite of the calm expressions observed by Baker, Truly, and Reid. A bus transfer allegedly found in Oswald's shirt pocket also proved his presence on the bus. Yet Oswald changed his shirt after he went to his rooming house after the bus ride. The official version, as Walt Brown pointed out, would have us believe that Oswald transferred the transfer from one shirt to another without putting the slightest crease in it.[22]

At about 12:44 P.M., Oswald supposedly departed the bus, walked four blocks to a Greyhound bus station, and caught a taxi driven by a man named William Whaley at 12:48. Whaley's log book reveals him picking up a passenger at the bus terminal at 12:30, a time that the Warren Commission said was inaccurate, because Oswald was shooting JFK at 12:30. Whaley said that Oswald wore either a gray jacket, a blue jacket, or both jackets. The commission decided that he wore no jacket because Mary Bledsoe claimed to have seen a hole in the elbow of Oswald's shirt on the bus, an impossibility if he wore a jacket. Whaley said that it took him at least nine minutes to drive Oswald to either the 500 or the 700 block of North Beckley Avenue, near his rooming house. Whaley identified Oswald at a police lineup on the afternoon of November 23. According to Whaley, the lineup was so stacked that "you could have picked him out without identifying him." No independent evidence exists to verify or refute Whaley's account. Neither the Dallas police nor the FBI bothered to dust Whaley's cab for prints for possible corroboration.[23]

The Warren Commission faced a formidable obstacle to its lone assassin thesis when it confronted the account of Dallas Deputy Sheriff Roger Craig. At about 12:45 P.M., or fifteen minutes after the assassination, Craig stood on the median between Elm and Main Streets. He saw a man run from behind the Book Depository building, race down the grassy incline to the street, and enter a Rambler station wagon driven by a dark-complected man. Before Craig could stop the vehicle, it continued west on Elm Street, under the underpass, then away from the plaza. Later that afternoon, at Dallas police headquarters, Craig entered the Homicide Bureau office of Captain Will Fritz, who was interrogating Lee Harvey Oswald. Spotting Oswald, Craig identified him to Fritz as the man he saw run from the Depository building and get into the station wagon. According to Craig, Oswald then stood up and exclaimed, "Everybody will know who I am now!" Obviously, if Craig's story had credibility, the commission would have been compelled to conclude that he had at least one accomplice, thereby opening up the undesirable reality of a conspiracy.[24]

The evidence strongly supports Craig's story. A professional law enforcement officer, Roger Craig had received training in observing people and objects, especially at the scene of a crime. Photographs taken in Dealey Plaza at 12:45 depict a Rambler station wagon headed west on Elm Street, just as Craig had stated. Another photograph depicts Deputy Craig in the homicide bureau office on the afternoon of November 22. Captain Fritz himself verified Craig's account of telling him that Oswald ran from the building and got into the station wagon, although Fritz did not recall Oswald's dramatic statement after arising from his chair. No evidence of any kind supports William Whaley's story of the taxi ride, especially because the authorities did not dust the cab for prints. The issue can never be resolved, but it provides a telling commentary on the Warren Commission's bias that it would give credence to Whaley's story while ignoring that of a trained law enforcement officer.[25]

The next sighting of Oswald took place shortly after one o'clock. Earline Roberts, the housekeeper at a rooming house at 1026 North Beckley Avenue, where Oswald rented a room, saw Oswald enter the house and go upstairs to his room. While Oswald was in his room, Roberts heard the honking of a horn and peeked out the window to see who had beeped the horn. She saw a Dallas police car parked in front of the rooming house, and she believed that it had the number "107" or "207" emblazoned on its side. A minute or so later, Roberts peeked outside, and the police car had left. Another minute or so later, she saw Oswald, wearing a jacket, leave the rooming house. Shortly afterward, Roberts again peeked out the window and saw Oswald standing in front of the house near a bus stop. About a minute later, the nosy Roberts peeked out again and saw that Oswald had left. Roberts's testimony disturbed the Warren Commission almost as much as did Roger Craig's. If indeed a Dallas police car had parked in front of the rooming house and beeped its horn while Oswald was there, the commission would be forced to give weight to a possible connection between Oswald and a member of the police department. After a perfunctory investigation established that cars numbered "107" and "207" were elsewhere at the time, the commission concluded that Roberts's testimony regarding the police car was mistaken. Interestingly, the commission gave full credence to Roberts's story about seeing Oswald enter the rooming house, then leave it a few minutes later.[26]

The Tippitt Killing: The Conspiracy Perspective

The next sighting of Lee Oswald took place at about the 700 block of North Beckley, when Elcan Elliott reportedly saw Oswald urinate in some bushes, without trying to hide. Elliott then followed the man and saw him wandering aimlessly, reversing direction several times and appearing disoriented. This story, which Elliott related to Gus Russo in 1994, hardly accords with the actions of the calm, collected man that Baker and Truly observed only a minute and a half after the assassination. If Oswald were disoriented, then lone assassin theorists have a difficult time explaining his presence on Lancaster Road. Supposedly, he wanted to catch a bus to the Texas-Mexico border, but no evidence exists to verify this speculation, especially because Oswald did not stay on Lancaster, but appeared on Tenth Street. This also conflicts with Oswald's presumptive timetable. According to the official version, Oswald left the rooming house on North Beckley at 1:04 or 1:05, then appeared on Tenth Street near Patton Avenue, nine-tenths of a mile away, at 1:15. This would necessitate him traveling nearly a mile on foot in ten or eleven minutes, an easy physical feat for a healthy twenty-four-year-old. However, if he stopped to urinate in bushes, then reversed his direction several times, as Gus Russo and Dale Meyers claim, these actions must be added to his time.[27]

Lone assassin theorists, of course, claim that Oswald murdered Dallas police officer J. D. Tippit. The emergency call to the police dispatcher about the shooting occurred at 1:16. It was made by T. F. Bowley, who used Tippit's police radio. Originally, Domingo Benavides tried to use the radio, but he did not know how, so Bowley made the call. But Benavides testified that after he saw a man shoot Tippit, he sat in his truck for "a few minutes" to make sure the killer had actually fled the scene. Only then did he get out of his truck and come to the aid of the fallen officer. When Bowley arrived at the scene, Tippit was already lying in a pool of blood next to his vehicle. It is obvious from the accounts of these two witnesses that the actual murder took place at least three minutes before the call to the dispatcher. This would require Oswald arriving at the scene at 1:13, or only eight minutes after he left his rooming house. To travel nine-tenths of a mile on foot in eight minutes demands running, or jogging at a fast pace. Yet the Warren Commission's star witness, Helen Markham, testified that the killer was leisurely strolling east on Tenth Street when Tippit stopped him.[28]

The evidence regarding the Tippit killing hardly implicates Lee Harvey Oswald as the perpetrator. The witnesses gave inconsistent and contradictory accounts. Helen Markham, for example, stated that she saw Oswald shoot Tippit across the hood of the police car, then run back toward Patton Avenue. Domingo Benavides saw a man shoot Tippit, but his recollection of the physical characteristics of the killer proved so hazy that the police did not even bother to have him view a lineup. Jack Tatum claimed that he saw Oswald administer the coup de grâce to the fallen officer by walking up to him and firing a shot into his head at point-blank range. No one else recalled such a dramatic incident. Apparently the police placed little credence in Tatum's story, for they did not even ask him to appear as a witness. Other witnesses, such as Mr. and Mrs. Frank Wright and Acquilla Clemmons, saw two men at the scene. Of all the people who heard shots fired, only Ted Callaway claimed to have heard five. Helen Markham stated that after the shooting, she, the only person to rush to the aid of the mortally wounded policeman, ran to Officer Tippit, cradled his head in her arms, and comforted him for twenty minutes before he died. Her account is a sheer fabrication, for the evidence proves conclusively that Tippit died instantly, that numerous people gathered at the scene within seconds after the shots, and that the ambulance arrived only three minutes later.[29]

The ballistics evidence contains equally contradictory aspects. Spectators recovered four cartridge cases near the crime scene. Not one was photographed in place, marked with the identifying initials of the law enforcement officers to whom they were given, nor in any other manner handled to connect them with the crime. They could not have been introduced as evidence in court. Four cartridge cases that allegedly were found at the crime scene appeared at police headquarters and were turned over to the FBI for ballistics testing. The tests proved that they came from Oswald's revolver, but again, there is no evidence to track them back to the crime scene. All four of the bullets recovered from Officer Tippit's body were too mutilated to ballistically match them to a particular weapon, although they were .38 caliber, the same as Oswald's Smith and Wesson revolver. Because Oswald's revolver had an oversized barrel, test bullets fired from it for ballistics purposes did not even match each other. Three of those bullets were of Winchester-Western manufacture, and one was Remington-Peters. Two of the cartridge cases were Winchester-Western, and two were Remington-Peters. No one has ever given a plausible explanation for this anomaly. The lone assassin theorists also make the ridiculous assertion that after shooting Tippit, Oswald, in a civic-minded attempt to leave incriminating evidence behind him, stopped, in full view of witnesses, opened the firing chamber of his revolver, manually ejected four empty cartridge cases from it, and gratuitously dropped them on the grass. It should be obvious that a competent defense attorney would easily have persuaded the presiding judge in a trial to reject most of the ballistics evidence in this case.[30]

Lone assassin theorists have offered no serious explanation for the presence of Officer Tippit near the intersection of Tenth and Patton at that time. Tippit received explicit instructions to patrol his assigned district, not the district in which he was killed. Nor can lone assassin theorists provide a credible explanation for Tippit's stopping Oswald. The Warren Commission said that because Oswald fit the description of the man wanted in the Kennedy assassination, Tippit stopped him. But the description—that of a white man of slender build, five feet, ten inches tall, and weighing one hundred sixty-five pounds—fit that of the average American man. Gus Russo and Dale Meyers speculate that Oswald had been headed west on Tenth Street, but reversed direction when he saw the police car, thereby calling attention to himself. In reality, virtually all those who saw Oswald near the scene of the crime stated that he headed east, and if he had indeed been heading west, additional time would have to be added to allow him to arrive at the scene in time for the murder. Oswald supposedly escaped by first discarding his jacket to leave yet another clue, eventually running to Jefferson Boulevard, the busiest thoroughfare in the area, then ducking into the lobby of a shoe store, then entering a movie theater without paying. It seems that he deliberately tried to call attention to himself, rather than trying to make a reasonable effort to escape.[31]

Oswald's motive for killing Kennedy remains one of the unknowns in this mystery. The Warren Commission asserted that Oswald had political motivation because of his strong endorsement of the communist system of government in the Soviet Union and his public support for Fidel Castro's regime in Cuba. Yet this hardly accords with Oswald's alleged attempt to murder Major General Edwin A. Walker in April 1963. Walker, an extreme right-wing fanatic, was on the opposite end of the political spectrum from John Kennedy, a liberal Democrat. The speculation offered by Gerald Posner that Oswald killed Kennedy to call attention to himself by eliminating the titular head of the society that had rejected him remains just that—speculation. Lee Harvey Oswald was one of countless misfits in American society at the time. None of the others made any serious attempt to attract publicity by assassinating the president.

As other chapters will discuss in detail, Fidel Castro, anti-Castro Cuban exiles, and organized crime all possessed not only the motive, but also the means for eliminating John Kennedy. By focusing exclusively on Lee Harvey Oswald, the Warren Commission allowed the opportunity to investigate these and other possible suspects to elapse. In its chapter on possible conspiracy, the Warren Report deals with Oswald and ignores the others. In a few pages, it dismisses the rumors of Jack Ruby's involvement with others in his slaying of Oswald. The House Select Committee on assassination, on the other hand, devoted considerable attention to an assassination conspiracy and even named Carlos Marcello, Santos Trafficante, and certain anti-Castro Cubans as primary suspects.

A final aspect of the case for conspiracy lies within a simple question. If Oswald did it all by himself, with no conspiracy, why was there a massive cover-up of the evidence? Newly released documents from the inquiry by the ARRB reveal that a deliberate, concerted effort to suppress the truth occurred. Documents were altered, such as Gerald

Ford's raising the actual location of the wound in Kennedy's back to his neck so it would fit the single bullet trajectory. Material evidence, such as John Kennedy's brain, was either destroyed or simply disappeared. Critical witnesses, such as Jack Ruby, were not allowed to testify. Autopsy photographs and x-rays, as well as other vital medical evidence, were suppressed or even altered. The Secret Service, the FBI, and the CIA all withheld hundreds of thousands of crucial materials from the public record. All this smacks of a concerted effort by various agencies of the federal government to conceal the truth about the assassination. None of this would have been necessary if it indeed had resulted from the action of a deranged, misguided social misfit.

5

Consensus: The Facts

Although the title of this chapter contains the word consensus, I doubt that anything approaching a consensus will ever be reached regarding the Kennedy assassination. The divisions between the lone assassin and conspiracy theorists remain so embroiled in both personal and professional disputes that it appears unlikely that any effort to offer an objective analysis of the basic facts of the assassination will satisfy either of the two sides. Nevertheless, history demands that the effort be made. Every previous study of John Kennedy's murder, including the one that I wrote more than twenty years ago, has fallen into either the "Oswald did it alone" category or that of multiple gunmen. For the first time, in this chapter, I shall look at certain aspects of the physical, scientific, medical, and ballistics evidence and examine them from an unbiased perspective. I shall do so by formulating certain questions and attempting to provide answers to them.

Is the Zapruder Film Authentic?

Yes.

Most Kennedy assassination researchers would agree that the Zapruder film constitutes the single most important piece of evidence in the entire case. Standing in precisely the right place to capture through his zoom lens the presidential limousine and its occupants throughout the shooting sequence and its horrifying aftermath, Abraham Zapruder instantly realized that his camera had recorded the murder of a president of the United States in graphic detail. Zapruder also quickly comprehended both the historical, evidentiary value of the film as well as its potential for making a lot of money. Therefore, immediately after the assassination, the Dallas clothing manufacturer hurried to two photographic laboratories to have the film developed and processed. After providing the Secret Service with a copy, Zapruder retained the original—the "out of camera" copy—and another first-generation copy for himself. Two days later, he would sell the original to Time-Life Incorporated for a total payment of $150,000 over six years.[1]

Although a few selected frames from the film were published in the Warren Report and in postassassination issues of *Life* magazine, the actual film remained unavailable to the public until New Orleans district attorney Jim Garrison subpoenaed it from the publishing company for showing at the 1969 trial of Clay Shaw. Garrison allowed bootleg copies to be made, and these were circulated among the research community for several years. In 1975, Robert Groden, a photographic analyst who had obtained a copy of the film, showed it on national television, and for the first time, the public could visualize the actual shooting sequence. The film shows President Kennedy and Governor Connally smiling and waving to the sparse crowd of spectators in Dealey Plaza as the limousine approached a street sign that briefly obscured it from the camera lens. As the limousine emerges from behind the sign, Kennedy reacts to the first shot by grimacing in pain and splaying his hands up toward his face. Three-quarters of a second later, Connally reacts to being struck by an apparent second shot by slumping his right shoulder sharply downward, with his right cheek filling with air and his hair standing up on his head. About seventy-five frames (four seconds) later, the right front side of Kennedy's head explodes in a burst of red and orange, and he flies violently backward and leftward until his head bounces off the rear seat a half second later. The film then depicts Jacqueline Kennedy desperately climbing onto the vehicle's trunk as Secret Service agent Clint Hill jumps onto the trunk from behind.[2]

The Zapruder film provides powerful visual evidence of an assassination conspiracy. It records the first two shots that struck Kennedy and Connally as having been fired too quickly to have both come from Lee Harvey Oswald's bolt action rifle. It also portrays Kennedy's violent backward and leftward movement in response to the head shot, a seemingly convincing visual evidence of a shot fired from the right front. Both of these topics will be treated later. For many years, hardly anyone questioned the film's authenticity. But in the late 1980s and early 1990s, certain students of the assassination, all of them conspiracy theorists, began to cast doubt on the film. In the late 1990s and early 2000s, many others joined the chorus of doubters. Among those who have questioned the genuineness of the Zapruder film are Harry Livingstone, David Lifton, David Mantik, James Fetzer, and Jack White. These researchers claim that the film contains so many anomalies, comes in so many differing versions, and leaves such a questionable "chain of evidence" that one can only conclude that the version commonly seen today is a fake.[3]

Proponents of the forgery thesis claim first of all that none of the eyewitnesses to the assassination saw Kennedy's head thrust backward and to the left after the fatal head shot, as the film depicts. In addition, several dozen witnesses saw the limousine come to a complete stop just before the first shot, but the film shows no such stoppage. The Zapruder film shows no damage to the back of Kennedy's head or to the back of his suit jacket, but virtually all of the medical witnesses, as well as law enforcement personnel, who saw the president's head at Parkland Hospital recalled a large, gaping wound in the rear, and photographs graphically reveal a huge bloodstain covering nearly three-quarters of the back of Kennedy's shirt and suit jacket. Second, forgery advocates assert that meticulous comparison of Zapruder film footage with countless other films and photographs of the assassination reveal startling discrepancies. Third, they maintain that the original film contained such incontrovertible evidence of a conspiracy that the CIA's National Photographic Center altered it to make it conform to the official lone assassin version. Finally, they contend that together with countless other pieces of evidence in this case, the "out-of-camera" original has disappeared, as has one of the first-generation copies, providing powerful evidence of an official cover-up.[4]

Among the most persuasive proponents of the authenticity of the Zapruder film are Josiah Thompson, Clint Bradford, and David Wrone. They argue first that the chain of evidence of possession of the film is airtight. From the moment he took the film, through the two processings, through his sale to Time-Life, Abraham Zapruder had the film in his possession at all times. It could not have been altered. Second, they claim that eyewitnesses are often mistaken. Many witnesses in Dealey Plaza, for example, gave faulty and contradictory accounts of what happened. The fact that some witnesses say the limousine came to a halt does not mean that it actually happened. Third, they assert that the photographic evidence is far more accurate and reliable than that of witnesses. The film depicts no large wound in the back of Kennedy's head, nor do any of the autopsy photographs. Finally, the Zapruder film has positively been authenticated by a thorough, painstaking examination by Roland J. Zavada, one of the world's leading experts in film production. Hired by his former employer, Kodak, to test the film for the Assassination Records Review Board (ARRB), Zavada concluded that its authenticity remains beyond dispute.[5]

Although I have great respect for the work of such forgery advocates as David Mantik, I must agree with the proponents of the Zapruder film's authenticity. I am persuaded first and foremost by the work of Roland Zavada, who has destroyed every argument made by the forgery theorists. His painstakingly detailed report confirms that the film contains no evidence of alteration, nor does it depict photographic anomalies that cannot be explained. Second, I cannot comprehend how certain government officials, say from the CIA, would alter the original film and release one that contains such graphic evidence of a conspiracy. Although Mantik and others claim that the backward head movement depicted in the film does not provide evidence of a shot fired from the right front, the vast majority of researchers argue to the contrary. Even more striking, the Zapruder film clearly shows President Kennedy struck by the first shot, then Governor Connally struck by the second, fired no more than 1.6 seconds later. Because Oswald's rifle could not be fired twice in less than 2.25 seconds, even without aiming, the film offers a graphic visual confirmation of two different assassins located behind the limousine. Any effort by nameless government officials to alter the film to conceal evidence of a conspiracy would hardly have resulted in the extant version. Finally, David Wrone's lengthy and exhaustive study of the history of the Zapruder film argues persuasively for its authenticity.[6]

Was President Kennedy Shot from the Front?

Yes.

This second question raises one of the most fundamental issues in the entire assassination controversy. Everyone agrees that both President Kennedy and Governor Connally were shot from behind. Yet vehement disagreements have been raised over the question of whether one or more shots came from the front. Lone assassin theorists argue first that the autopsy photographs and x-rays prove beyond dispute that all shots came from behind. Photographs of the back of Kennedy's head clearly reveal no massive, gaping wound of exit, as conspiracy theorists claim exists. The only wound visible in the back of the head is a small, oval wound of entrance near the cowlick. The photographs of the front of the president's throat likewise reveal a large wound of exit and no entrance wound, as posited by the conspiracy theorists. The x-rays also depict no exit wounds in the rear of the president's head or body. Lone assassin theorists have defied conspiracy advocates to produce one photograph or x-ray containing evidence of a shot from the front, and their challenge has not been met.[7]

Further evidence that the president and governor were shot only from behind comes from the detailed analyses and sworn testimony of numerous experts in forensic pathology, wounds ballistics, and similar specialties. These include such world-renowned authorities as Michael Baden, Marvin Fackler, Thomas Weston, and Vincent DiMaio. Furthermore, a substantial majority of the physicians at Dallas's Parkland Hospital have testified under oath and have stated on countless occasions that the Warren Commission's conclusion that President Kennedy was shot only from behind accords perfectly with their observations of the president's wounds in Trauma Room One. These include Drs. Malcolm Perry and Charles Carrico, and Marion Jenkins, Paul Peters, and others. Most recently, Dr. Robert Grossman, a neurosurgeon present in Trauma Room One, has publicly stated that his observations of Kennedy's head wound led him to conclude that Kennedy was hit by a shot fired from behind. No one, regardless of his position regarding an assassination conspiracy, has ever argued that Governor Connally's wounds came from anywhere except from behind him.[8]

Both the FBI and the Warren Commission found that President Kennedy's clothes contained evidence of rear-entering shots. The back of Kennedy's shirt and suit jacket had bullet wounds of entrance. The front of the collar, at the level of the tie knot, had holes that the FBI determined were exit holes. Two large bullet fragments were found on the front seat of the limousine, where they wound up after they exited the front side of the president's head. The backward movement of Kennedy's head, so evident on the Zapruder film, does not provide evidence of a shot from the front. Kennedy's head moved backward either from a neuromuscular reaction caused by the bullet destroying that part of his brain which controlled the central nervous system, or from a jet effect in which the head jerked backward because of the force emitted by the spray of blood and brain tissue out of the exit wound in the right front of the head.[9]

Conspiracy theorists disagree. They argue first that all of the medical personnel at Parkland and Bethesda who viewed Kennedy's corpse originally reported that he had a large exit wound in the back of his head. These include neurosurgeon Kemp Clark, surgeons Malcolm Perry, Ronald Jones, and Robert McClelland, and many others. Their descriptions of Kennedy's head wound, made contemporaneously, unanimously place a large wound in the occipital region, indicating a wound of exit in the rear of the head. Not one physician who viewed Kennedy's corpse on November 22, 1963, before the autopsy observed a wound of entrance in the back of the head. Even the official autopsy report, written at least two days after the assassination, did not claim incontrovertible evidence of a shot entering the rear of the president's head. The best that this document could do was to call the wound in the lower portion of the back of the head "presumably of entry."[10]

In a very similar manner, all Dallas medical personnel observed a tiny wound of entrance in Kennedy's throat. Drs. Malcolm Perry and James Carrico, for example, observed a small, four-by-six-millimeter entrance wound located just below the thyroid cartilage. Other doctors and nurses reported the same. At a press conference held an hour and a half after the shooting, Dr. Perry told the reporters that "there was an entrance wound in the neck." Kennedy's shirt appears to confirm these observations. Two slits are evident in the front of the collar—slits that could only have come from an entering bullet rather than an exiting one because they contain openings nowhere nearly as large as the gaping throat wound shown in the autopsy photographs. Contemporary notes made at Parkland by medical personnel reflect a unanimous opinion that the wound in Kennedy's throat was one of entrance.[11]

The backward and leftward movement of Kennedy's head at the instant of the fatal shot appears to virtually everyone that that shot came from the right front. Over the years, countless military veterans, law enforcement personnel, hunters, and other people with experience in gunshots have believed that at least one shot must have been fired from the vicinity of the Grassy Knoll. The argument of a neuromuscular reaction has been refuted by many neurosurgeons. The argument of a jet effect is utter nonsense. Regardless of Luis Alvarez's expertise in physics, he produced no credible evidence that his test firings of a rifle into a melon reproduced precisely the anatomical condition of Kennedy's head. The argument made by Itek Corporation and by David Mantik that the velocity of the head movement is far too great to have come from a rifle with a 2,000 feet per second muzzle velocity falls to the calculation that it could have been caused by a rifle with a much higher muzzle velocity. Real-life shootings, including the assassination of Dr. Martin Luther King Jr. and the execution of the Viet Cong prisoner by a South Vietnamese officer, captured so vividly on film by Eddie Adams, graphically reveal what virtually everyone instinctively knows: a person shot in the head will fall in the direction that the bullet travels.[12]

One of the things that has persuaded me that Kennedy must have been shot from the front is the carefully calculated effort to cover up the truth. If the Zapruder film revealed no evidence of a front-entering shot, why conceal it? The Warren Commission published poor-quality black-and-white frames from the film and actually reversed frames Z314 and Z313 to make it appear that Kennedy's head fell forward instead of backward. The autopsy photographs, so widely touted by lone assassin theorists, lack any serious evidentiary value because of the criminal manner in which they were handled. Today, more than four decades after the assassination, it is impossible to determine whether the current official set of autopsy photographs is the only set. Every qualified medical witness at both Parkland Hospital and at Bethesda observed a large wound in the rear of the president's head. Ordinarily, photographic evidence would be more reliable than that of eyewitnesses, but in this instance, highly qualified medical personnel, including a neurosurgeon, saw an exit wound in the rear of the head. That is precisely what White House photographer Robert Knudsen claimed when he told the House Select Committee on Assassinations (HSCA) that he photographed Kennedy's autopsy. That is precisely what navy photographic specialist Saundra Spencer told the ARRB when she claimed that she developed Kennedy autopsy photographs depicting a large hole in the back of the head.[13]

Could Bullets from Lee Harvey Oswald's Rifle Have Caused the President's Head Wound?

Yes.

Many conspiracy theorists, including myself, have argued that the massive damage to President Kennedy's head could not have been caused by the fully copper-jacketed Mannlicher-Carcano ammunition that Lee Harvey Oswald is alleged to have used. These theorists include Harold Weisberg, Howard Roffman, and James Fetzer. Their primary argument focuses on the copper-jacketed ammunition. This type of bullet, they maintain, is designed to penetrate into a body, inflict damage, and exit without losing much of its original mass. Fully jacketed ammunition does not explode and fragment, as did whatever kind of ammunition that struck Kennedy's head. The x-rays of the skull reveal massive damage to the brain, as well as extensive fragmentation of the bullet that struck it. Indeed, dozens of metal fragments are readily apparent on the x-rays. Therefore, Kennedy must have been shot in the head by some kind of ammunition other than that which Oswald supposedly used.[14]

Although I originally concurred with this thesis, I have since changed my mind for several reasons. First, we do not know what kind of ammunition Oswald may have used. Absolutely no evidence of any kind exists to prove that Oswald purchased any kind of ammunition at any time. One live round of ammunition, a fully jacketed Mannlicher-Carcano 6.5-millimeter cartridge, was found in the firing chamber of

Oswald's rifle when it was discovered on the sixth floor of the Depository building. Bullet 399, another fully jacketed round, was allegedly found on Governor Connally's stretcher at Parkland Hospital. Two large Mannlicher-Carcano fragments, the outer jacket and the inner core, were allegedly found on the front seat of the presidential limousine. These discoveries led the Warren Commission, together with its defenders and its critics, to conclude that Oswald had access to only one kind of ammunition. What none of us realized is that Mannlicher-Carcano ammunition came in many different varieties, each capable of being fired from Oswald's rifle. For example, I personally own five different kinds of 6.5-millimeter Mannlicher-Carcano ammunition: a round-tip, fully copper jacketed round identical to that presumably fired by Oswald; a round-tip, fully steel jacketed round; a round-tip bullet with a copper jacket and the lead tip exposed; a pointed-tip round, with a copper jacketing and the lead tip exposed; and a round-tip round, with a steel jacketing and the lead tip exposed. The last three types are commonly known as hollow-point ammunition and are specifically designed to penetrate into a body, then fragment extensively, causing considerable damage to the internal tissue and organs. It is entirely possible that Oswald fired a hollow-point Mannlicher-Carcano bullet into the rear of Kennedy's head. That bullet could have exploded inside the cranium and blown out a large portion of the right front and top of the head as it made its exit. This possibility naturally places the onus on Warren Commission's defenders to explain how Oswald managed to obtain two different varieties of this unusual ammunition without leaving a trace of his purchasing it.[15]

Second, wounds ballistics experiments conducted for the Warren Commission demonstrated that even the fully copper jacketed Mannlicher-Carcano ammunition fragmented when fired into human skulls filled with gelatin. As the bullets from the experiments entered the skulls, they drove through the simulated brain tissue, and upon exiting the skulls, they deposited several fragments outside. As renowned wound ballistics authority Dr. Joseph Dolce explained to me, the enormous intercranial pressures generated by the Carcano bullets as they coursed through the simulated brain tissue caused them to fragment upon exiting. Dolce elaborated that the pressures inside the brain of a living human being would have been far greater than those inside the experimental skulls, thereby causing an even higher degree of fragmentation. He also emphasized that the extensive fragmentation inside the cranium as depicted on the x-rays could only have come from a hollow-point bullet and not from the fully jacketed bullets that Oswald supposedly fired. Therefore, it is impossible for the fully copper jacketed ammunition Oswald is alleged to have used to have caused Kennedy's head wounds.[16]

Is the Single Bullet Theory Possible?

No.

Defenders of the Warren Commission stand on a house of cards when they try to promulgate the single bullet theory. Constrained by the parameters of the known speed of the Zapruder film (18.3 frames per second), by the minimum time necessary to fire two separate shots from Oswald's rifle, even without aiming, and by the reactions of both President Kennedy and Governor Connally to being struck, these lone assassin theorists maintain first that a bullet that went through Kennedy after striking him either in the upper back or in the back of the neck must have struck something else in the limousine. Because no person and no object in the limousine other than Governor Connally exhibited signs of being struck, the bullet that first penetrated Kennedy's throat must have hit Connally. Otherwise, where did it go? They also argue that neutron activation analysis (NAA) of Bullet 399 reveals the strong likelihood that it originally contained the fragments removed from Connally's wrist because NAA analysis of these fragments closely matched that of a piece removed from Bullet 399. They also maintain that various computer reenactments of the positions of the president and governor in the limousine demonstrate that they were aligned in such a manner as to make the single bullet feasible. Finally, they contend that most experts who have examined the medical evidence have concluded that it is quite likely that the same bullet that penetrated through Kennedy's neck caused Connally's wounds.[17]

These arguments fall to any serious, disinterested examination of the evidence. No one disputes that a bullet struck Kennedy in the back. The precise path of that missile through Kennedy's upper thoracic region cannot be ascertained because the autopsy pathologists were ordered not to dissect the wound. The possibility that it lodged in his body and was removed at autopsy, then destroyed to conceal evidence remains strong. When he was brought into the emergency room at Parkland, Kennedy had a tiny hole in his throat that had all of the appearances of a bullet wound of entrance. No exit wound existed in the front of the throat. Wounds ballistics experiments performed on goat skin, in which bullets fired from Oswald's rifle made entrance and exit wounds, demonstrated that that kind of ammunition left only one type of exit wound: one at least twice the size of typical entrance wounds. Because Kennedy faced forward at the time, the existence of a bullet wound of entrance in the front of his throat offers powerful evidence of an assassin firing from the front. In short, no evidence of any kind exists to prove that a bullet exited Kennedy's throat.[18]

Of equal significance is the nature of the bullet wound of entrance in Governor Connally's back. That wound was elliptical, 1.5 centimeters (0.6 inches) in its longest axis, with an abrasion collar of bruising that was heaviest in the upper right corner. Located about midway between Connally's right shoulder blade and right armpit, the wound exhibited all the characteristics of having been inflicted by a bullet that had not previously struck any other objects. This information comes from medical reports, testimony, and interviews with Dr. Robert Shaw, the thoracic surgeon who operated on Connally's back and chest. Dr. Shaw effectively debunked the phony claims of lone assassin theorists that the bullet that entered Connally's back had previously penetrated through Kennedy's throat and tumbled in midair as it left a 3.0-centimeter (1.2 inch) elongated entrance wound in Connally's back. They maintain that 3.0 centimeters is the exact length of a Mannlicher-Carcano bullet. Dr. Shaw stated emphatically that in its original condition, the entrance wound measured 1.5 centimeters, not 3.0 centimeters, before he debrided it. Also, Shaw, the former head of the thoracic surgery unit for the U.S. army in France during World War II, asserted that a tumbling bullet that had previously entered and exited from Kennedy's neck would not have left an abrasion collar of bruising around the wound's margins.[19]

Another critical issue raised by Dr. Shaw concerns the angle of the bullet track through Connally's back and chest. Shaw used a caliper to measure the downward angle of the bullet path simply by measuring the angle from the location of the entrance wound in the upper back to that of the exit wound in the chest, just below the right nipple. Shaw measured a downward angle of twenty-five degrees. Allowing for plus or minus two degrees as a margin of error, the twenty-three- to twenty-seven-degree angle through Connally's back and chest simply could not have been caused by a bullet that had previously gone through Kennedy's throat. Photographs and films distinctly reveal that both Kennedy and Connally sat upright in the limousine, and that neither man slumped forward until after he was hit. Nor could the bullet that hit Connally in the back have come from the southeast corner of the Depository building. Dr. Shaw confirmed to me that, on the basis of the nature of the bullet wound in his back, Governor Connally must have been struck by a bullet fired from an upper floor at the western end of the Texas School Book Depository building—that is, at the opposite end from which Oswald allegedly fired. This observation, based on careful medical analysis and precise measurements by a highly qualified thoracic surgeon, destroys the single bullet theory by itself.[20]

Finally, frames Z236 through Z238 of the Zapruder film distinctly show Governor Connally reacting to being shot. As the bullet strikes him in the right upper back and passes through his chest, collapsing the right lung and shattering the fifth rib, Governor Connally's cheek puffs with air, his right shoulder slumps sharply downward, and his hair flies upward on his head. Lone assassin theorists contend that these are delayed reactions to Connally's having been struck two-thirds of a second previously, at Zapruder frames Z223 or Z224. However, after carefully examining sharp, crisp individual frames of the film, the three physicians who operated on Connally, Drs. Shaw, Charles Gregory, and Thomas Shires, unanimously agreed that Connally was not in an anatomical position to receive the wounds he experienced before frame Z236. Therefore, because Kennedy was struck no later than frame Z224, and because Oswald's rifle could not fire two separate shots, even without aiming, in less than forty-two Zapruder frames, Connally must have been struck by a bullet fired from another weapon.[21]

Could Oswald Have Fired Two Separate Shots Striking Kennedy and Connally with Separate Bullets?

Yes.

Most studies of the assassination, including those made by the defenders and critics of the Warren Commission, assert that Oswald simply did not have sufficient time to fire two separate shots to wound Kennedy and Connally with separate bullets. Virtually all researchers have accepted the commission's analysis that an FBI reconstruction of the shooting revealed that the leaves of a live oak tree blocked Oswald's view of the presidential limousine before frame Z210 of the Zapruder film. Therefore, these writers argue, because Oswald fired no earlier than frame Z210, and because Connally was shot no later than frame Z238, the twenty-eight-frame difference, or 1.6 seconds, is less than the 2.25 seconds minimum time necessary to fire two separate shots from that weapon, even without aiming. These inescapable parameters required the conclusion that either Kennedy and Connally were struck by the same bullet—or they were shot by two different assassins firing from the rear.[22]

After examining the evidence, I have deviated from my original conclusion that agreed with the above hypothesis. My first reason lies in the lack of scientific validity of the FBI reconstruction. The FBI "reconstruction," conducted in May 1964, a time when climatic conditions clearly were different from those that prevailed on November 22, 1963, failed in several critically important matters. First, the FBI used a Cadillac convertible, rather than a Lincoln. The bureau's vehicle had only two seats, whereas the actual presidential limousine had folding jump seats between the front and back seats. The FBI stand-ins for President Kennedy and Governor Connally sat alone in the FBI vehicle (other than the driver), whereas on November 22, Kennedy and Connally sat with three people besides the driver. The FBI photographer who knelt at the sixth-floor window of the Depository building shot motion picture film from a camera through the telescopic sight of Oswald's rifle resting on a tripod. In the actual assassination, if Oswald indeed fired any shots from that window, he hardly used a tripod. The official version of the shooting maintains that he fired from either a sitting or kneeling position, with the rifle resting on book cartons. Therefore, the reconstruction lacked validity because it failed to reproduce the exact conditions that prevailed during the actual assassination. Therefore, just because the FBI photographer captured the live oak tree branches in his camera does not mean that the branches blocked Oswald's view of the motorcade. In fact, because the wind blew on November 22, it could easily have blown the leaves of the tree away from Oswald's view, thus allowing him time to fire the first shot at a much earlier time than most authorities believe. If he used the windowsill as a gun rest, Oswald would have had a much less obstructed view of Elm Street.[23]

My second reason for rejecting the claims of the lone assassin and conspiracy theorists that Oswald did not have sufficient time to fire two separate shots at Kennedy and Connally lay in our lack of knowledge of the precise conditions that prevailed during the gunfire in Dealey Plaza. The number of shots fired, for example, remains unknown. One shot, fired from an unspecified location in the rear, missed the limousine and struck the curb on Main Street near the underpass, with a fragment nicking James Tague's cheek. Another bullet fired from the front almost certainly struck Kennedy in the throat. Another struck him in the back. Yet another struck Connally in the back. Another may have struck Connally in the wrist. Two bullets, one fired from the front and the other from the rear, struck Kennedy in the head. Altogether, that adds up to seven shots. People can argue about the number of shots, but they have difficulty in explaining any scenario other than the seven-shot one posited here. However, it deserves mentioning that hardly anyone recalls hearing that many shots fired. No one today seriously questions the fragment from the missed shot that struck Tague. Everyone also agrees that one bullet struck Kennedy in the back and another struck him in the head. Most researchers assume that only one bullet struck Connally, but a careful examination of the Zapruder film demands revision of this hypothesis. As Drs. Shaw, Gregory, and Shires observed, a bullet struck the governor in the back at frame Z236 or Z237 of the film. Almost everyone assumes that that bullet, which exited his chest, went on to strike his right wrist. Yet as late as frame Z255, Connally can clearly be seen still grasping his Stetson hat in his right hand, a physical impossibility if his wrist had already been shattered. Drs. Shaw and Gregory both told me that in addition to causing a comminuted fracture of the radius, the bullet also severely damaged both the radial and ulnar bundles of nerves, which control the apposition of the thumb and fingers. Connally's wrist therefore must have been damaged by a shot different from the one that caused his thoracic wounds. And that shot came later than frame Z255 of the film.[24]

The Zapruder film restraints for Oswald firing separate shots at Kennedy and Connally thus have been dramatically expanded. If the leaves of the live oak tree did not block Oswald's view of the motorcade from the sixth-floor window, he could easily have fired one shot at frame Z210, striking Kennedy in the back, and had more than sufficient time to fire a second shot after frame Z255, striking Connally in the wrist. Some researchers believe that the first shot came as early as frame Z162; others argue that it came at frame Z189, thereby creating a much larger window of opportunity for Lee Harvey Oswald to fire more than one shot at the two men. Obviously, I do not mean to suggest that this proves that Oswald fired all of the shots. On the contrary, neither Oswald nor anyone else could have fired from different directions. Nor could Oswald have shot Kennedy from the sixth-floor southeast corner window of the building, then run to the western end and fired another shot that struck Connally in the back at frame Z236–Z237. He simply did not have enough time. Lee Harvey Oswald may have very well had more than sufficient time to fire separate shots at President Kennedy and Governor Connally, although he could not possibly have fired all of the shots.[25]

Did Lee Harvey Oswald Fire Any Shots?

Unknown.

The evidence accumulated against Oswald is impressive: his rifle was found on the sixth floor; empty cartridge cases fired from his rifle were discovered near the sniper's nest; a large homemade paper bag found near the southeast corner window contained two of his prints; a witness saw him fire a shot; Oswald left the Depository building three minutes after the assassination and murdered a Dallas police officer forty minutes later; Oswald's actions in the building after the shooting are compatible with his presence on the sixth floor at the time of the gunfire; a bullet fired from Oswald's rifle was discovered on a stretcher at Parkland Hospital; two bullet fragments fired from that same weapon were found in the front seat of the limousine. A loner, an outcast from society, a member of the extreme left wing, an outspoken critic of American policy toward Cuba, a former defector to the Soviet Union, Oswald had the motive, means, and opportunity to commit the crime of the century.[26]

Yet when examined critically and objectively, this case against Oswald falls apart. The rifle, cartridge cases, and paper bag could easily have been planted to implicate him. Not a single shred of evidence exists to prove that that rifle was fired on November 22. None of the law enforcement officers who discovered it carefully hidden inside a tall stack of book cartons smelled gunpowder, even though it had been supposedly fired less than an hour previously. All three of the cartridge cases contained markings that proved that they had been inside rifles other than Oswald's, and none contained any of his prints. The police did not photograph the paper bag where it was allegedly discovered, and FBI analysis of it revealed that it held no markings, oil smears, or any other evidence by which it could be linked to the rifle. According to the official story, Oswald must have carried this awkward, three-foot-long bag to Irving on the day before the assassination, yet none of the people who saw him—Buell Wesley Frazier, Marina Oswald, and Ruth Paine—observed him carrying such an obvious package. Howard Brennan, the witness who claimed to have seen Oswald fire a shot, has been severely criticized by many researchers. Brennan failed to pick Oswald out of a police lineup as the man he saw shoot the president. In FBI interviews, he changed his mind twice about whether he saw Oswald. Brennan claimed that he had super eyesight and was positive that Oswald was the sixth-floor assassin, yet his vision lacked the acuity to see the rifle either emit a flash of light or a puff of smoke, or recoil after it was fired. Oswald's rifle does all three. Brennan actually told Dan Rather in a television interview that he not only saw Oswald fire the fatal shot, he also saw the impact of the shot on Kennedy's head. Possessing superhuman powers à la Clark Kent, Brennan claimed that he could move his head faster than the speeding bullet.[27]

Police officer Marrion Baker and Depository building superintendent Roy Truly encountered Lee Oswald in a second-floor lunchroom no more than ninety seconds after the shots were fired. Both men testified that Oswald was not out of breath, agitated, or in any other manner acting abnormally. It seems virtually impossible for a man who had just killed the president of the United States and seriously wounded the governor of Texas, wiped his prints from the exterior surface of the gun, squeezed between tall stacks of fifty-five-pound book cartons, walked to the northwest region of the sixth floor, moved a stack of heavy cartons out of the way, laid the rifle on the floor, pushed the boxes back into position, then descended four flights of stairs, and, for some unknown reason, entered a lunchroom and stood in front of a soft drink machine, not to exhibit signs of apprehension, nervousness, fatigue, and breathlessness. It also challenges common sense that this man, the most wanted criminal in American history, purchased a Coke and walked at a leisurely pace toward the front of the building, when he could easily have escaped through one of the unguarded rear doors. Yet the official account demands that we accept that he exited through the heavily guarded front door of the building, walked seven blocks down Elm Street, and caught a bus headed back in the direction of Dealey Plaza. One might compare the official version of Oswald's movements with the known actions of John Wilkes Booth after he assassinated Abraham Lincoln. After jumping onto the stage at Ford's Theater, Booth hobbled out of the side door, got on a horse, and sped away across the Potomac River into Maryland. In short, Booth fled the scene of the crime as fast as he could, whereas Oswald, at a leisurely pace, actually caught a bus headed back toward the scene of the crime.[28]

I have already considered the other pieces of evidence against Oswald. The alleged discovery of Bullet 399 on Governor Connally's stretcher at the hospital has absolutely no substantiation. No one photographed the bullet at its point of discovery. The five men who saw and/or handled the stretcher bullet before it came into the possession of the FBI—Darrel Tomlinson, Nathan Pool, O. P. Wright, Richard Johnsen, and James Rowley—refused to identify Bullet 399 as the one they observed. Bullet 399 contained no blood, tissue, fibers, or anything else that could connect it to the wounds on Kennedy and Connally. The bullet fragments supposedly found on the front seat of the limousine also fail to meet the test of evidence. No one photographed them in place. The blood that they contained was washed off without comparing it to Kennedy's blood. In a court of law, a competent defense attorney would have successfully persuaded the presiding judge to disallow these items as evidence because the chain of evidence, so critical in criminal cases, lacked numerous links. The defense could just as easily have argued that both Bullet 399 and the limousine fragments were planted to frame Oswald.

None of this means that Oswald fired no shots. From a lower floor of the Depository building, he could have fired that shot that struck Kennedy in the back. Autopsy photographs reveal that the entrance wound in Kennedy's back had the greatest degree of bruising at the lower right margin, indicating a shot fired from a lower floor of the building. This scenario—Oswald firing from a lower floor of the building—is far more compatible with his discovery in the second-floor lunchroom only a minute and a half after the shooting. Oswald also could have fired the shot that struck Connally in the back from the fifth or sixth floors at the southwest end of the Depository building. This location would have given him ample time to descend the nearby stairs and enter the lunchroom before his encounter with Baker and Truly. This, of course, is speculation. Because in our criminal justice system the burden of proof lies with the prosecution to prove its case against a defendant, the onus lay with the Warren Commission to prove that Oswald fired shots. This the commission failed to do.

What Happened to the Bullets that Struck President Kennedy in the Front of the Throat and in the Back?

Unknown.

Rejecting the single bullet theory, conspiracy theorists have failed to provide a satisfactory answer to the above question. The detailed contemporaneous descriptions given by Dallas medical personnel of the wound in Kennedy's throat when he arrived in Trauma Room One leave little question that it was indeed a wound of entrance. Dr. Malcolm Perry, the surgeon who cut the tracheotomy through that wound and had a longer and better look at it than anyone else, told reporters at a press conference held less than two hours after Kennedy died that the president was shot in the throat from in front. Perry repeated that answer twice. Most conspiracy theorists have latched onto this entrance wound in the throat as positive proof of a conspiracy. Yet they have failed to give any serious explanation of the bullet's trajectory through the body, much less provide a credible explanation of the bullet's fate. Because Kennedy had no exit wounds anywhere in his body below the head, the bullet must have remained inside him. Likewise, the bullet that entered Kennedy's back must have lodged somewhere in his body because he had no exit wounds below the head.[29]

This leaves two bullets completely unaccounted for. Certain conspiracy theorists have argued that an FBI receipt for a "missile" removed from Kennedy's body during the autopsy explains one of these bullets. However, both FBI agents present at the autopsy, James Sibert and Francis O'Neill, have confirmed that the receipt for a "missile" actually referred to tiny bullet fragments removed from the president's head. Of all the conspiracy theorists, only David Lifton and Josiah Thompson have attempted to explain the lack of bullets. Lifton, of course, has given the most controversial analysis. He contends that before autopsy, John F. Kennedy's body was deliberately altered to conceal evidence of front-entering shots. The conspirators would have removed the bullets and simply destroyed them. Thompson contends that the bullet that entered Kennedy's back penetrated only a couple of inches, then fell out of his back onto the gurney. A hospital employee then picked up the bullet to save as a souvenir, but had second thoughts and deposited it on another gurney on the ground floor. Neither Lifton nor Thompson possess any proof that these scenarios occurred. Lifton cites the testimony of Dr. David Osborne that he saw a bullet removed from the body at the autopsy and actually held it in his hand, yet no one else present recalls such a dramatic incident. Thompson's scenario is sheer speculation. Because the back wound was never dissected, it is impossible to ascertain the track through the body, but it appears extremely unlikely that a bullet would have penetrated only a couple of inches, then fallen back out through the hole of entrance.[30]

Conspiracy theorists have a serious problem. They accuse lone assassin theorists of concocting ridiculous scenarios—such as the single bullet theory—without adhering to the hard evidence, but they themselves have fallen into the same trap. Where did the bullets that struck

Kennedy in the back and in the throat go? I have asked this question of several conspiracy theorists, including Harold Weisberg and Sylvia Meagher, and they simply could not provide a coherent answer to it. This question, in many ways central to a clear understanding of the essential facts of the assassination, remains unanswered. It does not, of course, refute the conspiracy thesis.

Did Oswald Shoot Officer Tippit?

Probably.

At around 1:13 P.M. on Friday, November 22, 1963, or about forty-three minutes after the assassination, Dallas police officer J. D. Tippit was cruising slowly east on Tenth Street in a quiet residential neighborhood nearly four miles from Dealey Plaza. As he approached the intersection of Tenth Street and Patton Avenue, Tippit observed a man walking east on Tenth. Tippit called the man to his car, and they engaged in a brief conversation. Tippit got out of the car, and as he walked to the left front wheel, the man pulled out a revolver and fired several shots into Tippit, killing him instantly. The killer fled to the corner, where he emptied by hand four cartridge cases from the revolver, reloaded the weapon, and ran down Patton. Domingo Benavides, who sat in his truck fifteen feet away from the murder scene, waited a couple of minutes to ensure that the cop killer had indeed fled the scene, then ran to the police car, where he attempted to use Tippit's radio, but he did not know how. T. F. Bowley drove up and ran to assist Officer Tippit, but he seemed beyond help. Bowley then took the radio from Benavides, called the police dispatcher, and reported the crime. The call came at 1:16 P.M. An ambulance arrived soon after and rushed Tippit to nearby Methodist Hospital, where he was pronounced dead.[31]

Another witness to the shooting, Helen Markham, stood at a bus stop on the corner of Tenth and Patton. Markham saw the man shoot Tippit and run back in her direction. As the gunman approached her, Markham got a good look at him and later identified him as Lee Harvey Oswald. Other witnesses, such as William Scoggins and Ted Callaway, identified Oswald as the man they saw fleeing the scene. Police cars arrived at the scene, and following descriptions given by witnesses, they pursued the perpetrator. Running from the scene, Oswald hid from his pursuers and wound up on Jefferson Boulevard, a major thoroughfare in the neighborhood. As police cars raced down that street, Oswald ducked into the lobby of a shoe store, as if to avoid being seen by the police. Johnny Brewer, a clerk in the store, saw Oswald and followed him down the sidewalk after the police cars had passed. Brewer saw Oswald go into the Texas Theater and asked the cashier, Julia Postal, to call the police. Postal did so, and the police converged on the theater and, after a brief scuffle, arrested Oswald.[32]

When arrested, Oswald had a .38-caliber Smith and Wesson revolver in his possession. Four cartridge cases found near the scene of the Tippit killing ballistically matched Oswald's revolver. However, the four bullets removed from Officer Tippit's body were too mutilated to be identified as having come from a particular weapon, although they were indeed .38 caliber and could have been fired from Oswald's gun. The positive ballistics match of the cartridge cases to Oswald's revolver, the positive identification of Oswald as the killer or as the man fleeing the scene of the murder, the discovery of Oswald's discarded jacket a couple of blocks from the murder scene, together with Oswald's ducking from the police, led the Warren Commission to conclude that he murdered J. D. Tippit. The HSCA also investigated the murder and came to the same conclusion. The committee even uncovered another eyewitness, Jack Tatum, who claimed that, after the first three shots, Oswald walked up to the fallen officer and fired another round into his head, as if to administer a coup de grâce. An exhaustive study of the Tippit killing by Dale Myers also concluded that Lee Harvey Oswald committed the crime.[33]

Impressive as the evidence against Lee Harvey Oswald as the person who gunned down J. D. Tippit may be, researchers have raised several troubling issues about the crime that remain unresolved. First, there exists a major discrepancy between the cartridge cases and the fatal bullets. Three of the bullets recovered from Tippit's body were made by Winchester-Western, and the fourth by Remington-Peters, but two of the cartridge cases were Winchesters and the other two Remingtons. Therefore, a Remington bullet is missing. The scenario, posed by the Warren Commission, has Oswald firing four bullets at point-blank range into Tippit's head and body, yet firing a fifth shot that missed and was never recovered. One witness, Ted Callaway, who stood around the corner from the scene, recalled hearing five shots fired. Despite the fact that no other witness heard that many shots, Dale Myers places great credence in Callaway's account because Callaway was a war veteran. Of course, Myers does not lend the same credibility to war veterans such as Phillip Willis, in Dealey Plaza, who provided earwitness accounts of a shot fired from in front of the limousine. It strains credibility that Lee Oswald, a crack shot who had just pulled off an extraordinary feat of marksmanship in Dealey Plaza, could fire four shots at point-blank range that struck their target, J. D. Tippit, but fired such an errant fifth round that no trace of it has ever been discovered. The mystery of the differing cartridge cases and bullets remains unsolved.[34]

Another problem lies in the broken chain of evidence. As with Dealey Plaza, the Dallas police failed to secure the crime scene, instead allowing spectators and reporters to roam all over Tenth Street and Patton Avenue, walk all over the sidewalk, and even touch and peer into Tippit's police car. Helen Markham even left a pair of shoes on top of Tippit's car. Myers's book contains numerous photographs of the lack of crowd control by the police. The four cartridge cases found near the murder site were picked up by civilians and handed over to police officers, who failed to mark them with their identifying initials. Three of the bullets recovered from Tippit's body lay in a file cabinet at Dallas police headquarters for several months. More significantly, none of the bullets fired from Oswald's revolver for ballistics testing matched each other. FBI ballistics expert Courtland Cunningham testified that because the bullets were slightly smaller than the diameter of the barrel of Oswald's revolver, the bullets received inconsistent markings when he test fired them. Therefore, because the test bullets themselves did not match each other, even though they were all fired from Oswald's gun, it was not possible to match them to the bullets removed from Tippit. It should be obvious that had Oswald stood trial for the murder of Officer Tippit, a competent defense attorney could have successfully contested the main physical evidence against him.[35]

Finally, a timing problem raises another question. The Warren Commission faced the problem of transporting Oswald from his rooming house at 1026 North Beckley Avenue to the Tippit murder scene, 410 East Tenth Street, a distance of approximately nine-tenths of a mile. Earline Roberts, the housekeeper at the rooming house, saw Oswald leave at approximately 1:04 P.M. Because Bowley's call to the police dispatcher came at 1:16 P.M., it is certain that the murder came before that time. The Warren Commission allowed only a one-minute leeway, but the evidence makes it clear that the actual time of the murder came before that. Domingo Benavides, for example, testified that he saw the man shoot the cop, then run to the corner. Afraid that the man might return, Benavides waited until he was sure that the man had indeed fled before he walked over to Tippit's vehicle and tried to use the radio. Bowley then drove up, went to assist Tippit first, then took the microphone from Benavides and called the dispatcher. From these eyewitness accounts, the only evidence we have, one can reasonably conclude that the murder probably occurred at 1:13 P.M. If Oswald left the rooming house at 1:04, then stood in front by a bus stop, as Roberts recalled, then he left the area of the rooming house at 1:05. This gave him eight minutes to travel the nine-tenths of a mile to the Tippit murder scene. Somehow, Oswald managed to travel that distance on foot without losing his breath, panting, or displaying any other signs of having just traveled almost a mile in eight minutes. We then have to add to that the time it took for Oswald and Tippit to hold their conversation. In addition, lone assassin theorists Dale Myers and Gus Russo claim that Oswald walked erratically back and forth, and even urinated into a bush, attracting Tippit's attention to him. This would compel us to believe that Lee Harvey Oswald traveled nine-tenths of a mile on foot in about seven minutes without running, a physical impossibility.[36]

In an interview with David Belin, the Warren Commission junior counsel in charge of the Tippit murder investigation, I mentioned these questions. Relying heavily on eyewitness identifications, Belin replied that Oswald had to have been able to travel the distance because there was no doubt that he was at the scene of the crime. Yet the only two witnesses to the actual shooting, Helen Markham and Domingo Benavides, have serious discrepancies in their accounts. Benavides told the police on the evening of November 22 that he did not believe that he could identify the man he saw shoot the policeman.

In testimony before the Warren Commission several months later, Benavides would only admit that a photograph of Oswald which he had viewed on television resembled the murderer. Markham did view Oswald in a police lineup the afternoon of November 22. As she testified before the commission, she failed to recognize anyone "from their face." After giving a series of responses to leading questions by the Warren Commission counsel, Markham finally responded to a blatantly leading question, "Was there a Number Two man there [in the lineup]?" with the famous reply, "Number Two was the man I saw shoot the officer. When I looked at him, I wasn't sure, but I had cold chills just run all over me." Nevertheless, Oswald was seen fleeing the murder scene by many witnesses, and when arrested in the Texas Theater, he had a loaded revolver and many rounds of ammunition on his person. The bulk of the evidence therefore supports the contention that Lee Harvey Oswald did indeed murder Officer J. D. Tippit.[37]

Are the Autopsy Photographs and X-rays Authentic?

Yes and No.

Many researchers have questioned the authenticity of the photographs and x-rays taken at President Kennedy's autopsy. Their chief argument against authenticity lies in the glaring contradiction between what the photographs and x-rays reveal and what the evidence proves regarding the wounds inflicted on the president. As already noted, virtually every medical witness at both Parkland and Bethesda testified that Kennedy had a large, gaping wound of exit in the back of his head. In addition to the Dallas doctors and nurses already cited, the following medical specialists at the Bethesda morgue also viewed an exit wound in the rear of the head: Drs. Calvin Galloway; John Stover; Robert Canada; George Burkley; Edward Kenney; John Ebersole, and David Osborne, together with medical corpsmen Paul O'Connor and James Jenkins. In addition, nonmedical observers also saw the exit wound in the back of the president's head: Secret Service agents Roy Kellerman, William Greer, and Clint Hill; FBI special agents James Sibert and Francis O'Neill; and photographers John Stringer and Floyd Reibe.

The autopsy photographs depict no such hole. Instead, they show only a wound high in the rear of the head near the cowlick, with the rest of the back of the head intact.[38]

Secret Service agents Kellerman and Greer, who had absolutely no jurisdiction, confiscated the undeveloped film, removed it from the morgue, and turned it over to Robert Bouck, the head of the Protective Research Section. Bouck ordered Kellerman to have the negatives developed, and Kellerman gave them to Secret Service photographer James Fox. Fox took the negatives to the Naval Processing Center in Anacostia, Maryland, where he watched navy photographic specialist Saundra Spencer develop the film. Fox returned the autopsy photographs to Kellerman, who told him to "make a set of these for yourself. They'll be history someday." Fox did so and retained his set of autopsy photographs until he sold it to David Lifton. The official set remained in the possession of Robert Bouck, who claimed that he kept the photographs and x-rays, together with other autopsy materials, in his safe in the Executive Office Building. Bouck guarded the autopsy materials zealously because Robert Kennedy had ordered him to do so. In 1965, Bouck complied with Kennedy's order to turn the materials over to Admiral George Burkley, who in turn handed them over to Evelyn Lincoln, John F. Kennedy's personal secretary. Lincoln then handed them over to Angela Novello, Robert Kennedy's personal secretary, who kept them in her office. In 1966, the Kennedy family turned the autopsy materials over to the National Archives under a "memorandum of agreement" that placed strict controls over access to them.[39]

This is the official version of the chain of evidence concerning the autopsy photographs and x-rays. It should be obvious that such haphazard, careless, and utterly illegal handling of this material destroys its evidentiary value. I asked Roy Kellerman why he confiscated the photographs and x-rays at Bethesda, and he replied that he simply followed orders from Bouck. When I asked Bouck why he ordered Kellerman to confiscate the materials, Bouck stated that his boss, Secret Service director James Rowley, had received strict instructions from Robert Kennedy to maintain custody over the materials. Both Bouck and Kellerman grew indignant when I asked them what authority Robert Kennedy held over the Secret Service, claiming that because Kennedy was the slain president's brother, he possessed legal jurisdiction over the autopsy evidence. When I asked Bouck about the discrepancies between the medical reports and the contents of the photographs, he hesitated, then stated, in quite cautious tones, that all of the autopsy materials have never surfaced, that the ones in the extant collection in the National Archives consisted only of those that tended to support the lone assassin thesis. This startling revelation implied that other autopsy materials that disproved that thesis did exist. Agents Kellerman and Greer both agreed with this hypothesis. Both men told me that they had seen autopsy photographs showing the exit wound in the back of President Kennedy's head, although they had no idea of the ultimate disposition of these photographs. Because both Kellerman and Greer viewed Kennedy's body at close range at both Parkland and Bethesda, their accounts must be given some credibility. Their accounts, of course, accord with the observations of medical personnel and with those of Saundra Spencer, who developed the original negatives. In addition, White House photographers Robert Knudsen and Joseph O'Donnell also saw photographs taken at the autopsy that depicted a large exit wound in the back of President Kennedy's head.[40]

Douglas Horne, the senior analyst for military records for the ARRB, added further to the sinister tale of the autopsy photographs. Official records reveal that Kennedy's brain was removed from the cranium during the postmortem examination and placed in a formalin solution for a supplemental autopsy several days later. With access to long-suppressed documents and interviews with key personnel, Horne concluded that the photographs of a brain in the extant official collection in the National Archives cannot be those of John Kennedy's brain for a number of reasons. First, photographer John Stringer testified under oath that he took pictures of the brain as it was being serially sectioned, yet none of the official photographs show such sectioning. Second, Stringer used unnumbered Kodak portrait pan film, whereas the official set in the archives contains only numbered Ansco film. Third, numerous medical personnel at Parkland and Bethesda saw severe damage to the president's brain. For example, neurosurgeon Kemp Clark, surgeons Malcolm Perry, Ronald Jones, and Robert McClelland, navy physicians Robert Canada and George Burkley, FBI special agent Francis X. O'Neill Jr., and mortician Thomas Robinson viewed severe damage to the cerebellum, located at the lower rear of the organ. Yet the official autopsy photographs depict an intact cerebellum. Fourth, Horne concluded that the examination of Kennedy's brain on November 25, only three days after the assassination, disclosed incontrovertible evidence that Kennedy had been shot in the head from behind. Therefore, according to Horne, this brain, the genuine organ, was destroyed, and a second autopsy was performed on another brain several days later, leading Dr. Pierre Finck, one of the autopsy pathologists, not present at the earlier supplemental examination, to conclude that only one shot struck the president from behind. Finally, Horne stated that the official weight of Kennedy's brain given at the autopsy and in a 1965 report that Dr. Finck wrote to his superior at the Armed Forces Institute of Pathology, Dr. Joseph Blumberg, was 1,500 grams. Because the average adult male brain weighs about 1,350 to 1,400 grams, and because Kennedy's brain suffered severe damage, it is inconceivable that it could still retain its normal weight.[41]

Dr. David Mantik, an eminent radiation oncologist, who has spent more time examining the autopsy photographs and x-rays than anyone else, has concluded that "the photographic collection has been deliberately manipulated to mislead." Mantik believes that after exhaustive measurements of the x-rays using optical densitometry, he has concluded that the anteroposterior x-ray of the president's head was altered through the insertion of a metallic fragment in the back of the skull to make it appear that a shot struck Kennedy from behind. In other words, this x-ray is a deliberate forgery. He also elaborated on an issue that has bedeviled assassination researchers for many years: the precise location of the so-called entry wound in the back of the head. The official autopsy protocol and numerous statements by the autopsy pathologists have placed this entry wound very low in the back of the head, either "slightly above" the external occipital protuberance, the bony knob at the base of the skull, or "slightly below" it. The official photographs and x-rays, however, show the entry wound four inches higher, near the top of the head, in the cowlick area. Not a single person, civilian or medical, who viewed the president's head at either Parkland or Bethesda has ever pointed to a red spot near the cowlick in a couple of the photographs as the point of entrance of the bullet. Officially appointed teams of medical specialists who have examined the autopsy evidence over the years have simply assumed that the entrance wound lay where it is depicted in the photographs and x-rays, yet no one who was present will verify this.[42]

It requires mentioning that the official autopsy x-rays and photographs have been extensively examined by experts who found no evidence of deliberate forgery. Douglas Horne himself took the materials to the Kodak facility in Rochester, New York, where their authenticity was proven beyond dispute. Defenders of the Warren Commission's lone assassin thesis also scoff at the discrepancies between the photographic evidence and the recollections of eyewitnesses. They contend that the witnesses who saw an exit wound in the back of the head were mistaken. The hard, scientific evidence of photographs clearly supersedes the faulty memories of eyewitnesses. In addition, careful examinations of the Zapruder film, even by conspiracy theorists, find no evidence of an exit wound in the rear of the head. From the available evidence, it appears that the autopsy photographs and x-rays in the official collection in the National Archives are authentic, but that other photographs and x-rays revealing evidence of shots fired from different directions have conveniently disappeared.[43]

Did Jim Garrison's Investigation Uncover the Truth behind the Assassination?

No.

In February 1967, the district attorney of Orleans Parish (New Orleans), Louisiana, Jim Garrison, admitted that a press account that his office was conducting an investigation into the Kennedy assassination was accurate. Garrison told the press that he had solved the mystery of John Kennedy's murder and that he would soon arrest some of the ringleaders behind the conspiracy. The towering district attorney flatly stated that the Warren Commission had deliberately distorted the facts to conceal the truth. He denounced the continuing cover-up and promised that he would bring those responsible for the crime of the century to justice. Garrison proclaimed that the assassination conspiracy was hatched right there in New Orleans during the spring and summer of 1963, that the conspirators used Lee Harvey Oswald as a scapegoat and carried out their nefarious plot against the president with a team of professional assassins.[44]

It is difficult to overstate the frenzied response to Garrison's sensational charges. From all over the nation—indeed, all over the world—reporters converged on New Orleans to cover the story. Pompous, arrogant, and publicity-seeking, Garrison relished the tremendous coverage he received and granted interviews to every imaginable organ of the press, including *Playboy* magazine. He even appeared as a guest on the popular *Tonight Show* and debated the assassination with Johnny Carson for more than an hour. From the beginning, Jim Garrison aroused adulation and contempt, his company coveted by such assassination researchers as Harold Weisberg and Mark Lane, with countless journalists trying to uncover evidence that would put the lie to his accusations. To this day, the Kennedy assassination research community remains badly divided over Garrison. Studies of his investigation fall flatly into the pro- or anti-Garrison camps, with no neutral ground between. Some thoughtful, responsible scholars like Jim DiEugenio and Joan Mellen look with admiration on Garrison, while other equally responsible researchers like David Lifton and Dave Reitzes consider him a charlatan.[45]

In March 1967, the Orleans Parish district attorney's office arrested Clay L. Shaw, a prominent business and civic leader, and charged him with conspiracy to murder John F. Kennedy. At the preliminary hearing, Garrison produced a witness, Perry Raymond Russo, who testified that he attended a party at the New Orleans apartment of David Ferrie. Both Clay Shaw and Lee Harvey Oswald also attended the party, in addition to several anti-Castro Cubans. David Ferrie held the guests spellbound as he launched into a verbal tirade against the Kennedy administration and voiced his intense desire to see President Kennedy, whom he labeled a communist, killed. Ferrie insisted that Kennedy could be assassinated as he rode in an open limousine, and that the way to kill him lay in catching him in a "triangulation of crossfire." Shaw, Oswald, and the Cubans listened to Ferrie's harangue and nodded in agreement, as if an assassination conspiracy had already commenced. Russo's sensational testimony persuaded the presiding judge to issue an indictment against Shaw. The other principal conspirator, David Ferrie, was found dead in his apartment on the very day that investigators from the district attorney's office arrived to arrest him.[46]

After considerable legal delays, the trial of Clay Shaw for conspiring to murder John F. Kennedy began in New Orleans in January 1969. For two months, the trial received massive press coverage. Garrison's office produced evidence, in the form of eyewitness testimony, as well as the first public airing of the Zapruder film, to prove that the assassination had resulted from a conspiracy. The prosecution produced witnesses, chief of whom was Russo, who repeated his story about the party at Ferrie's apartment. In cross-examination, the defense persuaded Russo to admit that his recollection of the party had been brought out through hypnosis. Seven witnesses from the town of Clinton, about ninety miles northwest of New Orleans, testified that they saw Shaw, Oswald, and Ferrie together there in late August or early September 1963. Other witnesses produced by the prosecution tried to demonstrate that Clay Shaw had often used the alias "Clay Bertrand," and that a man using that name had telephoned New Orleans attorney Dean Andrews on the night of the assassination and asked him to go to Dallas to represent Oswald. One prosecution witness, Charles Speisel, testified that he had also attended a party in New Orleans in August 1963 and heard Shaw, Ferrie, and Oswald discussing having President Kennedy assassinated. The defense destroyed Speisel and much of Garrison's case during its cross-examination. Defense attorneys got him to admit that he fingerprinted his daughter when she returned home from the holidays to ensure that aliens had not captured her and replaced her with a double. Clay Shaw took the witness stand for the defense and adamantly denied that he had anything to do with the assassination. The jury took only one hour to arrive at a unanimous verdict of not guilty.[47]

Jim Garrison deserves enormous credit for bringing the nation's attention to the many deficiencies of the Warren Report. He defied the Washington establishment and, quite accurately as it turns out, condemned the continuing suppression of vital evidence in the case. He generated a furious counterattack by the major organs of the press, with CBS going so far as to broadcast a four-hour special allegedly proving the lone assassin thesis. Garrison's investigation into the activities of Lee Harvey Oswald in New Orleans during the spring and summer of 1963 uncovered Oswald's connections with both Ferrie and Guy Banister and his possible links to Clay Shaw. Garrison also probed into the anti-Castro Cuban community's links to the CIA and unraveled some of the mysterious activities of certain splinter groups, such as the Information Council of the Americas (INCA), a right-wing anticommunist organization that spread propaganda throughout Central America. By adroitly using the tremendous publicity that he generated, Garrison helped to sway public opinion in the country behind the idea of a conspiracy in the Kennedy assassination.[48]

Despite these accomplishments, Jim Garrison went much too far. His prosecution of Clay Shaw took on the aura of a witch hunt, rather than a genuine search for justice. After the trial had ended, members of the jury proclaimed themselves astonished that the district attorney's office would offer such a flimsy case against the defendant. Garrison's witnesses included a genuine lunatic, Charles Speisel; a convicted heroin pusher and user, Vernon Bundy; and a convicted burglar, Perry Raymond Russo. It appeared that Garrison had a personal vendetta against Shaw, because he produced no credible evidence that Shaw had participated in an assassination conspiracy. He smeared Shaw's good name and forced Shaw to spend a fortune in legal fees to defend himself against the fundamentally baseless charges. Even after Shaw's acquittal, Garrison attempted to prosecute him for perjury, and it took a higher court to finally put an end to Garrison's persecution of the man.

Is It Possible to Reconstruct the Assassination?

No.

Over the years, countless attempts have been made to produce an exact duplication of the assassination. In 1963 and 1964, the Secret Service and the FBI used agents as stand-ins for President Kennedy and Governor Connally as open convertibles drove through the motorcade route. These efforts proved faulty. Both agencies used vehicles different from the actual limousine, and neither tried to duplicate the actual shots. Computer simulations of the motorcade have been made by various individuals and organizations. Lone assassin theorist Dale Myers developed a 360-degree computer simulation, as did *Nova* and ABC News. Most recently, a Scottish company has produced a video game entitled *JFK Reloaded*, in which, after downloading the game from the company's Web site (for a fee), the player fires at the simulated motor-cade from the simulated sixth-floor sniper's nest.[49]

One of the main purposes of these efforts at reconstruction lay in aligning the positions of Kennedy and Connally. Conspiracy theorists argue that because Connally sat directly in front of Kennedy, a bullet fired through the president's neck from above, behind, and to the right could not possibly have proceeded to strike Connally in the extreme upper right side of his back. Lone assassin theorists maintain that Connally actually sat much farther to the left, thus making the alignment for the single bullet trajectory possible. Furthermore, using carefully calculated measurements of the angles of the entrance wounds in both men's backs, both the Warren Commission and the HSCA projected backward from the wounds to pinpoint the region from whence the shot was fired. More recently, an Australian concern did the same, but they used gelatin-filled dummies to substitute for Kennedy and Connally.[50]

In reality, it is impossible to reproduce the precise conditions that prevailed during the assassination. The precise measurements of every part of the bodies of John Kennedy and John Connally remain unknown. Therefore, computer simulations can only approximate, rather than duplicate, their body dimensions. As forensic pathologist William Eckert told me, even the slightest mistake in reproducing such variables as the exact mass of Kennedy's upper back or Connally's fifth rib would result in an inexact simulation. In addition, no consensus exists among researchers as to the precise instant when the first shot was fired. Most researchers believe that the shot that struck Kennedy in his upper back was fired while a street sign blocked Zapruder's camera's view of the limousine. Therefore, Kennedy's exact position remains unknown. Furthermore, Dr. Eckert told me that even the slightest movement of Kennedy's right shoulder, or turn of his head, or any other movement of either man, would cause a drastic revision in the precise path of the bullet through the president's body. As we have seen, the autopsy failed to uncover that path, not only because of the gross incompetence of the autopsy pathologists, but also because high-ranking military and naval brass ordered them not to dissect the back wound. The absence of dissection makes it impossible to reconstruct that shot, because dissection is the only certain means of determining the path of a bullet through a body. Nor was Kennedy's brain dissected. In fact, it was preserved in a stainless steel container without being coronally sectioned. Therefore, the precise trajectory of the bullet through the president's head also remains unknown. It follows that tests purported to reproduce the exact conditions of the head shot cannot be actual reconstructions. The distinguished physicist Luis Alvarez, for example, fired shots from a rifle at a melon. Alvarez actually got the test results published in a peer-reviewed journal and made numerous speeches to physicists about how his tests "proved" that Kennedy's head could fly backward after having been struck from behind because of a "jet effect." Alvarez's test, of course, proved no such thing because he failed to prove that a melon wrapped in tape precisely duplicates a living human skull, or that the impact of a .30-caliber hunting round of ammunition on a melon exactly duplicated the impact of the actual assassination bullet on Kennedy's head.[51]

The most fundamental problem with efforts to reconstruct the assassination lay in the incompatibility of the reconstruction method with the actual event. The assassination, of course, took place in a three-dimensional environment, whereas the reconstructions have been based on two-dimensional records, most notably the Zapruder film. Even though hundreds of still photographs and motion picture films of the assassination have been studied, collectively, they fail to provide a comprehensive panorama of the event. No photographs or films taken from above the motorcade have ever surfaced, nor have any taken from such perspectives as the Dal-Tex building, located almost directly behind the limousine, or the County Records building, located behind and to the left of the motorcade at the time of the shots. In addition, climatic conditions differ. The result is that we cannot duplicate the assassination, and the efforts to reconstruct it have provided at best a distorted picture of the actual event.

Why Do Experts Disagree about the Facts of the Assassination?

Because it remains an unsolved mystery.

Few crimes in American history have attracted as much attention by experts in various fields as has the Kennedy assassination. For more than forty years, specialists in such fields as crime scene investigation, forensic pathology, wounds ballistics, questioned documents examination, photographic analysis, physics, chemistry, and marksmanship have devoted untold hours to studying different aspects of the assassination. That these authorities, many of them world renowned, have failed to arrive at a consensus provides a testimony to the enormous complexities of this crime. At a 2003 symposium commemorating the fortieth anniversary of the assassination, many such specialists presented their views, but it ended with "the great divide separating the partisans," as David Mantik phrased it, remaining as deep as ever.[52]

The earliest investigation by the experts came, of course, at the time of the assassination. The Dallas police, the Dallas County sheriff's office, the Secret Service, and the FBI conducted early investigations, each employing certain specialists to examine particular areas. The FBI conducted by far the most comprehensive examination of the evidence, and in nearly all areas, it employed its own experts to conduct that examination. J. Edgar Hoover's paranoid obsession with protecting the image of the bureau, together with the Warren Commission's presumption of Lee Harvey Oswald's guilt, precluded any serious, independent examination of any aspect of the evidence. In only two instances, using the Atomic Energy Commission's nuclear facility at Oak Ridge, Tennessee, to perform NAA on certain bullet fragments, and using an Illinois state police expert to examine the ballistics materials in the Tippit killing, did the FBI allow outsiders to review certain materials. With the publication of the Warren Report in September 1964, the federal government, as well as virtually all of the leading organs of the press and media, presumed that the final word on the assassination had been written.[53]

However, the publication of numerous books highly critical of the Warren Report by such authors as Mark Lane and Harold Weisberg, the outspoken criticism of the official conduct of the autopsy by such authorities as Milton Helpern and Cyril Wecht, and the enormous publicity surrounding the Garrison investigation generated public demand for an independent investigation. So concerned was he about the possibility that the Warren Commission may have erred that in 1967 attorney general Ramsey Clark appointed a panel of specialists led by forensic pathologist Russell Fisher to reexamine the autopsy evidence.

Although it ratified the Warren Commission's central conclusion that all shots came from behind, that panel's report fueled further controversy when it concluded that the autopsy pathologists proved so incompetent as to mistakenly locate the wound of entrance in the back of President Kennedy's head by four inches below its true location. Independent examinations of the autopsy materials by urologist John Lattimer and forensic pathologist Cyril Wecht yielded two diametrically opposite interpretations of the evidence, with Lattimer supporting the lone assassin thesis and Wecht believing that the evidence proved a conspiracy. Another examination by forensic pathologist E. Forrest Chapman in 1973 lent his expertise to the conspiracy side.[54]

In 1975 and 1976, the U.S. Senate Intelligence Committee conducted an investigation into allegations of U.S. government involvement in assassination plots against the leaders of foreign countries, and a subcommittee chaired by Senator Richard Schweiker probed the performance of the intelligence agencies in investigating the Kennedy assassination. This led to the appointment by President Gerald Ford of a commission headed by Vice President Nelson Rockefeller to delve deeper into the intelligence connection to the assassination. One aspect of the Rockefeller Commission's work lay in the appointment of a panel of medical specialists to reexamine the autopsy evidence. Because the president was himself a member of the Warren Commission and the chief counsel of the Rockefeller Commission, David Belin, had served as a junior counsel for the Warren Commission, it surprised no one that the commission's panel of experts concluded that Kennedy had indeed been shot twice from behind.[55]

Public opinion, fueled by the airing of the Zapruder film on national television, led to the appointment by the U.S. House of Representatives to appoint a House Select Committee on Assassinations to investigate the assassinations of John F. Kennedy and Martin Luther King Jr. The HSCA appointed a panel of experts in forensic pathology, firearms, photographic identification, acoustics, and other fields, together with consultants in radiology, wounds ballistics, and trajectory analysis to examine the evidence and report their conclusions back to the committee. In most instances, a majority of the panelists supported the Warren Commission's lone assassin conclusions, but usually, one or more of the panel members dissented from the majority report. The acoustics panel, however, touched off a controversy that continues to rage today when it concluded that the sonic wave length patterns produced by a Dallas police tape recording of the assassination proved that shots were fired from both behind and in front of the presidential limousine.[56]

Since the publication of the HSCA report in 1979, many experts have examined various aspects of the surviving evidence in the Kennedy assassination. Independent examinations of the medical evidence by emergency room physician Robert Artwohl, forensic pathologist Vincent DiMaio, ophthalmologist Gary Aguilar, and radiation oncologist David Mantik produced conflicting opinions, with Artwohl and DiMaio supporting the lone assassin thesis, and Aguilar and Mantik supporting the conspiracy thesis. The ARRB hired certain experts, including one from Kodak, to verify the authenticity of the Zapruder film and certain other material. Physicist Art Snyder has sharply criticized the NAA of certain ballistics evidence by Vincent Guinn, while oceanographer Kenneth Rahn has strongly supported Guinn's work. In its analysis of certain aspects of the evidence for a mock trial of Lee Harvey Oswald at the annual meeting of the American Bar Association, Failure Analysis Associates employed two experts to conduct tests. Wounds ballistics expert Marvin Fackler fired a Mannlicher-Carcano bullet into a human cadaver's wrist. The bullet, whose velocity had been deliberately slowed through Fackler's removing some of the gunpowder, supposedly to simulate the actual velocity of the slug when it struck John Connally's wrist, inflicted more damage on the cadaver wrist than Connally suffered, yet the test slug emerged in more pristine condition than Bullet 399. Roger McCarthy, the head of the company, fired shot into bottles filled with glycerin, supposedly simulating John Kennedy's head. In every instance, the bottles and the glycerin inside them flew away from the gun. In reality, neither test reconstructed the actual assassination scene.[57]

These represent but a few examples of the seemingly endless series of expert examination of the Kennedy assassination evidence. Undoubtedly all of these highly qualified individuals have arrived at interpretations of that evidence that reflects their honest, expert evaluation. Yet they cannot all be correct. Either one man fired all of the shots, or more than one man. Either Kennedy was struck only from behind, or also from the front. Perhaps famed crime scene investigator Henry Lee best summarized the only conclusion one can arrive at by listening to the experts when he proclaimed that he had investigated thousands of crimes in his distinguished career and could always arrive at a conclusion, but in the case of the Kennedy assassination, "I still don't know what happened."[58]

Lee Harvey Oswald

To all who have studied the assassination, regardless of their perspective, Lee Harvey Oswald clearly emerges as one of the most significant figures. For those who espouse the lone assassin theory, Oswald stands out as the man who committed the crime of the century. For those who espouse conspiracy theories, Oswald also stands out, either as a member of a group of assassins or as a patsy, the scapegoat employed to take the blame while the real assassins made good their escape. Only twenty-four years and one month old when he was gunned down by Jack Ruby, Lee Oswald led a life that to this day remains, to paraphrase Winston Churchill's famous remark about the Soviet Union, a mystery wrapped up in an enigma inside a puzzle. Despite the extraordinary amount of attention focused on that life, many aspects of it continue to befuddle researchers, and no definitive explanation of Oswald's precise role in the assassination can yet be given.

Lee Harvey Oswald was born in New Orleans in October 1939. Lee's father had died of a heart attack two months before he was born, leaving his mother, Marguerite Claviere Oswald, alone to raise Lee, his older brother Robert, and their older half-brother John Pic, the product of Marguerite's marriage to her first husband, John Edward "Eddie" Pic. Because she worked, Marguerite left the three boys to stay with relatives, and on occasion, Lee and Robert spent time in orphanages. When Lee was five, Marguerite moved to Covington, a small town on the north shore of Lake Ponchartrain (New Orleans is on the south shore), where Lee attended school for the first time. Marguerite then moved to Fort Worth, Texas, where she married her third husband, Edwin Ekdahl, a union that would soon dissolve. In the period 1945 to 1952, Marguerite moved more than a dozen times in the Dallas–Fort Worth area, and Lee found himself attending eleven dif-

ferent grammar schools. Clearly, the experience left the boy without
the stability of a place that he could call home, and he never had the
opportunity to develop lasting friendships. Some authors, such as Gerald Posner, argue that this continual mobility, combined with Marguerite's domineering personality and the lack of a man in the household,
had a profound impact on the impressionable young boy, prompting
him to withdraw into a shell of privacy and to isolate himself from society. This amateur attempt at psychoanalysis fails to account for the
fact that Robert and John Pic grew up under identical circumstances
and became perfectly normal adults.[1]

In 1952 Marguerite moved to New York City. There Lee, a young
teenager, found himself among strangers in school and often became
the object of his classmates' ridicule because of his Texas accent and
mannerisms. Frequently absent from school, he wound up in Youth
House for three weeks, during which time he underwent examination
by the chief psychiatrist, Dr. Renatus Hartogs, and by members of
his staff. Dr. Hartogs diagnosed Lee as suffering from "personality
pattern disturbance with schizoid features and passive-aggressive ten-
dencies." He labeled Lee as "an emotionally quite disturbed youngster
who suffers under the impact of really [sic] existing emotional isola-
tion and deprivation, lack of affection, absence of family life and rejec-
tion by a self-involved and conflicted mother." Another Youth House
staff member, Irving Sokolow, a psychologist, made Lee draw human
figures. On the basis of the drawings, Sokolow diagnosed Oswald as
"somewhat insecure" and "slightly withdrawn." He also believed that
Lee "exhibits some difficulty in relationship to the maternal figure
suggesting more anxiety in this area than in any other."[2]

The pseudo-Freudian nature of these interpretations of the thirteen-
year-old Lee Harvey Oswald's personality were emphasized by the
Warren Commission and Gerald Posner, both of whom depicted Lee
as quick to anger and displaying potential for violence. Posner, for example, notes how one day in New York, Lee pulled out his pocketknife
on John Pic's wife, at whose apartment he, Robert, and Marguerite
stayed. During the dispute, Lee punched his mother in the face. The
incident persuaded John Pic's wife to evict Lee and Marguerite, yet
it remains an isolated one in his life. There is no doubt that Marguerite Oswald was a difficult, obstinate, and domineering woman. She

and Lee certainly had numerous disputes, including some shouting matches. Yet could not the same be said of millions of other teenagers? Quarrels between teenagers and their parents are hardly uncommon, and Lee's relationship with Marguerite, however strained it might have been on occasion, stood the test of time. It should be noted that after Oswald's arrest for the murder of Officer Tippit and the assassination of President Kennedy, Marguerite Oswald steadfastly maintained her son's innocence. Far from harboring hostile feelings toward Lee, after his death, in testimony before the Warren Commission, and on many other occasions, she consistently championed his cause until her own death two decades later.[3]

In January 1954 Marguerite left New York and returned to New Orleans, where Lee finished the ninth grade. After working for a year, he enrolled in high school but left after a month, feeling that he did not need the education. He tried to join the marines, but the corps rejected him because of his age. As soon as he reached seventeen, in October 1956, Marguerite signed the papers allowing him to join the marines. Oswald's decision to join the marines has evoked considerable speculation because he had already supposedly developed a strong affinity for communism. Having read numerous works on Marxism and Leninism, he told friends that he was sympathetic to the Soviet Union. Why would a seventeen-year-old who exhibited pro-Marxist sympathies enlist in perhaps the most conservative, anticommunist branch of the service? Two reasons are commonly given. First, both John Pic and Robert had entered the service, and Lee naturally wanted to emulate them. Second, as John Pic expressed it, Lee enlisted "to get from out and under . . . the yoke of oppression from my mother." Neither reason appears satisfactory. Lee was never close to his brother and half-brother and certainly did not emulate them. Indeed, he hardly communicated with them. Joining the marines was a drastic step for a young man to escape his mother. All he had to do was simply leave home. It also should be noted that his alleged affinity with communism occurred during the height of the McCarthy era, and it is not unusual for a young teenager with above-average intelligence to try to satisfy his curiosity about the most common topic in the news. Whatever his motive, Lee did enlist in the marines and would stay there for the next two and three-quarters years.[4]

Leatherneck

In October 1956, Lee Oswald began the rigorous ten-week boot camp that all new marine recruits must undergo. He passed both the physical and mental challenges, experiencing the greatest difficulty in marksmanship. In January 1957, he underwent basic training, and after completing a course in radar, entered a class in aircraft surveillance at Keesler Air Force Base in Biloxi, Mississippi. There he frequently left base, ostensibly to visit relatives in New Orleans, only ninety miles away. In May, he was promoted to private first class and received a security clearance of "confidential." Some conspiracy theorists have speculated on Oswald's security clearance, but he held only the lowest and certainly did not have access to major military secrets, at least initially. However, in September 1957, Oswald was transferred to the Marine Air Control Squadron One (MACS-1) at the Atsugi base in Japan, one of the home bases of one of the cold war's most sensitive operations, the CIA-controlled U-2 spy plane flights over the Soviet Union and China. Oswald and the men in his radar unit tracked the U-2s as they took off and landed, although his unit did not have direct access to the highly classified aircraft. There is some evidence, although inconclusive, that while at Atsugi, Oswald made contact with Japanese communists. What they discussed remains unknown. In October, just over a month after it landed in Japan, MACS-1 was ordered to undergo maneuvers in the Philippines. Enraged at having to leave Japan so soon after he arrived, Oswald shot himself in the fleshy part of his upper arm to avoid having to ship out, but his ruse was easily uncovered, and he went to the Philippines anyway. Later, Oswald would be fined and demoted back to private for having an unauthorized firearm in his possession.[5]

After an extended tour in the Philippines, Oswald's unit returned to Japan in April 1958. In June he entered a bar and deliberately poured a drink over the head of the sergeant in his outfit because Lee blamed him for giving him extra mess duty. For this act of insubordination, he served a month in the brig. After a brief tour in Taiwan, Oswald was separated from his unit and returned to Japan. At Iwakuni, he impressed some of his comrades with his outspoken hostility toward the United States and his forceful advocacy of the communist system. It seems incomprehensible that the United States Marine Corps, one of the most hard-nosed, superpatriotic organizations in the world, would, during the height of the cold war, with the legacy of McCarthyism still heavily influencing American foreign and defense policy, allow one of its members to get away with such unpatriotic, almost disloyal remarks, yet for some unknown reason, the corps tolerated his behavior. In November 1958 Oswald left for the United States, where he visited with Marguerite and Robert. Stationed at a base at El Toro, California, he studied the Russian language intensively and became proficient in it. As in Japan, Oswald's comrades-in-arms were amazed at the marines allowing him to get away with his quite vocal sympathy for the Russian language and for the Soviet Union. Could Oswald have been recruited by some branch of American intelligence and ordered deliberately to pose as a pro-Marxist? No definitive evidence exists to answer in the affirmative, yet it offers the only explanation for the Marine Corps's otherwise inexplicable toleration of his nearly seditious demeanor. It further suggests that Oswald received training in Russian for some assignment by an intelligence agency.[6]

In August 1959 Lee Oswald applied for a hardship discharge from the marines because Marguerite had slightly injured herself at work and had applied for assistance. With alacrity, the marines gave Lee his discharge, without even bothering to check on Marguerite's story. In fact, Marguerite was neither disabled nor unemployed, and her son Robert lived close to her in Fort Worth at the time. Therefore, she did not need Lee's assistance. When Lee arrived in Fort Worth on September 14, 1959, he stayed with his mother less than two days, gave her $100, and departed for New Orleans. At no time did the marines investigate this obvious violation of his discharge request. In any event, with only $103 at his disposal, Lee booked passage to France on the SS *Marion Lykes*, a freighter, which sailed from New Orleans on September 20. On October 8, Oswald left the ship at Le Havre, France, and the following day traveled to Southampton, England. From London, he flew to Helsinki, Finland, and checked into an expensive hotel. How he afforded the transportation, lodging, and meals continues to puzzle researchers. Even in 1959, $103 could not possibly have paid the costs of travel to Europe and around the continent. Clearly, Oswald must have had another source of income, but no evidence of it has ever surfaced. On October 12, Oswald obtained a visa from the Soviet consulate in the Finnish capital, used his mysterious source of additional income to purchase $300 worth of Intourist (the Soviet tourist agency heavily infiltrated by the KGB) vouchers, and on October 15, took a train from Helsinki to Moscow, beginning another curious phase in his life.[7]

Life in the USSR

Oswald checked in at the Berlin Hotel in Moscow and immediately applied for Soviet citizenship. On October 21, he learned that the Russian government had rejected his request and ordered him to leave the country. Stunned, he tried to commit suicide by slashing his wrists. Discovered by his Intourist guide, he was rushed to a nearby hospital, given blood transfusions, and survived. Oswald's suicide attempt allegedly caused top-ranking Soviet officials to reverse their decision to deport him. Anastaysas Mikoyan, a powerful member of the Presidium, urged the KGB to reconsider granting the American defector asylum. According to Gerald Posner, the reason lay in the thawing of the relationship between the United States and the USSR and the desire by the Soviets to project a more humanitarian image by allowing the suicidal young man to remain in their country because the Russians under Nikita Khrushchev strongly desired to make a more favorable impression on other nations.[8]

It appears that the reason for the Soviet interest in Oswald lay more in his knowledge of certain aspects of the U-2 flights than in a most uncharacteristic display of altruism on the part of the Soviets. In his masterful study of the U-2 incident of May 1960, when an American spy plane was shot down over the Soviet Union and its CIA-employed pilot, Francis Gary Powers, captured, Michael Beschloss states that "Oswald undoubtedly revealed information [to the Russians] about the U-2," and he may have known "details about the plane, its rate of climb, cruising altitude and payload, the radar, the pilots, base security and how it might be circumvented." Beschloss, however, did state that had the Russians considered Oswald "valuable, they probably would not have left him within reach of western reporters for two months, and he might have gotten something better than a factory job." Gerald Posner dismisses out of hand the possibility that Oswald may have possessed information valuable to the Russians. In reality, Oswald did know a considerable amount about matters that would have interested the Soviets. The commander of Oswald's marine radar unit, John E. Donovan, told the Warren Commission that among other things, Oswald "had access to . . . all radio frequencies for all squadrons, all tactical call signs . . . the number and type of aircraft in a squadron . . . the authentication code of entering and exiting the ADIZ [Air Force (Defense) Identification Zone]. He knew the range of our radar." In short, Lee Harvey Oswald possessed a great deal of information relating to national security—information that the Russians apparently considered significant enough to allow him to remain in their country. It remains a most curious fact that only seven months after Oswald defected, the Soviets managed a feat they had previously proved incapable of performing: shooting down a U-2. In all probability, Oswald gave them some information that helped them accomplish the feat.[9]

Questions abound regarding Lee Harvey Oswald's two-and-a-half-year sojourn in the Soviet Union. One concerns the blatant contradictions contained within the writings commonly attributed to him. Gerald Posner claims that Oswald "appears to have been dyslexic" because of "numerous misspellings." Oswald did indeed misspell many words. Yet he could write with both accuracy and even refinement on certain occasions. When he discovered that the Russians were not eager to accept him, Oswald wrote in his so-called Historic Diary: "I am shocked!! My dreams !***I have waited for 2 yeare to be accepted. My fondes dreams are shattered because of a petty offial,***I decide to end it. Soak rist in cold water to numb the pain, Than slash my leftwrist. Than plaug wrist into bathtum of not water.*** Somewhere, a violin plays as I watch my life whirl away." Written on October 21, 1959, this diary entry clearly contains so many obvious misspellings and grammatical errors that one could hardly disagree with Posner's conclusion about Oswald's dyslexia. Yet only ten days later, Oswald wrote the following note, which he presented to the United States Embassy in Moscow:

> I have entered the Soviet Union for the express purpose of appling for citizenship in the Soviet Union, through the means of naturalization.
> I Lee Harvey Oswald do hereby request that my present citizenship in the United States of America, be revoked.

My request for citizenship is now pending before the Suprem Soviet of the U.S.S.R.

I take these steps for political reasons. My request for the revoking of my American citizenship is made only after the longest and most serious considerations.

I affirm that my allegiance is to the Union of Soviet Socialist Republics.

The two passages hardly seem to have been written by the same person. The diary entry contains such obvious misspellings of words like "wrist," "plunge," "bathtub," "fondest," "official," and "years," while the embassy note is quite literate and contains only two minor misspellings. None of the examinations of Oswald's handwriting by government-appointed experts has explained these and other glaring inconsistencies in his writings.[10]

Another puzzle entails Yuri Nosenko, who had previously contacted the CIA official at the U.S. embassy in Geneva about defecting. Only two months after President Kennedy was assassinated, Nosenko, a thirty-seven-year-old lieutenant colonel in the KGB, defected to the United States. After providing the CIA with sufficient details to convince the agency that he was indeed a high-ranking KGB official, Nosenko stated that his primary purpose lay in distancing the KGB from Oswald. He insisted that the Soviet secret police had not questioned Oswald, debriefed him, or made any contact with him during his two and a half years in the USSR. Under repeated interrogation by CIA experts, Nosenko clung to this obviously incredible story and vehemently denied any association whatsoever between Oswald and the KGB. Nosenko's allegations led to the most extensive shake-up within the CIA in the agency's history. Some, like famed counterintelligence chief James Jesus Angleton, believed Nosenko was a mole, insinuated into the agency to spread disinformation. Others believed him a genuine defector. The FBI also believed Nosenko because its spy, "Fedora," who worked in the Soviet delegation to the United Nations, informed J. Edgar Hoover that Nosenko was a real defector.[11]

Although Hoover wanted Nosenko to testify before the Warren Commission, powerful CIA figures did not. Acting with the full knowledge and consent of Attorney General Robert Kennedy, the CIA's deputy director for plans, Richard Helms, told Earl Warren that Nosenko lacked credibility. Warren accepted Helms's story, and nowhere in the voluminous materials published by the Warren Commission can one find Nosenko's name. It is curious that Helms would take orders from Robert Kennedy, who had absolutely no authority over the CIA, and indeed would soon resign as attorney general to run for the New York Senate seat. Helms in fact lied to Warren because he feared that allowing Nosenko to testify before the Warren Commission would tarnish the agency's image, which Helms would prove as paranoid in protecting as would Hoover the FBI's. Ultimately, Nosenko remained confined under extreme duress for seven years, and the CIA never did resolve its internal conflicts over whether he was a valid defector. The timing of Nosenko's defection, less than two months after the Kennedy assassination, as well as his stubborn, vehement insistence that the KGB had nothing to do with Oswald, obviously raises suspicions over the validity of his story. Because no one seriously thought that the USSR was behind the assassination in the first place, one can only wonder about the strange timing of Nosenko's defection and about his more than seven-year struggle to absolve the KGB of any connection with Lee Harvey Oswald.[12]

Another question concerns Oswald's treatment during his two and a half years in the Soviet Union. On January 7, 1960, Lee Harvey Oswald arrived in Minsk, where he was employed at an electronics factory. His salary as a metalworker, matched by the Red Cross, allowed him to earn as much as the factory's superintendent, which meant that he earned considerably more than the average Soviet citizen. In addition, Lee was rewarded with a large one-room apartment, a luxury the overwhelming majority of Russians could only dream of. If Oswald had no information of value to give the Russians, they would hardly have allowed him to live in such an elite—by Soviet standards—style. Furthermore, they allowed him freedom of movement around the country and even granted him permission to fire guns at a hunting club. The Russians made no attempt to publicize the defection of the former marine; on the contrary, they never allowed any publicity about him. Despite the release of numerous previously classified files from both American and Soviet archives, virtually nothing is known about Oswald's first year and a half in the Soviet Union. As mentioned previously, only seven months after his defection, the Russians shot down Francis Gary Powers's U-2 spy plane. Whether Oswald provided them with certain information about the plane remains unknown, but the possibility clearly exists.[13]

After dating several Russian women, Lee Oswald met Marina Prusakova, the niece of a Soviet intelligence official. Only a month after they met in the spring of 1961, Lee proposed, Marina accepted, and they were married a week later. Once again, the Soviets allowed Oswald greater freedom than they did their own citizens, for as the niece of a Soviet intelligence official, Marina needed permission to marry. Oswald had already visited the American embassy in Moscow to begin the preparations for his return to the United States because he had become disillusioned with life under communism. Marina apparently eagerly awaited their departure from her native land. Curiously, not only did the U.S. State Department lend Oswald the money for his voyage home, it also welcomed Marina with open arms. Even odder was the Soviet government's willingness to allow Marina to leave. This came at a time when it was almost impossible for ordinary Russians even to visit foreign countries, much less to emigrate to their government's avowed enemy, America. Nevertheless, in June 1962, Lee, Marina, and their baby daughter, June, departed the USSR for the United States, arriving there on June 13. Despite his defection to the Soviet Union and his two-and-a-half-year sojourn there, the CIA officially made no attempt to debrief, interview, maintain surveillance over, or in any other way keep track of Oswald after his arrival back in the United States.[14]

Back Home

The Oswalds settled in Fort Worth, and Lee got a job at a small welding company, where he would work for the next three months. In the summer of 1962, Lee became acquainted with Georges deMorenschildt, a Texas oil geologist, with a long and murky history of intelligence activities dating back to the pre–World War II era. DeMorenschildt's wife, Jeanne, also had a long history of working in intelligence and numbered among her friends and former fellow operatives in the CIA Richard

Helms, the agency's future director; James McCord, a close friend of Helms's and the future Watergate burglar; Hunter Leake, an agent who worked at the agency's large New Orleans office; and David Atlee Phillips, the head of the CIA's Western Hemisphere operations. At the time he met Oswald, Georges deMorenschildt was actively engaged in several clandestine operations involving the CIA's massive anti-Castro operation, code-named MONGOOSE. A veteran of the planning for the Bay of Pigs invasion of Cuba, in October 1962, when he first met Oswald, deMorenschildt used his employment as an oil geologist as a cover for smuggling arms, ammunition, and supplies to anti-Castro Cubans in Texas and Louisiana. One of the legitimate fronts that the CIA used for this activity was the large Schlumberger Well Company, an oil-drilling supply company, located near Houma, Louisiana. Hamilton Johnson, a Tulane University geologist who worked at Schlumberger Well at the time, recalled deMorenschildt, invariably accompanied by Cubans and by American intelligence agents, frequently visiting the company site in 1962 and 1963. Considering Oswald's own contacts with anti-Castro Cuban elements in both Texas and Louisiana in 1962 and 1963, his friendship with deMorenschildt assumes great significance in this story.[15]

In early October 1962, just before the outbreak of the Cuban missile crisis, Georges and Jeanne deMorenschildt visited Lee and Marina. The following day, Lee quit his job at the welding company, even though he had performed his work satisfactorily. A week later, he got a job at Jaggars-Chiles-Stovall, a company that produced topographic maps for the army and did other specialized photographic work. Interestingly, Oswald, the defector to the Soviet Union, got the job at the company, which did classified work. During the Cuban missile crisis, Oswald did not return home after work, and to this day, there exists no positive proof of his whereabouts from the time he left work until the time he began work the next day for nearly a month. It is strange that neither the company nor the Department of Defense made any attempt to check Oswald's credentials, even though he had access to the area where classified materials were processed. The possibility exists that Oswald and deMorenschildt performed certain undercover assignments during the Cuban missile crisis. In the summer of 1962, Lee and Marina became acquainted with members of the fanatically anticommunist White Russian community in the Dallas–Fort Worth region. This acquaintance, coupled with Oswald's close friendship with the equally fanatically anticommunist deMorenschildts, clashes sharply with his public image of a leftist and fanatical supporter of Marxism and Leninism.[16]

For the next six months, Lee Harvey Oswald worked regularly at Jaggars-Chiles-Stovall. He and Marina, having moved to a modest apartment in Dallas, maintained an ambivalent relationship. Working steadily, Lee earned enough money to pay off his loans from the State Department, and the young couple felt secure enough to plan another child, with Marina becoming pregnant in January 1963. On the other hand, they frequently argued, and Marina would later claim that Lee physically and mentally abused her. In addition to their friendship with Georges and Jeanne deMorenschildt, Lee and Marina also made the acquaintance of Ruth Paine and her estranged husband, Michael. Marina and Ruth would become especially close friends. Lee continued to tell friends about his experiences in the Soviet Union, and he sent the Soviet embassy in Washington a New Year's greeting in Russian. Yet he continued to hang around with Georges and Jeanne deMorenschildt, whose services to the CIA during Operation MONGOOSE hardly fit Oswald's public image of a pro-Marxist individual. All of this, of course, has fueled suspicions of Oswald's ties to American intelligence. Oswald also accompanied Jeanne DeMorenschildt to at least three meetings of anti-Castro Cuban exiles in the Dallas–Fort Worth region during the first three months of 1963.[17]

On January 27, 1963, Lee Oswald purchased, through mail order from a Los Angeles sporting goods company, a .38-caliber Smith and Wesson revolver with a short, two-inch barrel. On March 12, 1963, Oswald clipped a coupon for a used Mannlicher-Carcano rifle from the *American Rifleman* magazine, and sent it, together with a money order for $21.45, for the rifle and a four-power telescopic sight, to Klein's Sporting Goods in Chicago. Just as occurred with the revolver, the sporting goods company would send the rifle and scope to "A. Hidell," a common Oswald alias, at a Dallas post office box that Oswald allegedly had rented. That is the official version, but several matters need to be considered. Authorities on questioned documents, or handwriting experts, as they are commonly called, positively identified the writing on the coupon, the money order, and the envelope as Oswald's. The possibility of forgery, however, cannot be dismissed. Time and again, leading authorities on handwriting identification have been fooled by forgers, such as Clifford Irving's fake manuscript of the "autobiography" of Howard Hughes, positively authenticated by some of the nation's leading questioned documents experts, and the "Hitler diaries" authenticated by many of the world's leading handwriting experts. A second question concerns Oswald's purchase of ammunition for the weapon. He supposedly picked up the rifle at the Dallas post office box on March 20. Oswald must have purchased ammunition for it somewhere, but an exhaustive search of all gunsmith and sporting goods stores in the Dallas–Fort Worth metroplex uncovered absolutely no evidence that he had ever purchased Mannlicher-Carcano ammunition. Thorough searches of Oswald's room and possessions after the assassination also yielded not a single bullet of that readily identifiable type. Nor does any evidence exist regarding his purchase of ammunition for the handgun. Finally, absolutely no evidence exists to show where Oswald kept the revolver from the time he purchased it until the day he supposedly shot Officer J. D. Tippit with it.[18]

On April 10, 1963, Oswald allegedly fired a shot at retired U.S. Army Major General Edwin A. Walker while Walker sat in the dining room of his home in Dallas. The bullet grazed Walker's hair and lodged in the wall. The bullet suffered such mutilation that it never could be identified as having been fired from a particular weapon. Less than one hundred feet from Walker when he fired the shot, Oswald supposedly struck the wooden frame of the dining room window, with the wood deflecting the bullet just barely enough to miss Walker. Oswald's motivation for shooting at Walker lay in his hatred of Walker's notorious right-wing views and his desire to make a name for himself. Yet the evidence strongly suggests that Oswald did not, in fact, shoot at Walker. Oswald, supposedly a crack shot, missed a stationary target, yet in Dealey Plaza, he managed to strike a moving target two out of three attempts, the last at triple the range of the Walker attempt. A second factor militating against Oswald's complicity in the Walker shooting lies in the condition of the bullet. In the Kennedy assassination, Oswald supposedly fired the exact same type of bullet, which struck both President Kennedy and Governor Connally, shattered two thick bones, and emerged virtually intact. Yet in the Walker shooting, the bullet merely glanced off the thin window board, lodged in soft Sheetrock, and suffered severe deformation.[19]

Initially, the Dallas police department identified the bullet removed from the wall in Walker's home as a 30.06 caliber, a common hunting round of ammunition. How they made such a glaring mistake remains inexplicable. The 30.06 is easily identifiable, as my interviews with scores of hunters and gun shop owners demonstrated. Moreover, it is of a larger diameter (three-tenths of an inch) than the Mannlicher-Carcano (one-quarter of an inch). In addition, the Carcano ammunition, manufactured for firing in an obscure foreign weapon, would naturally raise suspicions by professionally trained ballistics experts in the police department. Billy Abel, the longtime owner of a sporting goods store that sold both 30.06 and Mannlicher-Carcano ammunition; Henry M. Morris, the former superintendent of the New Orleans police department; Robert A. Maurin Sr., who performed ballistics tests on the Mannlicher-Carcano for the U.S. Eighth Army in Italy during World War II; and Sidney Johnston, who conducted ballistics tests on the Mannlicher-Carcano for the Special Forces, are among the many authorities who have scoffed at mistaking one type of ammunition for the other. As Abel remarked, "Any cop, in fact, any hunter, would instantly recognize a .30 caliber bullet, and they would never confuse it with a 6.5mm [.25 caliber]." It is worth noting that several Dallas law enforcement officers misidentified the rifle found in the Book Depository building as a Mauser, and they claimed, in their initial police radio broadcast of the killer wanted for shooting the president and governor, that he was carrying a 30.06 rifle. Only after the Warren Commission began its investigation into Oswald's background did the Dallas police department produce a mangled Mannlicher-Carcano bullet and claim that it was the one recovered from Walker's home. It should be noted that the Dallas police did not charge Oswald with the attempted murder of General Walker because, as former Dallas police chief Jesse Curry told me, "We had absolutely no evidence to connect him to the case."[20]

A final argument against Oswald's being the gunman who fired at General Walker lies in the distance between his apartment and Walker's house. Because, according to the official version, Oswald did not drive, he must have traveled the nearly seven miles either on foot, in a bus, or in a taxi. The Warren Commission, Gerald Posner, David Belin, Max Holland, John McAdams, and many other lone assassin theorists have not even attempted to explain how Oswald managed to transport a rifle that measured thirty-six inches long when disassembled and weighed over ten pounds without being spotted. Citing Marina Oswald's story, Posner claims that several days before the Walker shooting, Oswald hid the rifle under his raincoat and walked to a nearby levee, where he practiced firing the weapon—although, like everything else Marina said about her husband's actions, they must be taken with a grain of salt. It would be inconceivable that Oswald would have walked the entire seven miles with the rifle concealed, perhaps in a handmade paper bag, from public view. It is equally inconceivable that he would have risked detection by passengers on the half-dozen different buses needed to convey him from his apartment to the vicinity of the Walker home. No taxi drivers ever reported picking up a passenger near Oswald's apartment on Neely Street and taking him to the area near the Walker home, in an entirely different section of Dallas. The possibility that someone had driven him to the crime scene, confirmed by witnesses who saw two men staking out the Walker premises two days before the shooting, and by a witness who saw two men drive away in separate vehicles from the scene after the shooting, would obviously have raised the certainty of a conspiracy in this murder attempt, so the Warren Commission did nothing to examine this possibility.[21]

Probably the most amazing aspect of the official story that Oswald fired a shot at Walker lies in his alleged escape from the crime scene. Presumably running away, Oswald, according to this version, stopped several blocks away and either hid the rifle among some bushes or buried it in the ground in an empty lot. Four days later, on Easter Sunday, he returned to the area, retrieved the rifle, and returned home by some mysterious means of transportation. The only evidence of this incredible scenario comes from Marina Oswald's account. It defies belief that only four days after the highly publicized assassination attempt against General Walker, Lee Harvey Oswald would travel by some unknown means to the place where he had concealed the weapon, recover the weapon, and return home in broad daylight without being seen by a single person. Seven months later, Oswald would presumably repeat the first part of this scenario by leaving the assassination weapon, the identical Mannlicher-Carcano, on the same floor of the Depository building from which he fired the shots.[22]

The most compelling evidence that Oswald did attempt to shoot General Walker comes from his widow's testimony. Marina recalled in detail how Oswald returned home the night of the Walker shooting quite agitated, and she described his rage at learning from newspaper and television accounts the next morning that he had missed. Marina also recounted seeing Oswald with the rifle and even told the Warren Commission that she had to lock him in the bathroom of their apartment to prevent him from trying to assassinate former vice president Richard M. Nixon during a Nixon visit to Dallas. Marina Oswald's various contradictory versions of events must be viewed in the light of threats made by the FBI, the Secret Service, and the Immigration and Naturalization Service to deport her back to the USSR if she did not "cooperate." In her earliest accounts, Marina related very different things to authorities than she did in later testimony. For example, in her earliest statements, she admitted that she did not know the difference between a rifle and a shotgun. Later, she testified under oath that the Mannlicher-Carcano rifle, a weapon so obscure that even experienced law enforcement officers mistook it for a Mauser, was the "fateful rifle of Lee Oswald." As early as February 1964, a Warren Commission staff declared Marina "cold, calculating, avaricious." It is therefore only with skepticism that we consider any of her versions of events, whether exculpatory of Oswald or pointing toward his guilt.[23]

The bullet provided by the Dallas police department to the FBI after the assassination was a badly mutilated Mannlicher-Carcano 6.5-millimeter slug. Because of the bullet's mutilated state, Robert A. Frazier, an FBI ballistics expert, testified that he could not state that Oswald's rifle had fired it. Frazier found nothing to preclude the bullet from having been fired from that rifle, but he could not connect it to the weapon to the exclusion of all other rifles. The Firearms Identification Panel of the House Select Committee on Assassinations (HSCA) agreed with Frazier, and neutron activation analysis tests of the Walker bullet could only conclude that it matched the general chemical composition of the nearly one million Mannlicher-Carcano bullets manufactured in 1943 during the same manufacturing run as Carcano ammunition recovered in the Kennedy assassination case. The Warren Commission claimed that a note written by Lee to Marina, in which he provided her with advice on what to do if he were arrested and taken to jail, was written just prior to the Walker shooting. Because the note is undated, that conclusion appears unwarranted. Several photographs of Walker's residence, taken by Oswald's camera, provide additional evidence that he did indeed attempt to kill the retired army officer. Finally, it should be noted that while in custody at Dallas police headquarters during November 22–24, 1963, Oswald was not charged with the attempted murder of General Walker. Indeed, Walker's extreme right-wing fanaticism, which incorporated both virulent anticommunism and vicious racism, placed him on the opposite end of the political spectrum from John F. Kennedy, and Oswald's alleged political motivation for killing Kennedy hardly concurs with his apparent political motivation for trying to kill Walker.[24]

Five Months in New Orleans

Having lost his job at Jaggars-Chiles-Stovall, Oswald decided to move, this time to his place of birth, New Orleans. The reason he gave to Ruth Paine and Marina lay in his inability to find a job in Dallas. This proved to be a false excuse. Dallas was experiencing an economic boom at the time, and a perusal of the city's newspapers for April 1963 reveals hundreds of classified advertisements for employment. If anything, New Orleans offered fewer job opportunities. In any event, Oswald took a bus to New Orleans on April 25 and moved in temporarily with his aunt and uncle, Lillian and Dutz Murrett. Much has been written about Oswald's uncle, Dutz Murrett, working as a bookie for Louisiana Mafia boss Carlos Marcello. In his study of the Mafia connection to the assassination, John Davis states that Oswald performed such chores for his uncle as collecting money from gamblers. Davis insinuates that Oswald therefore had connections to Marcello, one of the prime suspects in the assassination. In actuality, even if Oswald had performed chores for his uncle, it hardly connects him to Marcello, who remained carefully insulated from direct contact with the bookies in his organization. On May 9, Oswald got a job with the Reily Coffee

Company, manufacturers of one of New Orleans's favorite beverages, Luzianne coffee. The job, which paid $1.50 an hour, required Oswald to maintain the coffee-grinding machines by regularly oiling them. Oswald also rented an apartment on Magazine Street in uptown New Orleans and called for Marina and June to join him. On May 11, Ruth Paine transported them from her home in Irving, a Dallas suburb, to New Orleans.[25]

For the next four and a half months, Lee Harvey Oswald would lead a very strange life in New Orleans, a life in which he posed outwardly as a pro-Marxist supporter of Fidel Castro while covertly associating with people of precisely the opposite views. During the month of May he wrote to the national headquarters of the Fair Play for Cuba Committee, a pro-Castro organization, and ordered the printing of a stack of handbills with the heading, "Hands Off Cuba!" urging people to join the committee. In June he passed out the leaflets outside the place where the USS *Wasp* was docked. He maintained a steady correspondence with Vincent T. Lee, the national director of the Fair Play for Cuba Committee. Lee and Marina wrote letters to friends in the Soviet Union telling them how disenchanted they were with life in the United States. Oswald also corresponded with the Soviet Embassy in Washington, and he obtained an American passport to fulfill his intention of returning to the USSR. In August, Oswald got into a fight on the city's main thoroughfare, Canal Street, with a prominent anti-Castro Cuban leader, Carlos Bringuier, because Bringuier was infuriated at seeing Oswald, who had previously offered to assist Bringuier in his anti-Castro activities, pass out pro-Castro handbills. Oswald was arrested for disturbing the peace and spent a night in jail before being bailed out by a family friend, Emile Bruneau, who also had organized crime connections. Oswald also appeared on a couple of radio programs, in which he proclaimed his strong support for Marxism and his admiration for Fidel Castro.[26]

These activities reflected Oswald's alleged growing disillusionment with life in the United States and received emphasis in the Warren Commission's account of his five months in New Orleans in 1963. Yet he simultaneously led another life indicating that he had a deeper purpose than these superficial accounts have led us to believe. That purpose lay in Oswald's performing various undercover assignments for one of several intelligence operations that centered in New Orleans. Next to Miami, New Orleans served as the leading focus of the CIA's Operation MONGOOSE, a series of clandestine operations planned and activated after the abortive April 1961 Bay of Pigs invasion of Cuba and designed to foment insurrection in Cuba and ultimately to overthrow the Cuban dictator, Fidel Castro. Because it served as a place where large numbers of Cubans fled after Castro assumed power, New Orleans became a prominent center of anti-Castro activity. The CIA directed, administered, and financed many of these activities. According to Hunter Leake, a CIA agent based in New Orleans at the time and specifically assigned to serve as a liaison between the CIA and anti-Castro groups in Louisiana, these activities ranged from special operations, such as commando raids targeting Cuba's northern coast, gun-running missions, in which pilots flew illegally obtained weapons and other supplies to anti-Castro guerrilla fighters in Cuba, recruiting and training anti-Castro Cubans for a second amphibious invasion of the island, planned after President Kennedy won reelection in 1964, and even plotting to assassinate Fidel Castro.[27]

In several interviews, Hunter Leake provided information that, if accurate, would greatly enhance the intelligence aspect of Oswald's activities. Although the absence of substantive documentary evidence precludes the ability either to refute or confirm Leake's account, his version of events deserves recounting. Leake stated that Oswald came to New Orleans in April 1963 because the CIA office there intended to use him for certain operations. His job at the Reily Coffee Company merely served as a front for his actual role, and indeed, Oswald often left work for no apparent reason and so neglected his duties that he lost his job. One of his coworkers, Anthony Ponsetti, said that he was amazed that Oswald remained employed as long as he did because he failed to do his job from the time he began work. In any event, in May, Oswald first came to the attention of Guy Banister, a former FBI agent and former New Orleans police official. Banister, who, according to declassified CIA records, performed regular duties for the agency, was an extreme anticommunist and a vocal advocate of racial segregation. Several lone assassin theorists have denied the existence of an Oswald-Banister connection, and the HSCA concluded that it could find no credible eyewitness to the two men together. In fact, a number of witnesses saw them together. I myself saw Oswald and Banister when they visited the campus of Louisiana State University in New Orleans (LSUNO) when Banister condemned racial integration. I also saw them at a table in Mancuso's Restaurant, located in the same building as Banister's office. Banister's secretary, Delphine Roberts, saw them together. Gerald Posner and the HSCA did not deem Roberts's account worthy of belief because of her extreme, virulent racism. However, whatever her views, Roberts saw Banister daily. William George Gaudet, who had previously worked for the CIA, claimed that he saw Oswald and Banister talking together on a public sidewalk and saw them together in Banister's office.[28]

One person not previously mentioned in any of the accounts of Oswald's activities in New Orleans during the spring and summer of 1963 told me that she worked for Banister on a part-time basis translating documents from English into Spanish and vice versa. This person stated that Banister was heavily engaged in various anti-Castro operations and had numerous contacts among the Cuban exile community in New Orleans. Consuela "Connie" Martin said that on several occasions, Lee Harvey Oswald came into her office, located next to Banister's, handed her some documents, and asked her to type them into Spanish. Martin also stated that Oswald had her translate his infamous "Hands Off Cuba!" handbills into Spanish because he wanted to distribute them among the growing Hispanic community in New Orleans. Martin believed that because the handbills were pro-Castro, and because Oswald definitely worked for Banister, a vehemently anti-Castro provocateur, that Banister must have used Oswald to distribute the handbills in order to see how many of the city's many Cubans, Mexicans, Hondurans, and other Hispanic peoples displayed a sympathy toward the Cuban dictator. Martin stated that she saw Oswald in Banister's office at least half a dozen times in the late spring and summer of 1963. She further stated that on every one of these occasions, Oswald and Banister were together.[29]

These accounts accord perfectly with Oswald's giving 544 Camp Street as the address of the headquarters of his New Orleans chapter of the Fair Play for Cuba Committee. Some of the pro-Castro literature that Oswald distributed at various places contained that address. 544 Camp Street just happened to be the address of the building that housed Guy Banister's office. If no connection existed between Oswald and Banister, why would Oswald put the address of Banister's office building on his pro-Castro literature? No one has provided an adequate answer to that question. According to Connie Martin, Oswald stamped "544 Camp St." on some of his handbills because Banister had ordered him to in order to see if anyone would come to the building to sign up to join the pro-Castro organization. If they did, he or one of his agents would record that person's name, and Banister would then add it to his growing file of "suspicious" individuals living in the New Orleans area. Another responsibility that Banister had for Oswald was to "smoke out pro-Castro Cuban students in local universities and to discredit local leftwing or communist academics," a possibility raised by John Newman in his study of Oswald and the CIA. A fellow student at LSUNO, George Higginbotham, did precisely that type of work for Banister. Considering that Oswald accompanied Banister to the campus of LSUNO, and that Banister spoke to the members of the Young Democrats Club, itself under suspicion for fomenting left-wing causes, in Banister's paranoid mind, the possibility of Oswald being employed in that capacity cannot be eliminated. Oswald also probably performed the same undercover job at Tulane University, located near his apartment. Henry Mason, a left-wing political science professor, recalled seeing Oswald on Tulane's campus and still possessed one of the pro-Castro handbills he had distributed there. In addition, Banister knew that Oswald had visited the Quorum several times. Located on Esplanade Avenue, on the periphery of the French Quarter, the Quorum provided a convenient place for authors, artists, intellectuals, and others interested in promoting racial harmony to socialize and to discuss current events. Several former patrons of the Quorum recall seeing Oswald there. Almost certainly, Banister ordered Oswald to visit the Quorum and provide him with the names of the social club's regular visitors so he could add them to his list of "suspects."[30]

Hunter Leake stated that Guy Banister had arranged for the Cuban Revolutionary Council (CRC) to establish an office in the 544 Camp Street building. The CRC was an extreme anti-Castro organization, and its fundraising arm, the Friends of Democratic Cuba, headed by the anti-Castro leader Sergio Arcacha Smith until 1962 and after that by Frank Bartes, served as one of many CIA fronts in New Orleans at the time. Because Banister and Smith were convinced, quite correctly, that the Cuban community in New Orleans was heavily infiltrated with Castro's agents, they used individuals like Oswald to ferret out these double agents. One method they used lay in disseminating pro-Castro literature among Cuban and Latin American students at local universities and reporting their names back to Banister. Connie Smith stated that Oswald gave Banister lists of both native and foreign students that he believed were pro-Castro in their sympathies. In addition, Banister used Oswald to conduct surveillance of certain anti-Castro organizations to try to uncover Castro's agents. One such organization was the Cuban Student Directorate (DRE), which Oswald tried to infiltrate by visiting the store of a DRE leader, Carlos Bringuier, and telling him that he was willing to lend his support to the anti-Castro cause. In addition, Oswald joined other white Americans in guerrilla training exercises in which the DRE and other anti-Castro groups participated. The CIA organized, financed, and administered these exercises, conducted at various places along the north shore of Lake Ponchartrain, from Lacombe, about twelve miles from the Louisiana-Mississippi border, to Bedico Creek, a small inlet separating the parishes of St. Tammany and Tangipahoa. Oswald visited both of these training camps.[31]

Oswald, of course, was not the only gringo that the CIA used in these efforts. Another was William George Gaudet, who had provided the agency with information regarding Latin American activities between 1956 and 1961. Although Gaudet is not listed as an actual CIA employee, he himself stated that he had indeed been employed by the agency, a statement confirmed by Hunter Leake. The reader should note that the CIA often used pseudonyms for its employees and frequently simply omitted their names from official records. Therefore, the absence of Gaudet's name as an employee of the agency does not refute his assertion that he was indeed employed by it. Of extreme curiosity is the fact that on September 17, 1963, Lee Harvey Oswald went to the Mexican consulate in New Orleans to obtain a tourist permit to visit the country. Oswald received tourist permit #24085. The person to whom tourist permit #24084 was issued was none other than William George Gaudet. In an interview with Anthony Summers, Gaudet stated that his obtaining the tourist permit number just before Oswald's was sheer "coincidence." However, in an interview with me, Gaudet stated that he and Oswald were sent to Mexico City to survey the scenes at the Cuban and Russian Embassies and to report their findings to the CIA. Because Gaudet's official service to the CIA had ended in 1961, one might question why he still performed assignments for it two years later. As Jim Houghan has demonstrated in his analysis of James McCord's CIA connections, the agency frequently terminated an individual's employment publicly, only to continue to use him clandestinely. Because Oswald's New Orleans sojourn entailed connections with such other individuals who had proven CIA ties as Frank Bartes and Carlos Quiroga, and two active anti-Castro leaders, Carlos Bringuier and Guy Banister, Gaudet's sensational assertion cannot be dismissed out of hand. Nevertheless, because of the lack of documentation, neither can they be given full credence.[32]

It should be noted that no extant CIA records contain any reference to Lee Harvey Oswald's being employed by the agency, either directly as an agent or indirectly as a contact person. In his interviews with me, Hunter Leake explained this lack of documentation. Leake stated that on the day after the assassination, he was ordered to collect all of the CIA's files on Oswald from the New Orleans office and transport them to the agency's headquarters in Langley, Virginia. Together with other employees of the New Orleans office, Leake gathered all of the Oswald files. They proved so voluminous that Leake had to rent a trailer to transport them to Langley. Stopping only to eat, use the rest room, and fill up with gas, Leake drove the truck pulling the rental trailer filled with the New Orleans office's files on Oswald to CIA headquarters. Leake later learned that many of these files were, in the term made infamous by John Erlichman during the Watergate crisis, "deep-sixed." Leake explained that like the KGB, the CIA dreaded the release of any information that would connect Oswald with it. Leake speculated that his friend Richard Helms, the agency's deputy director for plans, was probably the person who ordered the destruction of the files because Helms had a paranoid obsession with protecting the "company." Leake asserted, in a quite definitive manner, that Oswald indeed performed chores for the CIA during his five months in New Orleans during the spring and summer of 1963. Leake personally paid Oswald various sums of cash for his services. Again, it is not possible either to confirm or to disprove Leake's story.[33]

In New Orleans in the summer of 1963, Lee Harvey Oswald also associated with two other men who had relationships with the CIA, David William Ferrie and Clay L. Shaw. An extreme anticommunist fanatic, Ferrie flew missions into Cuba between 1960 and 1963. He also helped organize militia units of anti-Castro Cubans in the New Orleans area and trained them at the training camps on the north shore of Lake Ponchartrain. Hunter Leake stated that Ferrie performed a series of tasks for the CIA: supplying weapons and munitions to anti-Castro guerrilla fighters in Cuba; training Cuban units for the Bay of Pigs invasion; conducting propaganda sessions among refugee units, thus reinforcing their hatred of the Castro regime; and serving as an intermediary between the CIA and organized crime. One job that David Ferrie held at the time entailed working for G. Wray Gill, one of Carlos Marcello's attorneys. Ferrie used this position as a front to allow him to enter into deals whereby he purchased large quantities of arms, ammunition, and explosives, and other munitions from Marcello's organization for Banister, Gaudet, and other CIA operatives to distribute among militant anti-Castro Cuban outfits. Ferrie also purchased weapons from the Chicago mob and transported them to Louisiana. One of his contacts in the Windy City was Homer Echevarria, the leader of a mysterious anti-Castro outfit named the 30th of November. Echevarria, whose father had supplied the FBI with information for years, smuggled arms and munitions he obtained from Sam Giancana's Mafia syndicate to CIA operatives such as David Ferrie in New Orleans and Dallas. Although all of this may indeed seem like a tangled web, it accords perfectly with the CIA's documented operations during the Eisenhower and Kennedy administrations.[34]

Clay L. Shaw, another of Oswald's associates in New Orleans, had served as the director of the city's International Trade Mart for a number of years before his retirement. In that capacity, Shaw came into contact with a host of business and political leaders from Latin America. In 1956, the CIA requested, and Shaw agreed, that he supply it with information he obtained from his Latino contacts. Even after his retirement, Shaw maintained a close, active relationship with many prominent Latin Americans. When the CIA began using New Orleans as a major base of its anti-Castro operations, it enlisted Shaw to assist it. Like Ferrie, Shaw made contact with anti-Castro organizations in

New Orleans, used his international connections to smuggle arms, munitions, and supplies to various anti-Castro guerrilla training camps in southeast Louisiana, and obtained funding for these activities through his network of such well-heeled anticommunist individuals as Dr. Alton Ochsner Sr., a prominent surgeon. Shaw and Ochsner formed a fund-raising unit that served as a conduit for both privately raised donations and appropriations given by the CIA. Shaw and Ochsner also had strong ties to the Information Council of the Americas (INCA), a vehemently anti-Castro organization that disseminated right-wing propaganda throughout Latin America.[35]

Both Ferrie and Shaw were homosexuals, and it was through this aspect of their personal lifestyle that they became associated with Lee Harvey Oswald. Although a married man and, indeed, an expectant father during the spring and summer of 1963 in New Orleans, Oswald associated with several gay persons. In his testimony before a Warren Commission counsel, a New Orleans attorney, Deans Andrews, related how one summer day Oswald, accompanied by several gay Latinos, walked into his office and asked him to perform some legal work. Because both before and after this curious incident Andrews had represented some of these Latinos, who had been arrested for cross-dressing, his description of Oswald's companions as gay appears accurate. On several occasions, Oswald was seen with Shaw and Ferrie. On one occasion, Perry Raymond Russo attended a party at Ferrie's apartment on Louisiana Avenue Parkway in New Orleans, and he saw the three together. Russo related this story in the context of Ferrie leading a discussion of how President Kennedy should be assassinated, an assertion that numerous researchers have challenged. Interestingly, no one has challenged Russo's story of seeing the three men together. Another man who attended that party at Ferrie's apartment, a Cuban refugee named Santos Miguel Gonzalez, while vehemently denying that Oswald, Shaw, and Ferrie discussed the assassination of President Kennedy, confirmed to me that the three men attended the party. Furthermore, Gonzalez stated that Oswald was well known among the Cuban exile community in New Orleans both as a provocateur for the CIA and as a homosexual. Hamilton Johnson also saw Ferrie and Shaw together, both in New Orleans and in Houma. In the late summer of 1963, several witnesses saw Shaw, Ferrie, and Oswald together in Clinton, Louisiana, a small town about one hundred fifteen miles north-west of New Orleans. Although several researchers have questioned the accuracy of the Clinton witnesses' observations, I believe that they told the truth. They had no reason to lie, and the minor discrepancies in their stories do not cast doubt on their essential accuracy.[36]

Much mystery surrounds Oswald's whereabouts in the first three weeks of September 1963. The record lacks reliable information re-garding virtually all of his activities at that time. From interviews, various individuals have suggested that he continued his assignments for the CIA and traveled to Dallas on at least one occasion. Anto-nio Veciana, the head of the militantly anti-Castro exile organization, Alpha 66, told the HSCA that in early September, he met in Dallas with his CIA case officer, Maurice Bishop. At the meeting, Bishop introduced Veciana to Oswald, and Veciana naturally assumed that like himself, Oswald was performing some kind of work for the intelli-gence agency—work that involved Bishop's area of specialization, anti-Castro activities. The HSCA questioned Veciana's veracity because he waited until 1978 to tell his story to the authorities and because he failed to make a positive identification of the man who called him-self Maurice Bishop. It appears, however, that Veciana told the truth. Hunter Leake told me that David Atlee Phillips, the head of the CIA's Western Hemisphere operations at the time, used the alias, a suspicion raised by the HSCA itself. Several other people, including Consuela Martin, William George Gaudet, and Santos Miguel Gonzalez, also heard the name "Maurice Bishop" used in reference to a high-ranking CIA officer involved in anti-Castro operations.[37]

The Mexico City Trip

During the summer of 1963, a curious incident occurred in the back-yard of the apartment house where the Oswalds lived. Several neigh-borhood children were shooting a BB gun at tin cans perched on a fence. Oswald came outside and asked if he could fire the gun. The children let him try to hit the cans, about fifteen feet from where he stood. According to Deborah Schillace, one of the children present, "he missed every shot. He couldn't hit the broadside of a barn."

Lee and Marina Oswald had experienced marital difficulties for a long time, and in mid-September 1963, they decided to separate. On September 24, Marina's friend, Ruth Paine, drove to New Orleans, loaded Marina's belongings into her station wagon, and drove Marina, eight months pregnant, and her daughter June back to Irving to stay with her. The next day, Lee abruptly left New Orleans and made a controversial and still quite mysterious trip to Mexico City. The ostensible purpose of the trip lay in Oswald's supposed desire to return to the Soviet Union via Cuba. However, intensive analysis of his Mexico City sojourn raises more questions than answers. Just as he did in New Orleans, Oswald led a double life during his brief, one-week stay in the Mexican capital. He—or at least someone claiming to be him—made several visits to both the Cuban and Russian embassies and attempted to secure the necessary visas and other papers to travel to the Soviet Union. Whether the individual in question was the real Lee Harvey Oswald or someone impersonating him remains the subject of lively debate.

Several Russians employed at the Soviet embassy in Mexico City at the time have recalled the real Lee Oswald visiting their office at least three times, showing them various papers relating to his pro-Castro activities in New Orleans, and demanding to be issued an expedited visa to enable him and his family to return to the USSR. Suspicious, they refused. Employees of the Cuban embassy, on the other hand, recalled that the "Oswald" they saw was about five feet, three inches tall, quite gaunt, with blond hair. Clearly, this description did not fit the real Oswald. The CIA compounded the confusion by releasing several photographs of a man it claimed entered the Soviet embassy. An agency memorandum of October 10, 1963, asserted that the man in the photograph, "Lee Henry [sic] Oswald . . . contacted the Soviet embassy in Mexico City." The photographs, however, depict a man about forty to forty-five years old, muscular, heavyset, with a squared-off jaw and a crew cut. In other words, the man in the photographs could not possibly have been Lee Harvey Oswald. The CIA acknowledged its mistake, attributing the mix-up to a bureaucratic error, but it has never identified the man in the photographs or produced any of the actual Lee Oswald entering or exiting either one of the embassies.[38]

Although he said different things to other researchers, William George Gaudet told me that he and Oswald went to Mexico City to look for pro-Castro spies among the large community of Cuban exiles living there. That is why Oswald stayed at the Hotel del Comercio, a well-known hangout for anti-Castro Cubans. There, according to Gaudet, Oswald met two Cubans, both prominent leaders of anti-Castro organizations and both working for the CIA, who told him to fly to Dallas with them to meet a woman who might prove a source of funding for their cause. Oswald accompanied the men to Dallas, and the three of them visited Silvia Odio, one of the central figures in the Oswald saga. The story that Odio herself related so unnerved the Warren Commission's chief counsel, J. Lee Rankin, that he ordered a special FBI investigation to determine the accuracy of her tale. Whether Gaudet's account of Oswald's transportation from Mexico City to Dallas is accurate will never be known, but Silvia Odio's story rocked the commission, for it posed the possibility of an assassination conspiracy.[39]

According to Silvia Odio, on a weekday in the last week of September 1963, the two Cubans and Lee Harvey Oswald visited her at her Dallas apartment. One of the Cubans, who called himself "Leopoldo," introduced Oswald to her as "Leon" Oswald. The Cubans asked Odio to assist them by providing financing for their cause, but she refused, and the three men left. The next day, Leopoldo called Odio and told her that Oswald was "loco," the Spanish word for crazy. Oswald had told Leopoldo that he thought that the anti-Castro Cubans were cowards and that they should have killed Kennedy after his refusal to back up the Bay of Pigs invasion with the full force of the American military. Oswald also stated that as an ex-marine, he was an expert marksman and could have done the job for them. When she heard the news of Kennedy's assassination in Dallas less than two months later and saw Oswald's picture on television, Silvia Odio fainted, for she realized that the man accused of killing the president had been a guest in her home.[40]

It need hardly be mentioned that the Warren Commission went to great lengths to discredit Silvia Odio's story, for, if true, it would have provided compelling evidence of an assassination conspiracy involving

Oswald and anti-Castro Cubans. According to Odio, the three men visited her on September 26 or 27. The commission concluded that Oswald arrived in Mexico City on the 27th, having spent virtually all of the 26th traveling via bus through Texas and Mexico. Therefore, he could not possibly have been in Dallas and in Mexico City simultaneously. The commission relied on shaky evidence to reach that conclusion. It accepted the testimony of two witnesses that they saw Oswald on a Continental Trailways bus, although none of the other passengers recalled seeing him on the vehicle. Her sister, Annie, who saw the three men in the apartment and remembered Oswald as one of them, substantiates Odio's story. Further, Silvia Odio told the story to her psychiatrist, who vouched for her credibility. Finally, the commission provided no substantive proof that Oswald actually arrived in Mexico City on September 27. The HSCA conducted a new investigation into the Odio incident and concluded that she told the truth, adding yet another mysterious element to the Oswald saga.[41]

Oswald left Mexico City on October 3 and arrived in Dallas the same day. He rented a room from Mary Bledsoe, who quickly developed an intense dislike for him. During the five days that he lived in her rooming house, Bledsoe heard Oswald speak in a foreign language on the telephone, ask her permission to put a container of milk in the refrigerator, and ate peanut butter, banana, and sardine sandwiches, all of which so irritated Bledsoe that she evicted Oswald two days in advance of the week that he had rented the room. Oswald then found a room to rent at 1026 North Beckley Avenue, in the Oak Cliff section of Dallas, where he would live until the day of the assassination. In the middle of October, he obtained a job as order filler at the Texas School Book Depository, and by all accounts, he performed steady, reliable work. It appears that he made a serious effort to reconcile with Marina because he visited her every weekend and gave her money from his wages. On occasion, he borrowed a car from one of the tenants at the rooming house to run some errands, but on the morning of November 22, he would ride to work in the vehicle driven by Buell Wesley Frazier.[42]

7

The Intelligence Connection

The mysterious trip that Lee Harvey Oswald made to Mexico City in late September and early October 1963 raised deep suspicions of an intelligence connection to the Kennedy assassination. Operating under the presumption of a lone assassin–no conspiracy interpretation of the assassination, the Warren Commission made no serious effort to untangle the web of intrigue surrounding that trip. The House Select Committee on Assassinations (HSCA), on the other hand, conducted a much more thorough investigation into the Mexico City trip, and its report brought to the surface all of the undercurrents that the commission had tried to keep submerged. The HSCA report, a three-hundred-page document entitled "Lee Harvey Oswald, the CIA, and Mexico City," written by staff members Edward Lopez and Dan Hardway and commonly referred to as the Lopez Report, documents the existence of at least one individual impersonating Lee Oswald in Mexico City and strenuous efforts by the CIA to steer the Warren Commission away from any path that would link Oswald to the intelligence agency.[1]

On November 23, 1963, the day after the assassination, John McCone, the CIA director, twice met with the new president, Lyndon Johnson. On both occasions, McCone informed Johnson about contacts that Oswald had in the Mexican capital with Valery Kostikov, a Soviet "diplomat," who, in the opinion of the Mexico City Station Chief for the CIA, Winston "Win" Scott, was in reality a sinister KGB agent who specialized in assassination. Undoubtedly, McCone alarmed Johnson by voicing CIA suspicions of the Soviets employing Oswald to assassinate Kennedy, possibly in retaliation for Kennedy's humiliation of the Soviet premier, Nikita Khrushchev, during the Cuban missile crisis of October 1962. Quite paranoid in his own right,

Johnson found his fears of a communist conspiracy reinforced by news provided him by FBI director J. Edgar Hoover in a telephone conversation of November 23 about Oswald in Mexico City. In the recently released tape of the conversation, Hoover stated, "We have up here the tape and photograph of the man who was at the Soviet Embassy [in Mexico City] using Oswald's name. The picture and tape do not correspond to this man's [Oswald's] voice, nor his appearance. In other words, it appears that there is a second person who was at the Soviet Embassy down there." On that same day, Hoover informed James J. Rowley, the head of the Secret Service, in a memorandum that the FBI agents in Dallas who had interrogated Oswald believed that the photographs and tape recording were of some other person—in other words, an impostor.[2]

This information must have stunned the new president. Both the news of Oswald's meeting with the notorious Kostikov, a KGB assassination specialist, and of someone impersonating Oswald at the Russian embassy in Mexico City raised the distinct possibility of a Soviet-led conspiracy. As a defector, Oswald had lived in the USSR for two and a half years, had married a Russian native, and had openly proclaimed his pro-Marxist sympathies as late as the summer of 1963. He would have been the perfect stooge for the Russians to use in their sinister attempt to eliminate Kennedy. It is little wonder that a few days later, when Johnson persuaded Chief Justice Earl Warren to chair the commission investigating Kennedy's assassination, he told Warren that the very real possibility of a nuclear war resulting in the deaths of forty million Americans could become a consequence of the assassination.[3]

On the afternoon of the assassination, a top-secret meeting took place in the United States embassy in Mexico City. At the meeting, U.S. ambassador Thomas C. Mann, Clark D. Anderson, the FBI's legal attaché, and Win Scott, the CIA station chief, discussed the fact that Oswald had visited the Cuban and Russian embassies in Mexico City. Shocked and outraged that the CIA had not informed the FBI about Oswald's visits to the embassies, Anderson demanded, and received, from Scott the photographs and tapes of Oswald. These materials were flown directly to Dallas and reviewed by FBI personnel who had been participating in the interrogation of Oswald at Dallas police headquarters. After listening to the tapes and reviewing the photographs, the

FBI agents concluded that the individual the CIA had identified as "Lee Harvey Oswald" must have been an impostor. The photographs depicted a man about forty years old, around six feet tall, with a stocky, muscular build, and sporting a receding hairline and a square jaw. The real Oswald, of course, fit none of these descriptions.[4]

After CIA director John McCone, his number two man, deputy director for plans Richard Helms, and the agency's legendary head of counterintelligence, James Jesus Angleton, learned of the FBI's conclusion that someone had impersonated Oswald in Mexico City, they developed a plan deliberately designed to further obfuscate matters and to deceive both the president and the FBI about Oswald's actual status. On November 26, the CIA sent copies of a highly classified message to the White House, the State Department, and the FBI. Ambassador Mann endorsed the contents of the message. The communication revealed that on September 18, 1963, Gilberto Alvarado, an agent of the Nicaraguan Secret Service, who had infiltrated the Cuban embassy in Mexico City, claimed that he saw an employee of that embassy give $6,500 to Lee Harvey Oswald. The payment, Alvarado stated, was for Oswald to carry out the assassination of an important American political figure. The news of Alvarado's startling revelations convinced Lyndon Johnson to appoint a presidential commission comprising men he trusted to investigate the assassination. Johnson feared that if news of the Nicaraguan's story had leaked, the popular reaction would have compelled him to retaliate against Cuba. This, in turn, might have led to a disastrous nuclear war between the United States and the USSR, Cuba's ally.[5]

Shortly after the creation of the Warren Commission, events proved Alvarado's story a poorly conceived hoax. Oswald was in New Orleans on September 18, and Alvarado himself admitted that he had made up the story to incite hostilities between the United States and Cuba. Nevertheless, both CIA director John McCone and Ambassador Mann continued to press the case against Cuba. Both received reprimands, and Thomas Mann was "promoted" to the position of ambassador to the Organization of American States in December. The CIA was provided with an advance copy of the FBI's report on the assassination, one that concluded that Oswald had committed the crime by himself and that no one else was involved. When confronted with this report, the CIA abruptly curtailed its own internal investigation and carefully followed both J. Edgar Hoover's and Lyndon Johnson's strong desire to adhere to the lone assassin interpretation. Both deputy director for plans Richard Helms and director of counterintelligence James Jesus Angleton made sure that no evidence damaging to the lone assassin–no conspiracy thesis would surface, especially evidence that might implicate the Central Intelligence Agency, or anyone associated with it. Helms, Angleton, and other leading CIA figures clearly preferred to blame the assassination on a "lone nut" than to allow a thorough investigation into matters their agency preferred to keep under the rug.[6]

The Cuban Problem

As intelligence officials well knew, the CIA as an agency had nothing to do with the assassination. Many of its leaders, such as Richard Helms and Desmond Fitzgerald, knew and liked John Kennedy, who, during his brief presidency, had showered lavish favors on their beloved "company." Kennedy's highly publicized sacking of Allen Dulles for his failure to successfully carry out the Bay of Pigs invasion of Cuba in 1961 had received considerable, although erroneous, publicity about Kennedy's desire to bring the renegade agency under his control. In reality, beneath the surface, John and Robert Kennedy had given the CIA vastly expanded resources and powers to carry out their desire to eliminate Fidel Castro. Under the watchful eyes of the Kennedy brothers, the CIA had flourished, mounting the largest clandestine operation in its history up to that time. This operation entailed shadowy figures, many recruited from the nether world of soldiers of fortune, conducting missions in conjunction with anti-Castro Cuban exiles. These covert operations included sabotage, the assassination of minor political leaders, the destruction of some aspects of the Cuban infrastructure, and more nefarious actions. This last category included no less than a sinister plot among high-ranking CIA officials and notorious mobsters to kill the Cuban dictator. Clearly, if word of these activities had become public, fears of an assassination conspiracy involving Cuba, and possibly its cold war benefactor, the Soviet Union, would have compelled Johnson to take retaliatory action, with a possible nuclear war resulting. In addition, the airing of this dirty laundry would undoubtedly have proven seriously damaging to an agency already tarnished because of its ineptness in masterminding the Bay of Pigs invasion.[7]

As we have seen, Lee Harvey Oswald had actively participated in several CIA-sponsored operations in Louisiana. The agency's hierarchy, McCone, Helms, Angleton, and several others, agreed that even if Oswald had indeed acted alone in assassinating President Kennedy, they must take drastic measures to ensure that nothing even remotely connecting the "company" to Oswald would surface. Richard Helms personally persuaded Lyndon Johnson to appoint former CIA director Allen Dulles to the Warren Commission and to allow him, Helms, to serve as the agency's liaison with the commission. That way, Dulles and Helms could prevent any leakage of potentially damaging information. In his testimony to the Warren Commission, Helms deliberately perjured himself to conceal the CIA's role in events that may have had a connection to the assassination. That role revolved around the Cuban issue.[8]

When John Kennedy took the oath of office as president in January 1961, he inherited from the administration of President Dwight Eisenhower the problem of dealing with the regime of Fidel Castro in Cuba. After he became head of the Cuban government in January 1959, Castro had followed an increasing anti-American policy. He confiscated the property of American business interests in the island, drove the Mafia out, and proclaimed his allegiance to the principles of Marxism. By the late spring of 1960, under extreme political pressure by the more than 100,000 Cubans who had emigrated to the United States since Castro came to power, Eisenhower, together with such leading members of his administration as CIA director Allen Dulles and Vice President Richard M. Nixon, decided to remove Castro from power and to replace him with a pro-American leader. Because an outright military invasion of Cuba would hardly have coincided with the fundamental principles of democracy, Eisenhower ordered the CIA to develop a covert means of removing Castro. The agency came up with a two-pronged approach: an amphibious invasion of Cuba by a brigade of anti-Castro Cuban exiles, financed, trained, and supplied by the CIA; and the assassination of Fidel Castro, also carried out by CIA operatives. For the remainder of Eisenhower's presidency, the CIA worked on both approaches.[9]

For more than two months after he took office, President Kennedy and his advisors debated the merits of the first option—the amphibious invasion. Despite clear warnings from many of his civilian advisors, as well as from the Joint Chiefs of Staff, who admonished the president that the only chance the invasion held of success lay in its backing by the full resources of the United States armed forces, Kennedy authorized the invasion, but adamantly refused to allow its backing by the navy and air force. The Bay of Pigs invasion of Cuba in April 1961 resulted in the most humiliating fiasco for the United States in the history of the cold war. Finding themselves abandoned by their American backers, the members of the Cuban brigade fought bravely but unsuccessfully as Castro's armed forces overwhelmed them. As they were paraded through the streets of Havana, the defeated Cubans and their friends and relatives in America felt betrayed. Their CIA case officers had promised them that the United States would lend its might to back up the invasion, but at the last moment, Kennedy had refused to give the order. The sense of humiliation and contempt that the anti-Castro Cuban exile community felt for John Kennedy persuaded them to support the Republican party, and they remain, more than four decades later, the only major Hispanic group that votes Republican in elections.[10]

John Kennedy believed that he, in turn, had been betrayed by the CIA hierarchy, who had led him to believe that once the invaders landed, the Cuban people would rise up in a popular uprising that would lead to Castro's overthrow. Instead, of course, the invasion served to solidify his hold on the popular imagination. To several politicians and journalists, Kennedy voiced his determination to bring the CIA under his wing, so another Bay of Pigs could not happen. The president did sack the director, Allen Dulles, and his deputy, Richard Bissell, to project the image of a strong, determined chief executive. To ensure that he would receive accurate intelligence regarding Cuba, he appointed his brother, attorney general Robert Kennedy, to head the White House's Cuban policy office. However, instead of reining in the CIA, the Kennedy brothers gave it vastly expanded powers and enormous sums of money to expand its anti-Castro activities. In all probability, the Kennedys had seethed with disgust after the failure of the Bay of Pigs invasion and became even more determined to settle scores with the Cuban dictator. They simply would not—nor, given their inherently competitive nature, could not—allow Castro to get away with his victory.[11]

The resulting actions, which fell under the umbrella of Operation MONGOOSE, entailed an amazing variety of James Bond–ish activities, some ludicrous, some sinister, others imbecilic, that made the term *intelligence* in the agency's name oxymoronic. Numerous authors have written about Operation MONGOOSE, and they will not be recounted here, except as they relate to the Kennedy assassination. One aspect of MONGOOSE was named "Executive Action," a top-secret operation specifically designed to remove foreign political leaders, with the ZR/RIFLE aspect of this focusing on actual assassination. Heading this covert action was William King Harvey, a hard-drinking, ruthless CIA operative, whose motto, emblazoned on a poster behind his desk, read, "The tree of liberty is watered with the blood of patriots," a variation of Thomas Jefferson's famous aphorism. Headquartered in Miami, MONGOOSE functioned from a building on the campus of the University of Miami, whence it carried out its JM/WAVE operations. Personally exhorting the participants in the anti-Castro activities, Robert Kennedy urged that "no time, money, effort, or manpower be spared" to fulfill its goal of overthrowing the Cuban leader.[12]

Between late 1961 and late 1963, Operation MONGOOSE involved more than 4,000 men in Florida, Louisiana, Texas, and even Illinois, engaging in a bewildering series of not-so-covert operations against Cuba. The operation consumed tens of millions of dollars of the taxpayers' money, involved selfless, patriotic Cubans fighting for the freedom of their native land to soldiers of fortune and other unsavory elements eager to accumulate a fortune, and the trafficking of enormous quantities of supplies ranging from small arms to powerful explosives to large quantities of heroin. The names of some of those involved read like a rogues' gallery of notorious individuals: E. Howard Hunt, James McCord, and Frank Sturgis of Watergate fame; David Atlee Phillips, Richard Helms, William King Harvey, Desmond Fitzgerald, Sheffield Edwards, and Hunter Leake of the CIA; Georges deMorenschildt,

Guy Banister, David William Ferrie, and others associated with Lee Harvey Oswald; Carlos Marcello, Santos Trafficante, Sam Giancana, Johnny Roselli, and Jack Ruby of organized crime. In short, MON-GOOSE had all the makings of a spy thriller, with a cast of characters that no Hollywood producer could possibly match. Because Fidel Castro remains alive and well forty-five years later, it need hardly be stated that MONGOOSE turned out a miserable failure.

The other phase of the CIA's plan to eliminate Fidel Castro took that directive quite literally and culminated in a series of elaborate plots to assassinate him. In 1960, the agency concocted several schemes so bizarre that they would have lacked credibility, except for the extensive documentation that exists. Under the overall direction of Richard Bissell, assisted by his deputy, Richard Helms, the CIA devised one plot to infest Castro's boots with a chemical that would cause all of his hair to fall out. Because, the theory went, the symbol of Castro's authority lay in his famous beard, the Cuban people would revolt against a bald, clean-shaven leader. Another fantastic scheme entailed an attempt to infect Castro with a hallucinogenic drug, such as LSD, that would render him incoherent during one of his long-winded tirades. The CIA's euphemistically named Technical Services Division plunged into the effort with a combination of inanity and ridiculousness so glaring that one wonders how the United States managed to win the cold war. This office started with poison cigars, so lethal that after only a couple of puffs, Castro would drop dead. It also infested a scuba diving outfit with a quite virulent strain of tuberculosis, and it even manufactured exploding seashells, to be planted in the area where Castro liked to scuba dive. These constitute the plots of which we have a record. One can only imagine the ones for which all of the evidence was destroyed![13]

By the fall of 1960, Dulles, Helms, and Bissell had grown wary of these inane schemes and made the decision to ask for assistance in killing Fidel Castro from those experienced in the business: organized crime. As their intermediary, they selected Robert Maheu, the right-hand man of reclusive billionaire Howard Hughes. In September 1960, Maheu met at Miami's Fountainbleau Hotel with Johnny Roselli, the mob's point man in Las Vegas, and Roselli's boss, Sam Giancana, the kingpin of organized crime in Chicago. Roselli and Giancana agreed to put the CIA in touch with Santos Trafficante, the Florida mob boss, who had extensive connections in Cuba. The following month, Giancana and Trafficante met in Miami with a high-ranking CIA official, who requested these notorious mobsters to help them eliminate the Cuban dictator. Trafficante agreed. The deal had been struck. The CIA quite literally took out a mob contract on the life of Fidel Castro.[14]

The meetings between the CIA and the Mafia continued in the Kennedy administration. Trafficante introduced CIA representatives to Antonio de Verona, a former prime minister of Cuba, and a leader of the Cuban Revolutionary Council (CRC). The CIA agents paid Varona a large sum of money and handed him several vials of poison, which one of Varona's Cuban contacts who worked in a Havana restaurant where Castro frequently ate would slip into Castro's food. The scheme called for Castro to consume the poison just as the Cuban exile brigade was landing at the Bay of Pigs, but it supposedly went awry when Castro stopped eating at the restaurant. On several other occasions, CIA officials met with Mafia leaders to discuss assassination attempts against Castro. William Harvey led the CIA negotiators, while Santos Trafficante spoke for the mob. Through Trafficante's extensive contacts with anti-Castro Cubans in Florida, Harvey and his comrades passed on to them various devices to be used in eliminating the Cuban leader: poison pills; explosives; rifles; handguns; and other lethal weapons. No evidence exists to suggest that anyone made a serious effort to actually carry out these assassination plots. Nevertheless, they did take place, and the evidence strongly indicates that the Kennedy brothers knew and approved of the plots to kill Castro. It also strongly suggests that Castro remained well informed about these assassination schemes.[15]

John and Robert Kennedy played a dangerous game of deception and duplicity. Both expressed personal aversion to the idea of assassinating the leaders of foreign countries while simultaneously authorizing such acts. In 1961, Tad Szulc, the Latin American correspondent for the *New York Times*, related the story of a conversation he had with President Kennedy during an interview about the new president's Cuban policy. Kennedy asked Szulc, "What would you think if I ordered Castro to be assassinated?" Horrified, Szulc replied that he opposed even the thought of such an action. Kennedy responded that he agreed, but that certain members of the "intelligence community" had been pressuring him to order the execution of the Cuban dictator. In another conversation, the president told his friend, Florida senator George Smathers, that CIA figures wanted him to dispose of Castro, but that he had refused to authorize such an immoral act. Kennedy proceeded to tell Smathers that he felt that the CIA had done too many things on its own, without informing him. Robert Kennedy also expressed surprise and disgust at the idea of having Castro murdered. In 1962, when CIA attorney Lawrence Houston informed Kennedy that the Justice Department should not prosecute Sam Giancana because Giancana had played a critical role in the previous CIA assassination plots against Castro, Kennedy appeared quite upset and ordered Houston to inform him if the agency ever tried to do business with the Mafia again. Later, Robert Kennedy told one of his trusted aides, Frank Mankiewicz, that he had learned that "some people" were plotting to kill Castro and that he had put an end to the scheme.[16]

Plenty of evidence exists to demonstrate that these remarks served as a subterfuge by the Kennedy brothers to conceal their close involvement in the Castro assassination plots. Former CIA officials have gone on record stating that the plots against Castro simply reflected the CIA's following orders. William Harvey, the head of the murderous ZR/RIFLE assassination campaign, told the CIA's inspector general that the agency's efforts to kill Castro were "developed in response to White House urgings." A former CIA case officer closely connected with the JM/WAVE project stated that Bobby Kennedy removed Harvey as head of the Cuban operations because "he wasn't having Castro killed fast enough." In New Orleans, CIA agent Hunter Leake heard the same thing. Leake told me that on one of his several visits to that city, Robert Kennedy ordered them to focus on "getting rid of Castro" and specifically declared that he did not care how that objective was accomplished. In an interview, Richard Helms asserted that in attempting to kill Castro, the CIA was strictly "following orders." Helms elaborated that "there was no way that we would have done such a thing without a direct presidential directive." I asked Helms if that statement applied to the Castro assassination plots undertaken during the Eisenhower and Kennedy administrations, and he replied in the affirmative. Another CIA operative, Sam Halpern, who served on the Cuban desk in the early 1960s, stated that Robert Kennedy himself ordered the CIA to provide a case officer to meet with notorious Mafia figures and that Kennedy himself supplied the underworld contacts for the agency. Richard Bissell, the former deputy director for plans, the second-highest position in the CIA, also confirmed that both John and Robert Kennedy knew of, approved, and ordered the assassination attempts against Castro's life, a statement that contradicted previous Bissell comments on the subject.[17]

The year 1963 witnessed an intensification of the Kennedy administration's efforts to eliminate Fidel Castro. Ironically, as part of the deal he made with Nikita Khrushchev to end the Cuban missile crisis of 1962, President Kennedy had made a promise never to invade Cuba, in effect acknowledging the permanence of the Castro regime. Covertly, however, Kennedy pressured the CIA to increase its anti-Castro activities, and the agency responded. In both Florida and Louisiana, teams of anti-Castro Cuban exiles trained under CIA supervision for another amphibious invasion of their homeland, supplemented by the contemporaneous assassination of the Cuban dictator. At these camps, located in the swampy marshes and inlets of the two states, specially chosen squads were given extensive training in various assassination techniques and given specific Cuban political officials as their targets. Everyone involved in these maneuvers believed that they would culminate in a second invasion of Cuba, this one occurring shortly after John Kennedy took the oath of office for his second term as president. Both Hunter Leake and Richard Helms told me that Robert Kennedy instigated these machinations and maintained a steady pressure on the CIA and its Cuban exile partners to do everything possible to put an end to the Castro regime.[18]

The Kennedys made a few minor efforts to give the impression that they had decided to end their hostility toward Cuba. On several occasions, they ordered the FBI to conduct raids on various exile training camps in Florida and Louisiana and confiscate their stashes of munitions. They also clamped down on some of the more militant anti-Castro organizations, such as Alpha 66. Of even greater significance, John and Robert Kennedy encouraged William Attwood in his efforts to reach an accord between the United States and Cuba. In September 1963, Attwood, a special advisor to the American delegation to the

United Nations, received a message that had been funneled through an African diplomat that Fidel Castro wanted to seek a reconciliation with the United States. President Kennedy personally authorized Attwood to meet with the Cuban ambassador to the United Nations, Carlos Lechuga, to discuss the subject. Attwood and Lechuga met twice, and it appeared to some that the prospect of repairing the strained relations between the two countries seemed quite real, that John Kennedy was making serious moves to restore peace in the Western Hemisphere and perhaps to bring Cuba back as one of America's strongest allies.[19]

The evidence suggests that the Kennedy brothers were, as Dean Rusk told Anthony Summers, "playing with fire." Simultaneous with the peaceful overtures toward Cuba came the most dangerous of all the assassination plots against the life of Fidel Castro, the AMLASH plots. AMLASH was the CIA code name for Rolando Cubela, a Cuban official and friend of Castro. The CIA first contacted Cubela in 1961 when he expressed disgust at the increasing Soviet presence in Cuba, but nothing came of the initial meetings. In September 1963, however, after renewing contact with Cubela, CIA agents discussed using him to kill Castro. Cubela had ready access to the Cuban dictator, and he indicated to his CIA contacts that if they could supply him with the proper type of weapons, he would seriously consider assassinating him. The most direct emissary the CIA used was the anti-Castro leader Manuel Artime, a personal friend of John and Robert Kennedy. In addition, the Kennedys employed two CIA officials they knew and trusted, Sheffield Edwards and Desmond Fitzgerald, to supervise the AMLASH plots. Two leading CIA officials, Richard Bissell and Richard Helms, confirmed that John and Robert Kennedy received personal updates on the AMLASH business from Artime, Edwards, and Fitzgerald. In early November 1963, Desmond Fitzgerald personally met with Cubela in Paris, and on November 22, the day of the Kennedy assassination, one of Fitzgerald's associates, Nestor Sanchez, met with Cubela and handed him weapons that he could use to kill Castro. Although the HSCA concluded that Rolando Cubela was not a double agent, reporting these schemes back to Castro, because he was sentenced to a lengthy prison term, one wonders if the "imprisonment" of Cubela served as a subterfuge to fool the committee members and staff who traveled to Havana. Fidel Castro would hardly have allowed a member of his government to live had he learned that this individual had been plotting to have him assassinated. The far more likely scenario involved Cubela pretending to plot against Castro while in reality providing the Cuban dictator with details of these plots against his life.[20]

Several other plots against Castro's life in 1963 also emanated from Miami and New Orleans. Manuel Artime told me that a special CIA team of assassins recruited from among the exile community in Miami had received intensive training for more than a year to slip into Havana and shoot the Cuban leader during one of his public appearances. Hunter Leake told me that one of the exile training camps on the north shore of Lake Ponchartrain served as the base for a special "hit team" of assassins, who would use explosives to kill Castro. Leake explained that although this activity was supposedly top secret, many people, including Guy Banister and David Ferrie, knew about it. Because Lee Harvey Oswald himself participated in some of the exercises at the guerrilla training camp at Bedico Creek, Louisiana, the possibility exists that he, too, learned of the Castro assassination schemes. Indeed, according to Silvia Odio, the anti-Castro Cuban named Leopoldo told her in late September 1963 that Oswald was proclaiming his great expertise as a marksman and his willingness to commit an assassination. This lends some small degree of credibility to the story told by Perry Raymond Russo, Jim Garrison's star witness, of hearing an assassination plot involving Ferrie, Oswald, Clay Shaw, and some unidentified Cubans.[21]

Another aspect of the intelligence connection to the assassination came in the story of Antonio Veciana, the head of the militant, violent anti-Castro exile organization, Alpha 66. In 1960, a high-ranking CIA official who used the alias "Maurice Bishop" contacted Veciana in Havana and enlisted him to participate in one of the agency's early efforts to kill the Cuban leader. The plot, hatched and carried out in the summer of 1961, entailed an attempt by a team of assassins recruited by Veciana to shoot Castro, which of course failed, Veciana having fled to the United States to avoid arrest by Castro's security forces. Upon his arrival in America, Veciana was recruited by "Bishop" to form an anti-Castro exile group and to staff it with volunteers fanatically determined to overthrow the Castro regime. Veciana formed the Alpha 66 group, which carried out a series of dangerous, violent attacks on the Cuban mainland. Lavishly financed—at one point, Veciana claimed a treasury of more than $100,000 given him by "Bishop"—Alpha 66 amassed a large quantity of boats and guns that it used for its forays into Cuba. Veciana claimed that "Bishop" constantly pressured him to engage in actions against Castro. In March 1963, Alpha 66 actually conducted a series of raids against Soviet ships in Cuban ports. Veciana stated that "Bishop" had planned and ordered these raids in a desperate attempt to foment a confrontation between the United States and the USSR over Cuba, a confrontation that would, "Bishop" believed, involve an American military invasion of the island.[22]

In late August, or perhaps early September 1963, "Maurice Bishop" introduced Antonio Veciana to Lee Harvey Oswald in Dallas. The meeting took place in the lobby of an office building in downtown Dallas. "Bishop" had called the meeting, and when Veciana arrived, he saw his CIA case officer talking to Oswald. The three men walked together toward a coffee shop, and then Oswald left, leaving Veciana and "Bishop" alone to talk. After the assassination, Veciana recognized Oswald's photograph in the newspapers as that of the man he had seen with "Bishop" in Dallas. In January 1964, "Bishop" met with Veciana in Miami. "Bishop" knew that Veciana's cousin, Guillermo Ruiz, held a high rank in Castro's intelligence service and was stationed in Mexico City at the time. "Bishop" asked Veciana to contact Ruiz and offer him a substantial amount of money to state publicly that he and his wife had met with Oswald during Oswald's trip to Mexico City in late September 1963. Veciana agreed, but he never could contact Ruiz, and several months later, "Bishop" told him to forget about it.[23]

The HSCA investigated Veciana's story regarding "Maurice Bishop" and concluded that Veciana lied. The committee claimed that Veciana waited fifteen years to tell his story, implying that, if the story were true, Veciana would have revealed it to the Warren Commission. In fact, the commission made no serious effort to unravel the tangle of secrecy and intrigue involving the Cuban connection, and it did not contact Veciana. The anti-Castro leader had been instructed in no uncertain terms to keep his mouth shut, and therefore he did not volunteer information. The HSCA also claimed that it could not identify the individual whom Veciana knew as "Maurice Bishop." In fact, several former CIA officials specifically recalled an agency employee by that name, although they did not provide further details. The speculation that "Maurice Bishop" may have been a cover name used by David Atlee Phillips, the high-ranking CIA officer heavily involved in Cuban and Latin American affairs during the 1960s, has never been positively proven or refuted. Phillips's vehement denials that he was "Bishop" do not, of course, lay the issue to rest. Sufficient documentation exists to prove that American intelligence, both military and civilian, held a strong interest in Veciana and Alpha 66 for over a decade. The HSCA also claimed that Veciana could not account for the $250,000 in cash that "Maurice Bishop" gave him when he terminated their relationship in the early 1970s. Obviously, the CIA wanted no paper trail that would lead back to it and gave the Cuban hard, untraceable, tax-free cash. It appears that Veciana told the truth, and his claim of being introduced to Lee Harvey Oswald by the CIA case officer, "Maurice Bishop," must be given considerable credibility.[24]

The CIA successfully concealed all of this from the Warren Commission, except, of course, commission member Allen Dulles. Those in charge in the intelligence agency carefully funneled the commission's investigation into Oswald's Cuban connections to his public pro-Castro, pro-Marxist stance, thereby deflecting and indeed preventing any in-depth investigation into his numerous anti-Castro acquaintances and activities. Both Richard Helms and his predecessor as deputy director for plans, Richard Bissell, stated that the last thing the agency desired was a probe into its Cuban programs. Understandably, Helms and Bissell feared that allowing commission staff access to their voluminous files covering its efforts to overthrow the Castro regime would inevitably have led to leaks to the press that would have damaged the agency beyond repair. In addition, they became apprehensive that had they disclosed the names of CIA operatives that Oswald had known and worked with—Hunter Leake, William George Gaudet, Antonio Veciana—the cover for many of their operations would have been blown. After all, the assassination plots against Castro would continue at least through 1972.[25]

For a brief time, high-ranking CIA officials remained content, for the publication of the Warren Report in September 1964 accomplished everything they wished. The Warren Commission blamed the

assassination on Lee Harvey Oswald, a disgruntled Marxian sympa-
thizer, an admirer and supporter of Fidel Castro. Nothing related
to Oswald's other side became public, for the commission never conducted a serious investigation into it. In 1967, this complacency by
the CIA changed to apprehension as Jim Garrison's investigation of
events in New Orleans during the spring and summer of 1963 threatened to blow the lid on the agency's carefully sealed cover. In his public remarks, Garrison named various individuals who had definite links
to the CIA's extensive operations in southern Louisiana as part of
Operation MONGOOSE: Guy Banister; David William Ferrie; Sergio Arcacha Smith; Clay Shaw; and, of course, Lee Harvey Oswald.
Recently released documents from agency files clearly reflect the nervousness of individuals like Richard Helms as they learned of probing
by Garrison's office into these matters. Guy Banister, for example,
had served as a key CIA liaison with many anti-Castro Cuban refugees
in southern Louisiana. Banister often handled details of the training
and supplying of various anti-Castro organizations. Typically, Hunter
Leake or another CIA agent from the New Orleans office would meet
Banister in Mancuso's Restaurant, located in the infamous 544 Camp
Street building. Other meeting places in New Orleans included Bart's,
a popular seafood restaurant near Lake Ponchartrain, the bar at the
St. Charles Hotel, in the central business district, and the Napoleon
House, a bar in the French Quarter. Leake claimed that he provided
Banister with substantial sums of cash, and Banister would use the
money to purchase needed supplies and to pay the salaries of the men
working in certain anti-Castro operations.[26]

One person that Guy Banister employed was David Ferrie. Not
only was Ferrie an experienced pilot willing to fly dangerous missions
into Cuba, he also possessed a personal hatred of communism at least
as intense as Banister's. Ferrie often lectured groups of Cuban refugees in the New Orleans area about the urgency of eliminating Castro.
He personally participated in a number of training exercises at one of
the guerrilla camps located on the north shore of Lake Ponchartrain.
In addition, Ferrie also served as an intermediary between Banister
and the Carlos Marcello–organized crime syndicate in southern Louisiana. One of his principal missions lay in obtaining weapons from
Marcello's people and transporting them to Banister, who, in turn,

would distribute them to various exile groups. Like his counterparts Santos Trafficante in Florida and Sam Giancana in Chicago, Carlos Marcello did not want to become directly involved in these transactions, so he used agents to secure the weapons from the international arms smuggling trade and sell them, for handsome profits, to Ferrie or one of Banister's other agents. Marcello provided Ferrie and Banister with small arms, artillery, armored vehicles, explosives of every type, antiaircraft and assault weapons, ammunition and other munitions, as well as huge caches of clothing, food, medical supplies, camping equipment, and the like. Banister, of course, reported directly to his CIA case officer or his case officer's underling, Hunter Leake.[27]

One facility served as the central supply house for these operations. The Schlumberger Well Company, which provided oil companies drilling in the Gulf of Mexico, with equipment and supplies, was located in Houma, Louisiana, about sixty miles southwest of New Orleans and only thirty-five miles from Marcello's camp in Jefferson Parish. Hamilton Johnson, a geologist who later served on the faculty at Tulane University, worked at Schlumberger Well in the early 1960s. Johnson stated that on numerous occasions, he observed Guy Banister, David Ferrie, various anti-Castro Cubans, and agents of both the CIA and FBI on the company's premises. On at least two occasions in the summer of 1963, Lee Harvey Oswald accompanied Banister and Ferrie to Houma. Johnson stated that it was an open secret among company employees that the federal government was using the large facility for intelligence activities. Johnson observed a steady stream of munitions and other supplies being transported to and from the plant. Large trucks would deliver the supplies to a large warehouse and Cubans would unload them. Usually, within a couple of weeks, more trucks would arrive, and Cubans would load them back onto the trucks. Johnson saw such supplies as guns, ammunitions, hand grenades, howitzers, bombs, land mines, propellers, backhoes, tractors, and vast quantities of canned foodstuffs, blankets, pillows, medical supplies, and much more. On several occasions, Cubans told him that they were using the equipment for "training exercises for another invasion of Cuba."[28]

Hunter Leake verified Hamilton Johnson's story about Schlumberger Well. Leake stated that the company was paid handsomely to provide storage space for the equipment. He also confirmed that

Banister, Ferrie, and even Oswald visited the camp from time to time. From the Schlumberger Well facility, the supplies would be transported to various training camps in Lacombe, at Bedico Creek, and in Lafourche, Terrebonne, St. Bernard, and Plaquemines Parishes because of the numerous swamps, marshes, and inlets to give the Cuban guerrilla fighters the proper kind of terrain to train on for an amphibious invasion. Leake said that Oswald's role in this was relatively minor, and that he visited Houma primarily as an observer, rather than as a participant. Oswald did, however, actively participate in a couple of training exercises at guerrilla camps, and in New Orleans, he made contact with several of the anti-Castro organizations there.[29]

Guy Banister employed Oswald to uncover pro-Castro Cubans and other Latinos in New Orleans. At that time, New Orleans served as the place of residence not just of Cuban exiles, but also of large numbers of Hondurans, Nicaraguans, Mexicans, and other Central Americans. Fidel Castro enjoyed a high degree of personal popularity in Central America, and Banister grew suspicious that some of these pro-Castro Latinos would try to infiltrate the anti-Castro Cuban exile groups with which he had worked. In addition, the ever-paranoid Banister harbored deep suspicions about the large numbers of university students and faculty in New Orleans, as well as the city's large community of artists and musicians. These groups, he believed, held left-wing views on all issues and wanted the United States to seek a peaceful accommodation with Cuba. That is why Banister employed Oswald to distribute pro-Castro literature among Latin Americans in New Orleans and to pass out his famous "Hands Off Cuba!" leaflets a few blocks from Banister's 544 Camp Street headquarters. Consuela Martin explained that she translated some pro-Castro literature into Spanish so Oswald could disseminate it to Hispanics in the city. Martin said that she observed Oswald in Banister's office at least half a dozen times, and that Oswald personally ordered her to do the translating.[30]

One unusual aspect of Oswald's five-month stay in New Orleans during the spring and summer of 1963 that has not been disclosed previously concerns his visits to the Quorum. The Quorum was a social club located in a house on Esplanade Avenue, on the outskirts of the French Quarter. It served as a gathering place for artists, writers, musicians, academics, and others who went there to socialize and discuss current issues. The Quorum became one of the first social clubs in New Orleans to allow blacks and whites to mingle freely. Undoubtedly this enraged Banister, a rabid defender of racial segregation and a vehement critic of the civil rights movement. According to Consuela Martin and William George Gaudet, Banister hired Oswald to go to the Quorum, pretend to be a fervent supporter of Castro's, and provide Banister with the names of the people who sympathized with his views. On several occasions, Henry "Hank" Kmen, a Tulane history professor and an avid jazz musician, saw Oswald at the Quorum in the summer of 1963. In other words, Banister employed Oswald to spy on people, to allow him, Banister, to add their names to his constantly growing list of those he considered to be "security risks." Banister himself had personally gone to Louisiana State University in New Orleans, located on the shore of Lake Ponchartrain, and Tulane and Loyola Universities, adjacent to each other across from Audubon Park. According to Henry Mason, a political science professor at Tulane, and Charles O'Neill, Society of Jesus, a history professor at Loyola, Banister gave virulently anticommunist speeches to groups of students and faculty during the early 1960s. On one visit to Tulane, Lee Harvey Oswald accompanied Banister.[31]

William George Gaudet, himself a CIA contact person heavily involved in Operation MONGOOSE activities in southern Louisiana, confirmed the important role that Guy Banister played. Banister's previous service with the FBI and with the New Orleans police department gave him many contacts in both organizations that gave him access to information that ordinarily would have been classified. Gaudet recalled seeing Banister pick up the telephone and place calls to "high placed individuals" in New Orleans and even Washington, D.C. Even though Banister had a record of heavy drinking and had a violent temperament, Gaudet said that the CIA used him in its anti-Castro operations in New Orleans because of his contacts and because Banister brought to the cause the dedication of a true disciple. As noted, Banister employed David Ferrie and others to purchase weapons and munitions from Carlos Marcello's organized crime syndicate. Banister also used his contacts with right-wing groups such as the Information Council of the Americas (INCA) and even the White Citizens Council to raise funds for the anti-Castro missions. Gaudet claimed that Banister raised money from Dr. Alton Ochsner, the prominent surgeon, the prominent segregationist leader Leander Perez Sr., and other well-heeled contributors to anticommunist causes. This money he used primarily to pay the salaries of certain Cuban leaders.[32]

Henry Morris, who served as chief of the New Orleans police department, knew Guy Banister well and verified Gaudet's account. Morris recalled Banister's ties with INCA, as well as his close connections with anti-Castro activities in New Orleans during the early 1960s. Morris stated that the police department paid no attention to Banister's smuggling of illegal munitions because it had been "instructed to stay away" from him. Morris explained that the police often cooperated with the FBI and on occasion, the CIA, when these agencies conducted operations in New Orleans. "We knew Guy was smuggling arms from Marcello," Morris said, "but we also knew that he was doing what the feds wanted." Interestingly, Morris stated that the man who bailed Lee Oswald out of jail after his altercation with Carlos Bringuier, Emile Bruneau, was not only a bookie employed by the Marcello organization. Bruneau also performed work for Guy Banister, and in all probability, Banister ordered Bruneau to put up the bail money so Oswald could get out of jail. "Guy had connections to the [anti-Castro] Cubans," Morris said, "but he also was close to some of Marcello's men." According to Morris, one of Carlos Marcello's attorneys, G. Wray Gill, hired David Ferrie to perform private investigative work for him because Banister had recommended Ferrie to Marcello. Morris also said that Oswald did work for Marcello, probably acting as a runner, collecting money and running errands. This enabled Oswald to collect additional income at a time when his sole source of legal income came from unemployment funds.[33]

None of this is intended to exaggerate the significance of Lee Harvey Oswald's activities in New Orleans during the spring and summer of 1963. Oswald never played more than a minor role in any of these activities. At best, he was a minor figure in a cast of thousands. Nevertheless, he did participate in some of these events. Like many other people in New Orleans at that time, Oswald touched, either directly or indirectly, the FBI, the CIA, and organized crime, and each of these organizations had its own reasons for suppressing the truth about his relationship to them. For example, when parking garage owner Adrian

Alba stated that Oswald left messages on FBI vehicles parked in his garage, the bureau denied it. The CIA vehemently denied ever communicating with Oswald at any time. Yet Hunter Leake specifically remembered the agency's voluminous files that mentioned Oswald, and he vividly recalled the panic in Richard Helms's voice when Helms ordered him to transport all of those files to Langley right after the assassination. Needless to state, organized crime never even bothered to mention Oswald, even though Oswald's uncle, Dutz Murrett, worked as a bookie for Marcello, and Oswald associated with Ferrie, Banister, and occasionally Emile Bruneau, all of whom had proven connections to Carlos Marcello.[34]

When Lee Harvey Oswald left New Orleans in late September 1963, he made his famous trip to Mexico City—the trip that generated such consternation among the CIA hierarchy when news of it surfaced soon after the assassination. As noted above, the agency not only supplied the FBI with blatantly phony photographs of "Oswald" entering the Russian embassy in the Mexican capital, it also fabricated the story of the "agent" witnessing a Cuban embassy employee giving Oswald a lot of money to assassinate a prominent political leader. Why did the CIA concoct such fables? It had a great deal to hide, and its leaders probably figured that the Warren Commission and the FBI would spend so much time unraveling the truth behind the photographs and the planted "Cuban assassination plot" story that they would have no time to conduct a thorough investigation. By the time the HSCA did investigate Oswald's sojourn to Mexico City, it could only hint at the truth. In reality, Lee Oswald had made several trips to Mexico City in 1963 to carry out missions for Guy Banister and Hunter Leake. Leake alleged that the two men sent written communications to anti-Castro Cuban leaders in Mexico and used Oswald as a courier. They trusted neither telephone nor telegraph communications because of the extensive networks of agents that Castro and his Russian allies had in Mexico City. On the trip that he took on September 25, Oswald arrived in the Mexican capital, checked into the Hotel Comercio, a well-known hangout for anti-Castro Cubans, and met with William George Gaudet later the next day. The sources for this new information include interviews with Hunter Leake, William George Gaudet, and Richard Helms, as well as Anthony Summers's interview with Guy Banister's secretary,

Delphine Roberts. Whether these sources were telling the truth or dissembling remains uncertain.[35]

Acting on orders from Win Scott, Gaudet ordered Oswald on September 27 to fly to Dallas to meet a couple of anti-Castro Cubans and accompany them to the home of a Cuban woman who might invest money in the anti-Castro crusade. The result, of course, was the famous Silvia Odio episode, still the subject of controversy among Kennedy assassination researchers. Silvia Odio and her sister, Annie, had recently moved to Dallas to join that city's anti-Castro community. Their father, a wealthy Cuban, was imprisoned on the island. Silvia and Annie had helped organize Junta Revolucionaria (JURE), a left-wing anti-Castro organization. One evening in late September 1963, three men visited Silvia to discuss her providing funding for some of their anti-Castro activities. Two of the men were Hispanic, and the third was American. One of the Latinos introduced him to the Odio sisters as "Leon Oswald." When Silvia refused to give the men the funding they sought, they left. The next day, one of the Hispanic men, Leopoldo, telephoned Silvia and asked her what she thought of the American, and she responded that she had not formed an opinion about him. Leopoldo said that Oswald was a former marine and an expert marksman. "He's kind of loco, kind of nuts. He could go either way. He would do anything—like getting underground in Cuba, like killing Castro." Leopoldo went on to say that Oswald told him that "we Cubans don't have any guts. He says we should have shot President Kennedy after the Bay of Pigs. He says we should do something like that." Less than two months later, Silvia and Annie Odio both heard about the Kennedy assassination and recognized the photographs and films of Lee Harvey Oswald on television as those of the man who had visited their apartment in Dallas.[36]

The Warren Commission rejected Silvia Odio's story because Lee Harvey Oswald was in Mexico City at the time she claimed that he visited her apartment. The HSCA, however, believed Odio, although it failed to ascertain how Oswald could possibly have traveled from Mexico City to Dallas, then back to the Mexican capital. On balance, Silvia Odio's story rings true. It fits perfectly with Oswald's associations with anti-Castro Cubans in New Orleans just before his departure for Mexico City. Leopoldo actually told Odio that the three men had just driven to Dallas from New Orleans, and she believed him because they seemed exhausted. William George Gaudet's story about Oswald flying to Dallas to meet the two Cubans cannot be verified or refuted, but it appears factual. Gaudet, it should be recalled, had received his Mexican tourist card on the same day, at the same time, and in the same place as Oswald. Both men conducted various missions for CIA-sponsored individuals and organizations. Both men went to Mexico City to find out about pro-Castro infiltrators in anti-Castro groups. Clearly, some government agency, be it CIA or FBI, had some reason to cross out the name of the person—Gaudet—who received his Mexican tourist card right after Oswald.[37]

In Mexico City, either Lee Harvey Oswald or someone claiming to be him visited both the Cuban and Russian embassies. The man wanted to obtain a visa to travel to Havana, whence he would fly to Moscow. Over the years, employees of both embassies have given disparate accounts of the visits, with some people stating that the man was the real Lee Oswald, while others stated that the visitor was an impostor. Complicating the topic is a curious teletype that the CIA sent to the FBI, the State Department, and the navy, on October 10, 1963:

> Subject: Lee Henry [*sic*] Oswald
>
> 1) On 1 October 1963 a reliable and sensitive source in Mexico reported that an American male, who identified himself as LEE OSWALD, contacted the Soviet Embassy in Mexico City. . . . The American was described as approximately 35 years old, with an athletic build, about six feet tall, with a receding hairline.
>
> 2) It is believed that OSWALD may be identical to Lee Henry [*sic*] OSWALD, born on 18 October 1939 in New Orleans, Louisiana.

Obviously, the individual described was not the real Lee Harvey Oswald. Yet the CIA persisted in its attempts to foist such a palpable impersonation on its fellow government agencies. Both the photographs of Lee Henry [*sic*] Oswald that the CIA provided to the FBI and the tapes of its wiretaps of the telephone lines of the Soviet embassy pointed to someone other than the genuine Oswald. The real Lee Harvey Oswald, of course, was twenty-three-years old, had a slender build, was five feet, nine inches tall, and did not have a receding hairline. Although the FBI instantly spotted the deception, it could do little about it. The CIA alone possessed the critical information regarding Oswald's Mexico City trip, and it obviously wished to conceal evidence of it. Neither the Warren Commission nor the HSCA managed to unravel the web of deception that the CIA wove, although the HSCA at least went to great lengths to uncover the truth.[38]

The HSCA investigation concluded that an impostor calling himself Lee Harvey Oswald was in Mexico City at the same time as the real Oswald. David Atlee Phillips testified before the committee, but he carefully hid information detrimental to the agency. The CIA's duplicity concerned not only the fact that Oswald visited the Mexican capital to carry out an agency mission, but also to obfuscate other activities which it preferred not to disclose. One such category of activities concerned continuing assassination plots against the life of Fidel Castro. Several of these plots originated with Robert Kennedy himself. The attorney general placed persistent and continual pressure on various CIA employees to eliminate Castro. In his book, *Live by the Sword,* Gus Russo documented many of these efforts by Kennedy, efforts that lasted right up to the time of his brother's assassination. Certainly the most dangerous of these involved the aforementioned AMLASH plots. AMLASH, it will be recalled, was the code name for Rolando Cubela, a Cuban diplomat who had close ties to Fidel Castro. In the summer and fall of 1963, high-ranking CIA officials, including Nestor Sanchez, the personal emissary of Desmond Fitzgerald, the head of the agency's Special Affairs Staff, and a close personal friend of both John and Robert Kennedy, commenced the actions that would culminate in the AMLASH plot. Beginning in September and continuing through November, Sanchez, and on at least one occasion Fitzgerald himself, met with Cubela as part of an assassination plot personally ordered by Robert Kennedy.[39]

Kennedy partisans bitterly dispute any involvement by either the president or the attorney general in plots to kill Castro. Russo, however, has provided impressive and irrefutable documentation proving their involvement. Hunter Leake, Richard Bissell, and Richard Helms have also confirmed Robert Kennedy's imprimatur over the AMLASH scheme. This brings us to one of the most controversial and still unresolved theories in the Kennedy assassination: the theory that

Fidel Castro was the mastermind behind it. Why? To retaliate against Kennedy for the repeated assassination attempts against his own life. It would be a grievous understatement to say that it was merely coincidental that the very first meeting that Nestor Sanchez had with Rolando Cubela occurred on the same day that Castro gave his famous warning to American leaders that "they themselves would not be safe" if they persisted in their terrorist attacks against the lives of Cuban leaders. "Let Kennedy and his brother Robert take care of themselves since they too can be the victims of an attempt which will cause their death." Coming as it did only two and a half months before John Kennedy's assassination, this warning clearly demonstrates that Castro knew about the plots against his life.[40]

In the meeting that Nestor Sanchez held with Rolando Cubela in Brazil on September 7, Cubela stated that he would participate in a coup against Castro. Sanchez immediately informed his boss, Desmond Fitzgerald, who told Robert Kennedy about it. On September 12, Bobby Kennedy's Cuban Coordinating Group met and decided to pursue the AMLASH operation. In early October, Cubela informed Sanchez that he would assassinate Castro as part of a broader operation to overthrow the communist regime in Cuba. Cubela gave Sanchez details of the kinds of rifles and explosives that he needed to carry out the assassination. Fitzgerald informed Bobby Kennedy and received permission to meet with Cubela to give him the "full assurances of United States support if there is a change of the present government in Cuba." On October 29, Fitzgerald personally met with Cubela in Paris and gave him that assurance. Three weeks later, on the very day that John Kennedy would be assassinated in Dallas, Nestor Sanchez provided Rolando Cubela with the weapons he had requested. This CIA operation, code-named AMLASH, did not occur in a vacuum. No CIA official would take such extraordinary steps without permission from higher-ups. Both Richard Bissell and Richard Helms confirmed that John and Robert Kennedy not only knew of these undertakings, they approved and authorized them. Des Fitzgerald acted on behalf of Robert Kennedy when he supervised the AMLASH schemes.[41]

In their eagerness to see Fidel Castro assassinated and his regime in Cuba replaced by a pro-American government, John and Robert Kennedy overlooked the obvious: that Rolando Cubela acted as a double agent, reporting everything back to Castro. The Cuban dictator had penetrated the anti-Castro exile community in the United States with many double agents, and he had solid intelligence about virtually every CIA-sponsored attempt against his life. Cubela had close ties to both Fidel Castro and to Castro's compadre in American organized crime, Santos Trafficante. It appears beyond belief that CIA officials did not warn the president and attorney general that Cubela might be playing them for fools to see just how far they would go in their efforts to have Castro killed. The chief of counterintelligence for Desmond Fitzgerald's Special Affairs Staff, a man known only as "Joseph Langosh," warned Fitzgerald that Cubela was a double agent and would tell Castro about the plots. Ted Shackley, chief of the CIA's JM/WAVE station, the operational headquarters of MONGOOSE in Florida, also warned Fitzgerald that Cubela's loyalties lay elsewhere than with the United States. Whether Fitzgerald even gave serious consideration to these warnings from two of his most trusted advisors remains unknown, but he ultimately ignored them.[42]

The HSCA rejected the theory that Fidel Castro masterminded John Kennedy's assassination in retaliation for Kennedy's repeated attempts on his life. The committee argued, first, that there existed prospects for restoring friendly relations between the two countries in late 1963, as evidenced in the approaches made by William Atwood. However, the Atwood moves served only as a subterfuge and not as a genuine effort by Kennedy to end hostility between the United States and Cuba. Second, the committee stated that Castro would never have risked the retaliation of the full might of the American military by having Kennedy assassinated. As powerful as this argument may seem, it falls to the fundamental instinct that drives all humans: the instinct of survival. Castro provided the details of at least twenty-four attempts on his life by the United States, most of them during Kennedy's administration. After finding out from his friend, Rolando Cubela, that the United States was continuing to try to have him killed, Castro issued his famous public warning of September 7. It was a warning that the Kennedys utterly ignored, for the record shows that they intensified the AMLASH plots in September, October, and November of 1963. Although Castro had a very efficient security force, which thwarted several of the assassination attempts, he may very well have concluded that sooner or later, the Kennedys would get lucky and one of their hired assassins would kill him. Therefore, to ensure his own survival—to save his own neck—Fidel Castro had John Kennedy murdered. To carry out that murder, he turned to his companion in the international heroin trade, Mafia boss Santos Trafficante.[43]

The Organized Crime Connection

"I want to tell the truth, and I can't tell it here," exclaimed Lee Harvey Oswald's killer, a Dallas nightclub owner named Jack Ruby. Ruby's statement came during an extraordinary interview that he gave to two members of the Warren Commission, Chief Justice Earl Warren and Congressman Gerald Ford, and to the commission's chief counsel, J. Lee Rankin. The interview took place in June 1964 at the Dallas County jail, where Ruby was incarcerated after his conviction for Oswald's murder. During the interview, on several occasions, Ruby pleaded with the chief justice to allow him to testify under federal protective custody in Washington because he was afraid to tell the truth in Dallas. During his testimony, Ruby said, "Gentlemen, my life is in danger here." He followed up by asserting that "my whole family is in jeopardy. My sisters, as to their lives." Ruby also said, "Unless you get me to Washington, you can't get a fair shake out of me."[1]

Chief Justice Warren flatly rejected Jack Ruby's repeated pleas to allow him to testify in Washington. Ruby, probably the single most important witness to provide testimony in the Kennedy assassination case, clearly felt apprehensive and feared for his life and for those of his beloved sisters. After delaying Ruby's testimony until near the very end of its investigation, the Warren Commission placed such little importance in what Ruby had to say that just two of its seven members interviewed him in Dallas. Those two members, Warren and Ford, clearly had no intention of delving beneath the surface of Ruby's background. During the interview, Ford asked Ruby, "Is there anything more you can tell us if you went back to Washington?" Ruby responded with a simple, "Yes," then added plaintively, "Are you sincere in wanting to take me back?" The answer, of course, turned out negative. The commission did not allow Ruby to testify in Washington, as Ruby wanted. The reason lay in Ruby's extensive background of close ties to members of organized crime, as well as the possibility that Ruby testifying under protective custody would open up unwelcome questions about exactly how he managed to enter the basement of Dallas police headquarters.[2]

Born in Chicago in 1911, Jacob Rubenstein grew up in the city's ethnic neighborhoods. Never a good student, he took to the streets and got into trouble, spending his early teenage years in a series of foster homes. In 1926, Jack Ruby, as Jacob Rubenstein called himself, made the acquaintance of Barney Ross, a prominent prizefighter and an associate of mobsters. One place that the teenager hung out was Dave Miller's gym, where Ross trained, and where such notorious mobsters as Al Capone, Frank Nitti, and Tony Capezio often visited. Barney Ross himself told the FBI that the youths with whom he associated ran "innocuous errands" for Capone. In 1937, Ruby, now twenty-six years old, became active in Local 20467 of the Scrap Iron and Junk Handlers Union. Two years later, the local's founder, Leon Cooke, was murdered, and Ruby's friend, Paul Dorfman, who had close ties to the Chicago mob, took control of the union. The police questioned Ruby in connection with the murder, but they released him because they could not uncover evidence against him. In 1941 Ruby became heavily involved in Chicago's liquor, narcotics, and striptease operations, activities that the underworld had dominated for many years.[3]

After serving in the military from 1943 to 1945, Ruby moved to Dallas in 1947 as part of an elaborate attempt by the Chicago mob to bribe the newly elected sheriff of Dallas County, Steve Guthrie, to allow it to take over various nightclubs and restaurants in the city. Sheriff Guthrie refused to accept the bribes, but he would later specifically mention Jack Ruby as the man the Chicago mob had selected to run a high-class restaurant in the city. In 1947 Ruby moved to Dallas, where he managed the Silver Slipper nightclub, which quickly became a hangout for notorious mobsters. During the 1950s, Ruby operated several night spots in Dallas, including the Sovereign Club, which he later renovated and renamed the Carousel Club. This establishment became a popular club, which served beer and champagne, and featured striptease shows. The Carousel served as a meeting place for many Dallas policemen, as well as mobsters. Gambling was quite evident at the

Carousel, with patrons placing bets on sporting events and going to Ruby's "warehouse" to play illegal slot machines. According to associates, Ruby had connections with gambling interests in New Orleans, Shreveport, and Tulsa, in addition to the Dallas–Fort Worth region. Ruby was also involved in narcotics and prostitution.[4]

The Warren Commission concluded that no evidence existed to prove that Ruby "ever participated in organized criminal activity." To substantiate that conclusion, the commission actually had the audacity to cite the statements of such individuals who had well-documented ties to the Mafia as Lenny Patrick, a hired syndicate hit man; Joseph Campisi, a leading member of the Dallas branch of the mob; and Irwin Mazzei, a union official with underworld ties. In reality, as the House Select Committee on Assassinations (HSCA) documented, its investigation supplemented by the research of David E. Scheim, throughout his adolescent and adult life, Jack Ruby had extensive, close relationships with numerous individuals connected with organized crime in America. These included Barney Baker, who had worked with such famous Mafia figures as Benjamin "Bugsy" Siegel and Meyer Lansky. Only two weeks before the Kennedy assassination, Baker called Ruby from Chicago, and Ruby called Baker from Dallas the next day. Joseph Campisi, a close associate of Dallas mob boss Joseph Civello, was close friends with Louisiana Mafia boss Carlos Marcello, whom Campisi visited many times. Joseph Campisi was one of Jack Ruby's closest friends in Dallas and actually visited Ruby in jail less than a week after he shot Oswald. Another associate of Ruby's, Frank Caracci, became a "major figure in the Marcello organization." Caracci had been heavily involved in various efforts to bribe public officials in Louisiana and managed some of Marcello's gambling operations in Louisiana and Texas. In the summer and fall of 1963, Jack Ruby visited one of Caracci's nightclubs in New Orleans, made several telephone calls to Caracci, and met personally with Caracci at least once.[5]

One of Jack Ruby's friends, Joseph Civello, headed organized crime in Dallas. Civello reported to Carlos Marcello, and he accompanied Marcello's brother Joseph to the infamous organized crime meeting in Apalachin, New York, in 1957. Bobby Gene Moore, who worked at Ruby's Vegas Club in Dallas in the 1950s, told the FBI that Ruby frequently visited and associated with Civello, for whom Moore worked in the early 1960s. Another mobster with whom Ruby associated was Lewis McWillie, who worked for organized crime bosses Sam Giancana, Meyer Lansky, and Santos Trafficante. In 1959, when Ruby made his famous trip to Havana, he and McWillie visited frequently. In 1963, Ruby shipped a revolver to McWillie in Las Vegas and telephoned him at least eight times. Ruby also telephoned Murray "Dusty" Miller, a Teamsters official connected with the syndicate; Lenny Patrick, an associate of Chicago mob boss Sam Giancana; and Johnny Roselli, closely connected with mob figures ranging from Al Capone to Sam Giancana. Roselli also handled significant mob business in Las Vegas and Los Angeles. In summary, as the HSCA extensively documented, Jack Ruby did in fact have a long history of intimate friendship with and business dealings with numerous figures in organized crime in America. In the three-month period before the assassination, for example, Jack Ruby made more than seventy long-distance telephone calls to persons involved in organized criminal activities.[6]

At 11:21 A.M. on Sunday, November 24, 1963, two days after President Kennedy's assassination, tens of millions of Americans watched in horror as their television sets broadcast the image of a well-dressed man suddenly bolting out from a crowd of reporters and police officers to fire one perfectly aimed shot into Lee Harvey Oswald's abdomen. The bedlam that ensued—Oswald, still handcuffed to his police escorts, falling to the ground in obvious pain, throngs of police officers grabbing the gunman and subduing him, the utter astonishment of the television commentators—shocked the nation almost as much as did the assassination itself. When Dallas police chief Jesse Curry announced the name of the man who shot Oswald, few people outside of Dallas had heard of Jack Ruby. At the time, Curry had little idea that dozens, if not hundreds, of members of the police force he headed knew Ruby, nor did he know of Ruby's suspicious actions leading up to his assassination of Oswald.

On the night before the assassination, Ruby stopped by the Egyptian Lounge, owned by Joseph Campisi. Before that Ruby had met with his friend, Lawrence Meyers, at the Carousel Club. Later, after dinner together, Ruby visited with Meyers at the Cabana Motel in Dallas. That night, Meyers had a guest, Jean West, whose apartment phone in Chicago David Ferrie had called two months previously, a "coincidence" that no one has satisfactorily explained. Ruby stayed at the Cabana until nearly three o'clock in the morning of November 22. After going to his apartment and sleeping for a few hours, Ruby dressed and drove to the Carousel Club. Then he walked to the offices of the Dallas *Morning News*, where he remained for the rest of the morning. Lone assassin theorists claim that Ruby shot Oswald because of his overwhelming grief at the loss of his beloved president and because of his deep sympathy for John Kennedy's widow and children. Yet when the motorcade arrived at Dealey Plaza, Ruby was nowhere to be found. Lone assassin theorists cannot explain why Ruby failed to walk two blocks from the newspaper office to the plaza to see the president he supposedly loved so deeply.[7]

After the assassination, Ruby drove to Parkland Hospital, where he bumped into his friend, Seth Kantor, a reporter for the Scripps-Howard newspaper chain. They ran into each other in a hospital corridor at 1:30 P.M. Kantor stated that Ruby appeared quite upset and even had tears in his eyes when Kantor told him that the president was dead. Ruby then asked him if he should close his nightclubs out of respect, and Kantor replied that he should. Ruby vehemently denied driving to Parkland Hospital after the assassination, and the Warren Commission believed him, rather than Kantor, whose account of seeing Ruby at the hospital was corroborated by Wilma Tice. The commission argued that Ruby simply did not have the time to drive from his Carousel Club on Commerce Street to Parkland Hospital because of all the traffic congestion in Dealey Plaza. In fact, as films clearly show, traffic proceeded smoothly, and Ruby had ample time to drive to the hospital to arrive there by 1:25. Seth Kantor was a well-respected reporter, and for the Warren Commission to place more credence in the account of Ruby, a convicted murderer, than of Kantor provides yet another indicator of its bias.[8]

Throughout the afternoon and evening of Friday, November 22, Jack Ruby roamed the halls of Dallas police headquarters. Numerous witnesses, including detectives, police officers, reporters, and others, saw Ruby on various floors of the building. That evening, a reporter saw Ruby actually try to open the door to the homicide bureau, where Captain Will Fritz was interrogating Oswald, but a police officer stopped him by saying, "You can't go in there, Jack." At midnight, having obtained press credentials from one of his many friends in the police department, Ruby appeared at a press conference, where reporters briefly questioned Oswald. Shortly after, Dallas district attorney Henry Wade gave the assembled press, with Ruby still impersonating a journalist, a briefing on Oswald's background. When Wade stated that Oswald belonged to the Free Cuba Committee, an anti-Castro organization, Ruby shouted, "Fair Play for Cuba." How Ruby knew this detail of Oswald's life has never been satisfactorily explained. Lone assassin theorists contend that while driving his car, Ruby had listened to an obscure radio station that had given the correct organization. This constitutes sheer speculation, because no evidence exists to prove Ruby's automobile radio listening habits. A far more plausible explanation is that Ruby already had knowledge of Oswald's background from his organized crime sources. Why, Warren Commission defenders ask, did Ruby not shoot Oswald at the midnight press conference if he had been ordered to do so? The answer lies in Ruby's awkward placement, standing in the last tier of the press row, separated from Oswald by several rows of reporters, as well as by numerous cameras and microphones.[9]

Although nearly a dozen witnesses saw Ruby at Dallas police headquarters on Saturday, November 23, Ruby claimed that he did not visit the building again until Sunday morning. His appearances on Saturday would enhance the theory that he stalked Oswald, waiting for the opportunity to silence him. Ruby would also assert that throughout Friday, Saturday, and Sunday morning, he was consumed by an overweening grief, out of sympathy for Jacqueline Kennedy and her children. In fact, Ruby fabricated this story to assist in his insanity defense. A note that he gave attorney Joe Tonahill read: "Joe, you should know this. Tom Howard [Ruby's original lawyer] told me to say that I shot Oswald so that Caroline and Mrs. Kennedy wouldn't have to come to Dallas to testify. O.K.?" At 10:19 A.M. on Sunday, November 24, Jack Ruby received a phone call from Karen Carlin from her Fort Worth home. Carlin, a stripper at Ruby's Carousel Club, asked him to send her some money so she could buy groceries. Taking his beloved dog, Sheba, with him, Ruby drove to the Western Union office located only half a block from the basement parking garage of Dallas police headquarters, rather than to Western Union offices located closer to his apartment. After wiring $25 to Carlin at 11:17, Ruby walked the short distance to the basement, entered it, and joined a throng of reporters and law enforcement officers awaiting Oswald's appearance. As Oswald, accompanied by two detectives, walked into the basement at 11:21 A.M., Ruby dashed from the crowd and fired one perfectly aimed shot into Oswald's abdomen. The .38-caliber bullet penetrated through the liver, pancreas, spleen, kidney, and aorta. Oswald fell to the ground, quickly falling into shock from the massive internal hemorrhaging. When a police officer asked Oswald to own up to shooting Kennedy because he was fatally wounded, Oswald refused, then lapsed into unconsciousness. He died on the operating table at Parkland Hospital shortly after 1:00 P.M.[10]

The slaying of Lee Harvey Oswald by Jack Ruby had all the hallmarks of an organized crime hit, as spectacular and sensational as the St. Valentine's Day Massacre in Chicago in 1929, the murder of Albert Anastasia in a Park Avenue barbershop in broad daylight in 1957, the double shooting of Joe Colombo and his gunman before a large crowd in 1970, and the gunning down of Paul Castellano in midtown Manhattan at rush hour. Ruby made the perfect gunman—a man without close family ties, a minor figure in the syndicate who could not be directly connected to any particular mob boss, someone who had fallen under intense pressure from the Internal Revenue Service to pay his back taxes, someone who lived a life of relative obscurity and who now had a chance to make a name for himself, someone whose devotion to his sisters would provide the opportunity to ensure that he would keep his mouth shut. To a far greater extent than the theory that Ruby acted out of impulse, the theory that he killed Oswald to silence him neatly coincides with the organized crime conspiracy theory.

Under the direction of chief counsel G. Robert Blakey, the HSCA conducted a thorough investigation into the possible involvement of organized crime in the Kennedy assassination. Unlike the Warren Commission, which whitewashed every possible hint of an assassination conspiracy, the HSCA concluded that certain organized crime bosses, specifically Carlos Marcello of New Orleans and Santos Trafficante of Florida, "had the motive, means, and opportunity to have President John F. Kennedy assassinated." From the moment he became attorney general, Robert Kennedy targeted Marcello as a prime candidate in his crackdown on organized crime in America. Kennedy established an organized crime division in the Justice Department and ordered it to place illegal wiretaps on the telephones of Mafia leaders and to place equally illegal listening devices in their homes and places of business. Kennedy showed little regard for legal niceties when in April 1961, he ordered agents at the Immigration and Naturalization Service offices in New Orleans to arrest Marcello and deport him. This they did, handcuffing him, putting him on a plane, and flying him to Guatemala, where they dumped him in a remote jungle. Infuriated, Marcello made his way back to Louisiana and loudly proclaimed his hatred for the Kennedys to virtually anyone who would listen. His feelings only intensified when the Justice Department secured indictments against him on charges of fraud, perjury, and illegal reentry.[11]

The attack against Carlos Marcello formed only a small part of Robert Kennedy's war on organized crime. The attorney general greatly increased prosecutions against mafiosi all over the country. FBI agents monitored telephone and personal conversations among mobsters. Although the information gathered could not be used in court, it provided the federal government with an unprecedented knowledge of the inner workings of the syndicate. Some of the conversations monitored reflected the growing animosity of Mafia bosses against the Kennedy brothers. For example, Stephano Maggadino, the Mafia boss of Buffalo, fumed that "they should kill the whole [Kennedy] family." In Chicago, Sam Giancana uttered the same sentiments, especially because he had used his vote-getting prowess on the city's west side to roll up a huge vote for Kennedy in the 1960 election. In Philadelphia, Angelo Bruno and Willie Weisberg conversed about killing John Kennedy in the White House itself. On one visit to New Orleans, Santos Trafficante voiced the desire to see Robert Kennedy killed to his close friend, Carlos Marcello.[12]

Another figure in the organized crime theory is the notorious Teamsters Union president, Jimmy Hoffa. Infuriated by Hoffa's hostile testimony during the McClellan Committee hearings into labor union racketeering, in which, as chief counsel to the committee, Bobby Kennedy had questioned Hoffa and had received vituperative responses, Kennedy harbored a personal vendetta against the head of the nation's largest labor union. Shortly after he became attorney general, Bobby Kennedy shifted scarce funds from the civil rights division to a special "Get Hoffa

Squad" that he established in the Justice Department. Flouting the very concept of justice, Kennedy refused to apply the same standards to numerous other labor unions in the country that had connections to organized crime because they gave their support to Democratic Party candidates. Instead, he focused on securing a successful prosecution of Hoffa by whatever means necessary. Aside from his deep personal hatred of Hoffa, Kennedy also had a political motive, for at the time, the Teamsters were the only significant labor union in America that supported Republican candidates. Kennedy ordered extensive wiretapping of Hoffa's telephone conversations and electronic surveillance of his personal ones. These, of course, were strictly illegal at the time, but Kennedy disregarded the law in his determination to put Jimmy Hoffa behind bars.[13]

In 1962, Jimmy Hoffa held a series of conversations with one of the most powerful Teamsters officials in Louisiana, Edward Grady Partin. In Baton Rouge, Partin's home, and in Washington, Hoffa's base of operations, as well as over the phone, Hoffa repeated his desire to see the attorney general assassinated. According to Partin, Hoffa said, "Somebody needs to bump that son of a bitch off." He went on to explain that he would like to use someone with no connections to the Teamsters who would use a high-powered rifle, similar to Hoffa's own .270 hunting rifle, and shoot Kennedy while he rode in an open convertible. Partin, who was already plotting to betray Hoffa to the federal authorities, informed a federal investigator, Hawk Daniels, of the assassination plot. Daniels listened to a telephone conversation between Hoffa and Partin and heard Hoffa repeat the plot. Daniels informed the Secret Service, which gave President Kennedy himself the information about it. The similarities to the actual assassination are obvious. The HSCA investigated but ultimately concluded that Hoffa did not play a part in the Dallas tragedy. However, in interviews, both Edward Grady Partin and Hawk Daniels insisted that they believed that Hoffa meant the threat seriously—that he actually intended to kill Robert Kennedy, and possibly his brother. Partin and Daniels said that after his convictions on embezzling union pension funds and jury tampering, Hoffa vowed to "get the Kennedys." In the spring of 1963, Hoffa voiced the same sentiment to Frank Ragano, one of Santos Trafficante's attorneys.[14]

Jimmy Hoffa included both Santos Trafficante and Carlos Marcello among his friends and business associates. He had become acquainted with them in the 1950s during the great expansion of Mafia operations in Cuba. Because of Florida's proximity to Cuba, Trafficante served as the mob's main liaison in Havana, owning wholly or partly several gambling casinos and dominating the growing narcotics traffic that flowed through the island on its way to the United States. Marcello owned part of a gambling hall in Havana, allied with Trafficante in the narcotics trade, and took to smuggling arms to Cubans fighting against the regime of Fulgencio Batista. Jimmy Hoffa became involved in an arms smuggling operation that transported weapons from Florida to Cuba. One individual heavily involved in the arms deals was Robert McKeown, a Texas gunrunner who had supplied Fidel Castro with large quantities of munitions in his guerrilla campaign against Batista. After Castro took power in January 1959, he publicly expressed gratitude for the assistance McKeown had given him. In that same year, 1959, Jack Ruby approached McKeown and asked him to provide a letter of introduction to Castro and offered him $25,000 for the favor. Although McKeown did not accept the offer, Ruby did make several highly controversial trips to Havana in the summer of that year. In August, he spent over a week in the Cuban capital, visiting with Lewis McWillie, a close confidant of Trafficante's. McWillie managed the Tropicana, a gambling establishment that included the famous mobster Meyer Lansky as one of its owners. Much speculation has centered on the issue of whether Ruby served as a bagman bribing Cuban officials to get Trafficante sprung from jail. It is documented that Ruby left Havana on September 11, flew to New Orleans, returned to Havana the following day, then departed, this time for good, on September 13. The obvious implication is that Ruby obtained the funds necessary to free Trafficante from Carlos Marcello.[15]

Not long after Trafficante was released from prison in Cuba, Fidel Castro began cracking down on mob activities there. By early 1961, he had closed down the casinos and whorehouses and had run virtually all syndicate men out of Cuba. Although this action enraged many mafiosi, including Meyer Lansky, Santos Trafficante looked to Castro in much the same fashion he had Batista, a Cuban leader whom he could bribe to allow him to continue the increasingly lucrative narcotics trade through Cuba and thence to Texas, Louisiana, and Florida. Trafficante cared nothing about Castro's politics, for the Cuban dictator readily agreed to continue the arrangement that Trafficante had with Batista. Much to Trafficante's astonishment, he learned from the Chicago mob boss, Sam Giancana, that the Kennedys wanted to have Castro assassinated. When he was hauled into the CIA plots against Castro's life, Trafficante pretended to assist. He told his CIA contacts that he had many friends in Havana who could slip poison into Castro's food or drink. When that scheme did not succeed, Trafficante offered to send a team of hired assassins into Havana to shoot Castro. Johnny Roselli believed that Trafficante had indeed tried to carry out the assassination of Castro, but that Castro's security forces proved too tough to crack. In reality, Trafficante never made an attempt to kill Castro. Instead, he kept Castro informed about the plots on his life. The Florida Mafia boss wanted the heroin trade, which Castro played a vital role in maintaining.[16]

John and Robert Kennedy, however, had determined to eradicate the Mafia from the United States. As the HSCA documented, under Attorney General Robert Kennedy, Justice Department prosecutions of leading organized crime figures multiplied many times over their number during the tenure of President Eisenhower's attorney general, Herbert Brownell. Trafficante saw his friends Jimmy Hoffa, Carlos Marcello, and others become the subjects of intense investigations and prosecutions. These actions enraged the Florida mafioso. In several parts of the country, organized crime had actually provided assistance to Kennedy during the close 1960 campaign. Trafficante thus felt betrayed and was determined to do something about it. He also wanted the Kennedys to stop interfering with Cuba because he had made a nice arrangement with Castro. Because of his geographical location and his many connections with anti-Castro Cuban exiles in Florida, Trafficante learned of many details of Operation MONGOOSE and detested the whole business. After being asked to participate in the assassination plots against Castro by Johnny Roselli and Sam Giancana, Trafficante decided that things had to stop to return to normalcy.[17]

Within this context came the famous conversation that Santos Trafficante had with the wealthy Cuban exile, Jose Aleman, in September 1962. Trafficante and Aleman, who were already friends, had participated in several business ventures together. At a Miami hotel, the mobster and the Cuban started talking about a large sum of money that Trafficante would obtain from Jimmy Hoffa to lend to Aleman. Trafficante began ranting about the Justice Department's ongoing investigation of Hoffa and the Teamsters Union, stating that the Kennedys were not doing the right thing by putting pressure on Hoffa. Trafficante asserted that the Kennedy brothers were dishonest. In an apparent reference to Sam Giancana's infusion of large amounts of cash into John Kennedy's treasury during his campaigns for the nomination and election, Trafficante fumed that the Kennedys "took graft and they did not keep a bargain." He also stated, in an ominous tone, "Mark my words, this man Kennedy is in trouble, and he will get what is coming to him." When Aleman said that he thought Kennedy would win reelection, Trafficante replied: "You don't understand me. Kennedy's not going to make it to the election. He is going to be hit." Coming from the mouth of one of the most feared Mafia bosses in America, these words—that John Kennedy was "going to be hit"—meant only one thing. Santos Trafficante knew about a plan to kill the president, and he gave Aleman the distinct impression that Jimmy Hoffa would be the ringleader of the plot.[18]

Nearly fifteen years later, Jose Aleman related the above story to investigators of the HSCA. The committee staff probed the story and could not come to a conclusion about its veracity. Aleman told the committee that he had told his FBI contact, but the FBI had no record of the conversation. This, of course, does not mean that the conversation did not occur, simply that the FBI could find no contemporaneous record of it. The committee also raised the question of why a major Mafia boss like Trafficante would reveal such a plot to someone like Aleman. It is impossible to answer this legitimate question. Perhaps Trafficante had too many drinks and talked too much, as he was wont to do on occasion. For example, on the evening of November 22, 1963, while much of the nation mourned, Trafficante and some select friends held a public party at a nightclub, where they celebrated the death of President Kennedy. Certainly Aleman believed the story. When he testified in public before the HSCA in September 1978, Aleman said that although Trafficante said that Kennedy would be "hit," he thought that he meant only that Kennedy would be "hit" by many Republican votes in the 1964 presidential election.[19]

Another mob boss, Carlos Marcello, also voiced similar sentiments in the fall of 1962. According to Edward Becker, who had worked in the casino industry, Marcello met with himself and two other men at Churchill Farms, his rural house in Jefferson Parish, near New Orleans. After a few drinks, Marcello began raving about Robert Kennedy, shouting that he "would be taken care of." In his native Sicilian tongue, Marcello said, "Livarsi na petra di la scarpa [take this stone from my shoe]." He referred to Bobby Kennedy as the tail of a dog, with John Kennedy as the dog's head. Marcello stated that if you cut the dog's tail off, it will continue to bite, but if you cut off its head, it will stop biting. Marcello elaborated that he would be delighted to see President Kennedy killed, and he believed that the best way to accomplish the feat lay in using a "nut" to carry out the assassination. None of the three men with Marcello at the time said anything.[20]

As with Trafficante's remarks to Aleman, the HSCA had serious reservations about Edward Becker's story. Because Becker himself had ties to organized crime, the committee doubted his truthfulness. The committee also raised the question of whether a tight-lipped Mafia leader like Carlos Marcello would actually speak of having President Kennedy assassinated before Becker and the others. Ordinarily, this would make sense, but Marcello had a reputation for having a big mouth, especially after consuming alcoholic beverages. He also was cocky, never dreaming that Becker would actually betray his confidence. Marcello often boasted of his feats, and in fact, it was his bragging that led to his eventual conviction and incarceration. In 1981, Marcello talked for many hours to Joseph Hauser about his illegal deals made with the state of Louisiana involving computer and hospital contracts. Unbeknownst to Marcello, Hauser was wired by the FBI and their conversation recorded, and the United States attorney's office in New Orleans used the information on the tapes to secure Marcello's conviction on several counts of criminal conspiracy.[21]

The HSCA concluded that Trafficante and Marcello were the most likely suspects in the Kennedy assassination, but that it did not have sufficient evidence to prove their guilt. In its study of the organized crime connection to the assassination, the committee virtually ignored the role played by John Martino. For a long time in the 1930s and 1940s, Martino had worked for various mobsters, including Frank Costello, "Dandy Phil" Kastel, Carlos Marcello, and Sam Carolla, as an electronics whiz who knew how to program mechanical slot machines and pinball machines to give the highest payouts to their owners. In the mid-1950s, Martino worked for Santos Trafficante and Meyer Lansky in a casino in Havana. After Castro came to power in 1959, Martino was caught trying to sneak out of Cuba with a large sum of cash on him. He remained in a Havana prison until 1962. After his release, Martino returned to the United States, where he participated in the CIA-Mafia assassination plots against Castro. He also participated in several ultra-high-secret clandestine operations that the CIA controlled. He became, for example, an integral figure in one covert operation involving former U.S. ambassador to Cuba, William Pawley, an operation deliberately designed to foment trouble between the United States and the USSR during the Cuban missile crisis of October 1962.[22]

In 1963 John Martino seemed to be everywhere. He made regular visits to Santos Trafficante's home in Tampa. He spent several weeks in New Orleans during the summer of that year. Both William George Gaudet and Consuela Martin saw Martino in Guy Banister's office at the infamous 544 Camp Street address. Henry Morris recalled that the New Orleans police department, as well as the Jefferson Parish sheriff's department, maintained surveillance on Martino while he was in New Orleans. He visited several establishments owned by Carlos Marcello and met with Marcello himself at the Town and Country Motel in Jefferson Parish. In addition, Martino became involved in several of the CIA-sponsored anti-Castro operations centered in New Orleans. Together with Banister, David Ferrie, and some Cubans, Martino ran guns from Chicago and Miami. At least twice, Martino went to the CIA's huge depot at the Schlumberger Well Company in Houma. Hamilton Johnson saw him there both times, in either July or August 1963. In September 1963, Martino showed up at an anti-Castro meeting in Dallas, where he announced that he knew a prominent anti-Castro Cuban, who just happened to be the father of Silvia Odio.[23]

Of all the sightings of John Martino in Texas, Louisiana, and Florida in 1963, by far the most significant came in August of that year when several persons saw him hanging around Curley's Corner, a well-known hangout in New Orleans for persons connected with sports betting, especially on boxing matches. Located at the corner of Poydras Street and St. Charles Avenue, Curley's Corner featured a bar and a boxing ring where many local fighters trained. According to Allen "Black Cat" Lacombe, a local character with a Runyonesque personality and manner of speaking, and a habitué of the establishment as well as of the city's Fair Grounds racetrack, John Martino visited there several times in August 1963, and on every occasion, he was accompanied by one or more of Carlos Marcello's confidants. Two of those people were Dutz Murrett and Emile Bruneau. It will be recalled that Murrett was Lee Harvey Oswald's uncle and that Bruneau had bailed Oswald out of jail after his arrest following his altercation with Carlos Bringuier. Both Murrett and Bruneau could frequently be found at Curley's Corner, serving as brokers for the incessant gambling that occurred there. On several occasions in the spring and summer of 1963, Black Cat Lacombe saw Lee Oswald at Curley's Corner, running errands for his uncle Dutz and for Bruneau. Lacombe thought nothing of it at the time, because both men frequently hired young men as runners to collect money and serve as gophers. Henry Morris confirmed Lacombe's sighting of Martino at Curley's Corner in 1963. According to Morris, "we [the New Orleans police department] kept an eye on the place, but we never busted them." As Morris explained, one of the police officers responsible for patrolling the area where Curley's Corner was located, a cop named Joe Burke, was "paid off" to look the other way regarding the illegal gambling that took place there.[24]

The significance of these sightings cannot be overemphasized. John Martino, a man with proven connections to both Carlos Marcello and Santos Trafficante, associated with two of Marcello's men at an establishment located only two blocks from the notorious 544 Camp Street building that housed Guy Banister's office and the offices of several anti-Castro Cuban exile groups. Martino appeared almost to serve as a courier, conveying messages between Trafficante and Marcello and hanging around a known sports betting establishment. John Martino also appeared to have inside knowledge of the assassination. As Anthony Summers disclosed, in 1975, Martino told a Texas business associate that the "anti-Castro people put Oswald together. Oswald didn't know who he was working for." Martino went on to state that Oswald bungled his planned rendezvous with the assassination conspirators at the Texas Theater, so "they [organized crime] had Ruby kill him." Martino also reportedly told his wife and son on the morning of the assassination that President Kennedy would be killed that day. He also told John Cummings, a reporter for *Newsday*, that two men, working for anti-Castro Cubans, had committed the assassination. He also confessed to Cummings that he himself had been part of the broader assassination conspiracy.[25]

Given the passage of time and the fading trail of evidence, it is impossible to determine the exact extent, if any, of John Martino in an assassination conspiracy. I tend to believe that Martino did indeed possess inside knowledge of the crime. He had indisputable connections to various mobsters, but could not be linked directly to anyone of significance in the Mafia's pecking order. Therefore, he made a perfect candidate for a conveyor of information. Martino's associations with Marcello and Trafficante, as well as his active involvement in various CIA-sponsored anti-Castro activities and his close links to men who knew Oswald give him a much greater role to play in the assassination saga than he has been credited with. It is also quite possible—indeed, plausible—that after the assassination, Martino tried to link the crime to the anti-Castro community in order to draw suspicion away from organized crime. It may be sheer coincidence, but not long after the assassination, Martino came into a lot of money that enabled him to live comfortably for the rest of his life.[26]

Johnny Roselli was another leading mobster who played an important role in the intrigue surrounding the Kennedy assassination. During the latter part of the 1950s and in the 1960s, Roselli served as the Mafia's main man in Las Vegas. He had close connections to Sam Giancana in Chicago, to Santos Trafficante in Florida, and to mobsters throughout the country. After the CIA contacted him about arranging a meeting with certain mob leaders, Robert Maheu turned to Roselli for assistance. Roselli brought CIA officials and Giancana and Trafficante together in Miami Beach in 1960 and again in 1961. Later Roselli actually turned over vials of poison, to be used in an attempt to kill Fidel Castro, to one of Trafficante's Cuban associates. In 1966 Roselli faced the possibility that he would be deported because, although he had lived in the United States for many decades, he was technically an illegal alien. To avert this, Roselli turned to his CIA friends, Sheffield Edwards and William Harvey, with whom he had worked in the Castro plots. Not satisfied with their help, Roselli told his lawyer, Edward Morgan, about the plots to kill Castro. Morgan informed his friend, Jack Anderson, who fed the information to his mentor, Drew Pearson, for Pearson's political gossip column. Pearson also informed President Lyndon Johnson, who was startled by the news. In a recorded telephone conversation with Attorney General Ramsey Clark, Johnson bellowed, "It's incredible! . . . They have a man [who] was instructed by the CIA and the attorney general [Robert Kennedy] to assassinate Castro after the Bay of Pigs." Johnson went on to explain that Castro's security forces captured his would-be assassins, tortured them, and ordered them to kill Kennedy. Johnson even said that Castro "called Oswald and a group in" and told them to kill Kennedy. This information Johnson got directly from Drew Pearson.[27]

Johnny Roselli knew a lot about many things that his syndicate friends preferred to keep quiet. For example, Roselli knew Judith Campbell, an attractive young woman whom he introduced to Sam Giancana in 1959 and who became one of Giancana's mistresses. In February 1960, shortly after he announced his candidacy for the presidency, Senator John F. Kennedy visited Las Vegas, as he was wont to do. At a casino bar, Kennedy's friend, Frank Sinatra, introduced him to Campbell, and the two became lovers. During the campaign, Kennedy used Campbell to convey messages to Giancana, whose financial and political support would prove critical in the campaign. After he became president, Kennedy again used Campbell to convey messages to Giancana, and this time, the messages concerned new assassination plots against Fidel Castro. Judy Campbell kept her friend from Las Vegas, Johnny Roselli, fully informed about all of this. Sam Giancana enjoyed his communications with President Kennedy, and he intended to use them as blackmail if Robert Kennedy ever tried to have him indicted. Campbell's relationship with Kennedy lasted through the year 1962, and she estimated that she traveled from Chicago to Washington and back at least three dozen times during the first two years of the Kennedy administration. Even after J. Edgar Hoover learned of the president's relationship with Campbell, Kennedy continued to see her.[28]

In 1963 Johnny Roselli continued his meetings with Santos Trafficante and several other persons involved in the Castro assassination attempts, including the infamous Washington, D.C., detective, Joseph Shimon. Roselli also visited New Orleans several times during the year to observe the anti-Castro machinations there. Hunter Leake recalled Roselli meeting with Guy Banister and David Ferrie in Banister's office on Camp Street. On one occasion, both Johnny Roselli and John Martino met with Carlos Marcello in New Orleans. Another participant at this meeting was none other than Orleans Parish district attorney Jim Garrison, whose ties to organized crime have been documented extensively. It should be mentioned that Garrison's involvement concerned only his standing line of credit at several mob-controlled casinos in Las Vegas. Together with Martino, Roselli made the arrangements to smuggle arms from the Chicago mob to New Orleans to equip the anti-Castro guerrillas being trained there. Jack Ruby also played a role in the shipment of illegal arms and munitions in 1963. The Dallas nightclub owner made several trips to New Orleans in June, July, and August, ostensibly to make arrangements for strippers from Bourbon Street establishments to perform at his Dallas clubs. In reality, Ruby met with Roselli, Martino, and Nofio Pecora, one of Marcello's top aides, to set up arms trafficking from Texas to Louisiana.[29]

In the mid-1970s, the Senate Intelligence Committee, chaired by Senator Frank Church of Idaho, conducted an investigation and held hearings on various issues involving the connection and performance of American intelligence agencies in the investigation of the Kennedy assassination. Because Senator Church desperately wanted to whitewash the committee's final report in order to preserve the image of John F. Kennedy as a wholesome family man, he refused to allow the publication of anything that smacked of a Mafia connection to the president. Both Johnny Roselli and Sam Giancana had volunteered to provide the committee with evidence of Kennedy's relationship with Judith Campbell, but Church refused to allow it. To prevent Roselli and Giancana from talking, Santos Trafficante ordered them murdered. In June 1975, Roselli's decomposing and hacked-up torso was found in an oil drum floating in a bay near Miami. In 1976, a gunman walked into Giancana's heavily guarded mansion and shot him numerous times around his mouth as a warning to others to keep their mouths shut. Both Roselli and Giancana were scheduled to testify before the Intelligence Committee.[30]

The day after the assassination, the Chicago office of the Secret Service learned from an informant a story involving the same kinds of illegal arms deals that Roselli, Martino, and Ruby had made. On November 21, 1963, a Cuban exile named Homer Echevarria, who had often voiced his hatred for the Kennedy administration, told a friend, who happened to be an informant for the Chicago Secret Service, that he would be ready to conclude an illegal arms deal. Echevarria told his friend that he had "plenty of money" and that he would finalize the arrangement "as soon as we take care of Kennedy." Needless to mention, this information rocked the Secret Service, and the agency went to great lengths to follow through. It discovered that Paulino Sierra Martinez, a Cuban exile with close ties to both the Chicago and the Florida Mafia, had financed Echevarria's weapons smuggling operation. The Secret Service further learned that Echevarria had associated with Juan Francisco Blanco-Fernandez, the military director of the Cuban Student Directorate (DRE), the organization that Oswald had contacts with in New Orleans. Unfortunately, this promising lead became part of the assassination's voluminous cold case files because on November 29, 1963, President Johnson designated the FBI as the main federal agency to investigate Kennedy's murder. The Secret Service turned over its files on Echevarria to the FBI, which abruptly decided to end the investigation into this obvious lead. In all probability, J. Edgar Hoover himself ordered the bureau not to pursue the Echevarria clues for two reasons. First, Echevarria's father, Homer Echevarria Sr., had served as an FBI informant. Second, the longtime bureau chief did not want even the possibility of his own ties to various organized crime figures brought out.[31]

Had the FBI followed through on this lead, it would have discovered close links between Paulino Sierra and organized crime. In the spring of 1963, Sierra moved to Miami from Chicago, and he immediately began trying to persuade anti-Castro leaders in Florida to join him in an operation designed to overthrow the Castro regime. Sierra claimed that he had lavish financing from a group of Chicago businessmen who wanted to replace Castro with a Cuban leader willing to allow American business interests to invest in the island. Sierra made little headway among most anti-Castro Cuban leaders in Miami, but he did display evidence of having access to large amounts of money. He purchased impressive quantities of guns, which he distributed to various Cuban groups. Sierra told associates that mobsters in Las Vegas, probably Johnny Roselli acting for Sam Giancana, and in Cleveland, controlled by Moe Dalitz, wanted to establish casinos in Havana again. Sierra told friends that he had access to $30 million in mob money that would be used to finance the new invasion of Cuba. In addition to contacting some of the most militant exile leaders, such as Antonio Veciana, Sierra did establish connections to members of Giancana's syndicate in Chicago, Marcello's in New Orleans, and Trafficante's in Florida. He also made a special effort, ultimately successful, to reach a deal with Homer Echevarria because of Echevarria's outspoken hatred for President Kennedy. According to a source, Sierra believed that Echevarria, or one of his companions in the mysterious 30th of November exile group, would actually try anything to eliminate Kennedy, thus paving the way for a renewed effort to overthrow Castro.[32]

The trafficking in illegal weapons obtained from various Mafia syndicates in the country involved many persons considered prime suspects in the Kennedy assassination. This trade made lots of money for the mob, and it helped to cement the connection that the mob had made with the CIA in its Castro assassination plots. The CIA, not willing to provide the weapons itself, turned to the mob to supply the exile groups actively functioning during Operation MONGOOSE. Individuals such as Jack Ruby, Johnny Roselli, Paulino Sierra, John Martino, Jimmy Hoffa, and a host of others with established ties to organized crime engaged in this illegal arms trade. In New Orleans, the trade flourished throughout 1962 and 1963. Even though the FBI made a well-publicized raid on an arms depot at an exile training camp in Lacombe, on the north shore of Lake Ponchartrain, it devoted little attention to the many other caches of munitions and supplies that the mob had created in the region. It was clear that the bureau, aware of Hoover's obstinate refusal to crack down on the Mafia, tried to steer clear of this business as much as possible.[33]

In addition to the trafficking in illegal arms, the Mafia also increasingly focused on smuggling contraband narcotics into the country. Both Santos Trafficante and Carlos Marcello were heavily involved in this trade. Both Florida and Louisiana offered numerous opportunities for bringing the drugs to trucks waiting near swamps and bayous. As social mores grew more liberal in the 1950s and 1960s, the demand for illegal drugs escalated, and the two mafiosi saw another opportunity to make large sums of money. Because the drugs came from the Far East, shipped through such Mediterranean countries as Lebanon, through Corsica, thence through Marseilles, the mob needed a reliable staging area in the Gulf of Mexico for the further shipment to the United States. They found this in the island of Cuba. Both Fulgencio Batista and Fidel Castro proved amenable to allowing heroin and cocaine to be transported through Cuba in return for a hefty cut of the profits. Kennedy's war against Castro alarmed Marcello and Trafficante, for it threatened to eliminate this lucrative source of income. Trafficante became closely involved in the abortive CIA assassination plots against Castro so he would remain fully informed about them. Furthermore, there is every reason to believe that Trafficante told Fidel Castro about these plots, so the Cuban dictator could take the necessary precautions. With the threats against Castro continuing into 1962 and 1963, both mob bosses decided to join forces with their Cuban drug-smuggling ally to stop Kennedy before he succeeded in his efforts to eliminate Castro.[34]

A partial confirmation of this story comes in the 1992 disclosures made by Frank Ragano, a longtime counsel and confidant of Santos Trafficante's and a friend of Carlos Marcello's. According to Ragano, in the spring of 1963, he met with Jimmy Hoffa in Washington to discuss various Teamster dealings with the mob. When Ragano told Hoffa that he would shortly fly to New Orleans to meet with Trafficante and Marcello, Hoffa told him to tell them to have President Kennedy killed. A couple of days later, Ragano met Trafficante and Marcello at the Royal Orleans hotel in New Orleans's French Quarter. Ragano, approaching the two mob chieftains, said that Jimmy Hoffa wanted them to kill the president. Neither man said anything, but the manner in which they looked gave Ragano the distinct impression that Trafficante and Marcello had already formulated plans to have Kennedy assassinated. On November 22, 1963, Ragano's fears of a Mafia plot to kill the president were confirmed by conversations he had with the three men. In a telephone call, Jimmy Hoffa exclaimed to Ragano, shortly after Kennedy's death was announced, "They [Trafficante and Marcello] got the son of a bitch. This means Bobby is no longer attorney general!" That night Ragano dined with Trafficante, and they drank toasts celebrating the death of John Kennedy. A few days later, Carlos Marcello told Ragano that Hoffa "owes me, and he owes me big," implying that he had masterminded the assassination.[35]

Frank Ragano's suspicions of a Mafia assassination conspiracy were confirmed by a deathbed conversation he had with Santos Trafficante. In late 1986, Trafficante, gravely ill from heart and kidney disease, called Ragano to his home in Tampa, where they had a long conversation, primarily reminiscing about their past relationship. Ragano claims that Trafficante began criticizing John and Robert Kennedy for their continual interference in his "business activities." Then Trafficante began to discuss the assassination itself. In words that could not be mistaken, Trafficante said, "Carlos fucked up. We should not have killed Giovanni. We should have killed Bobby." Although some researchers place no credence in Ragano's story, I find it plausible. He could have been in Tampa at the time, and he and Trafficante were certainly close enough for the dying mobster to confide in him.[36]

Carlos Marcello contributed to this story in a series of conversations that he had with FBI informant Joseph Hauser in 1980. The text of many of the conversations, secretly taped by Hauser, was used to convict Marcello on various charges and send him to the federal penitentiary. However, the presiding judge, Morey Sear, refused to allow the disclosure of three of the tapes, as well as some of the material obtained by the FBI from bugging Marcello's office in Jefferson Parish. These conversations touched on the Kennedy assassination. In his usual braggadocio manner, Marcello boasted that he had taken care of those "goddamn Kennedys," implying that he had ordered the assassination of the president, which soon resulted in Bobby giving up the position of attorney general. Carlos's brother, Joseph, also told Hauser that "we took care of them [the Kennedys], didn't we?" Judge Sear remarked that after listening to the tapes, as well as reading the transcripts, he had no doubt that Marcello had masterminded the assassination. Marcello had previously acknowledged knowing Oswald and his uncle, Dutz Murret, as well as David Ferrie. Considering Marcello's openly professed hatred for the Kennedy brothers, as well as the fact that Dallas fell within his sphere of influence, it is not unreasonable to harbor deep suspicions about his involvement in the conspiracy.[37]

On November 9, 1963, only two weeks before the assassination, a chilling conversation took place in Miami. Joseph Milteer, a wealthy anticommunist, segregationist extremist, told a friend, Bill Somerset, that someone would shoot John Kennedy with a high-powered rifle from an office building. Just hours later, the police, Milteer predicted, would arrest someone "just to throw the public off." Milteer's friend happened to be an informant for the Miami police department, and when he gave the police the tape of the conversation, Kennedy's planned motorcade through the streets of Miami was canceled when he arrived there on November 18. Instead, he flew by helicopter to give his speech, then back to the airport. The reason lay in the Miami police's fear of the threat on the tape. After the actual assassination occurred, Milteer, who claimed to be in Dallas on November 22, returned to Miami the following day. He told his friend that he had been correct—that an assassination was "in the works." The Miami police gave this information about Milteer to the FBI, but the bureau did nothing with it. Another promising lead went unprobed.[38]

Although this Milteer story has been related numerous times in studies of the assassination, no one has pursued his background in sufficient depth. In reality, Joseph Milteer had close connections to Santos Trafficante. Both played prominent roles in the anti-Castro movement in Florida, and both were involved in the illegal arms and narcotics trafficking that flourished at the time. Milteer also had close connections to Guy Banister, for both men shared identical extremist views on communism and race, as did Trafficante and Marcello. As part of Operation MONGOOSE, Milteer made several trips to New Orleans in 1963, arranging arms deals and joining Banister and David Ferrie for meals and drinks. Milteer also knew Paulino Sierra, for they both played roles in the arms smuggling operations. Interestingly, Milteer had worked with Jack Ruby in both the arms and narcotics trade, which is why the two men made trips between Miami and Dallas in 1963. Both men also traveled to New Orleans in the summer of 1963, where they consorted with some of Marcello's associates, such as Nofio Pecora. In April, Milteer had attended a meeting of the Congress of Freedom, Inc., a mysterious extreme right-wing organization that openly advocated the violent overthrow of the United States government. Headquartered in New Orleans, this group included among its members several extremists known for their virulent anti-communism and their equally vicious racism. David Ferrie and Guy Banister also attended meetings of the Congress of Freedom, Inc. because they shared its ultra right-wing views.[39]

Two persons who saw Milteer in the company of Banister and other right-wing elements in New Orleans were Bernard Eberle, the manager of the city's Confederate Museum, and Samuel Wilson, a prominent French Quarter architect. Eberle knew Banister and claimed that on several occasions, he saw the men together. On one such occasion, Banister introduced Eberle to Milteer, and the three men had a friendly discussion about their distaste for the Kennedy administration. Wilson had a similar experience. At a popular French Quarter watering hole, Wilson saw Milteer and Banister together. Knowing Banister from the mid-1950s, when Banister served as an assistant superintendent of the New Orleans police, Wilson was well aware of his extremist views. He was not surprised when Milteer joined Banister in venting his hatred for the Kennedys because they were "soft on communism" and because of their racial policies. Because of his interest in and work with the restoration of various French Quarter structures, Sam Wilson also came to know Clay Shaw quite well. Like Shaw—and, for that matter, Banister and Milteer—Wilson was tall and had white hair. Wilson stated that over the years, Shaw had voiced right-wing sentiments very similar to those of Banister and Milteer and was not surprised when Jim Garrison's investigation linked Shaw and Banister. Wilson saw Shaw and Banister together and believed that he saw Milteer with them once. Finally, several times in 1963, Wilson saw Banister, once accompanied by Milteer, conversing with some of Marcello's people in the French Quarter. Wilson emphasized that he had no knowledge of anything connected to an assassination conspiracy, but his numerous contacts with right-wing elements in New Orleans during the early 1960s led him to believe that they probably were implicated.[40]

None of this proves an organized crime connection to the Kennedy assassination, but the possibility exists that Santos Trafficante and Carlos Marcello jointly ordered the execution of the president. Both men harbored deep personal hatred for John and Robert Kennedy.

Marcello detested Robert Kennedy because of his humiliation at being kidnapped on Kennedy's orders and forcibly deported to Guatemala. He knew David Ferrie; Clem Sehrt, a longtime politico closely connected to Governor Earl Long; Dutz Murrett, Oswald's uncle; and Emile Bruneau, the man who bailed Oswald out of jail. Marcello personally knew David Ferrie, and because he liked Ferrie's graphically violent hatred of the Kennedys, he allowed Ferrie to work as a private investigator for him. Marcello also knew Jack Ruby, and when Ruby made several trips to New Orleans in the summer of 1963, the two men met at Marcello's Town and Country Motel on the Airline Highway, just outside New Orleans. Marcello's territory included Texas, and any planned mob hit on John Kennedy in Dallas would have to meet with his approval. Carlos Marcello, however, almost always shunned violence, preferring the Louisiana tradition of bribery. It is therefore unlikely that he would have resorted to breaking with that tradition in the most sensational manner possible.[41]

Instead, Marcello would have turned to his Mafia compadre, Santos Trafficante, who had no hesitation in employing violence to achieve his aims, to pull off the actual assassination. As we have seen, Trafficante had become heavily involved in the international narcotics trade, and he was determined to protect his interest in this lucrative source of illegal income. In the fall of 1963, two of Trafficante's associates, Lewis McWillie and Johnny Roselli, met with Jack Ruby in Miami and Dallas. Ruby's final meeting with Roselli came only a month before the assassination. In all probability, they made the necessary arrangements with Ruby for the scenario that would be worked out after the assassination. The actual assassins themselves Trafficante probably imported from abroad, or he used hit men from the national organized crime commission's list. It is even possible that Trafficante employed several of Fidel Castro's own squad of assassins to pull off the cross fire in Dealey Plaza. Castro certainly had the motive to eliminate Kennedy because of Kennedy's repeated attempts on his own life.[42]

Given the dearth of concrete evidence and the passage of time, it is impossible to determine the extent of organized crime's involvement in the Kennedy assassination. Several factors militate against it. First, the Mafia ordinarily did not try to kill politicians. Two of the best-known prosecutors of organized crime figures, for example, Thomas

E. Dewey and Rudolph Giuliani, remained free of violence. Mobsters preferred to employ bribery and other nonviolent means to gain the support of politicians. Those political leaders who prosecuted them they left alone. Second, had evidence of organized crime involvement in the assassination surfaced, the full force and fury of the federal government would have been brought down on the national syndicate.

Nevertheless, the organized crime theory remains one of the strongest. Perhaps Jack Ruby summarized it best when he remarked to a television interviewer, "The only thing I can say is [that] everything pertaining to what's happened has never come to the surface. The world will never know the true facts of what occurred, my motive in other words. I am the only person in the background to know the truth to everything relating to my circumstances." Asked whether he thought that the truth about the assassination would ever be revealed to the public, Ruby replied, "No, because unfortunately these people, who have so much to gain and have such an ulterior motive to put me in the position I'm in, will never let the true facts come aboveboard to the world." Shortly after his conviction on the murder of Lee Harvey Oswald, Jack Ruby said, "They're going to find out about Cuba. They're going to find out about the guns, find out about New Orleans, find out about everything." He never elaborated on these intriguing statements.[43]

Conclusion

In my four decades of researching, writing, studying, and teaching about the assassination of President Kennedy, by far the most common question that people ask me is the identity of the assassins. In other words, "Who killed JFK?" I wish that I could give them a good answer to that question, the one that the Warren Commission never asked. Unfortunately, I must tell them—to their great disappointment—that I do not know the answer to that most fundamental question of all. As time has elapsed, as virtually all of the principal characters in this great American tragedy have died, the likelihood of finding an answer diminishes. Contributing to this mystery is the continuing refusal of certain agencies of the United States government to release all of the information relating to the assassination. Both the CIA and the Secret Service, for example, have proven especially reluctant to allow public access to their materials. The wholesale destruction of important evidence, such as the Defense Department's intelligence files on Lee Harvey Oswald, has made a solution to the crime of the twentieth century in American history unlikely.

This destruction and suppression of evidence has fueled countless conspiracy theories about the CIA, the FBI, or the military-industrial complex killing Kennedy to prevent him from trying to extinguish the flames of the cold war, as he suggested in his stirring American University speech of 1963. Although I do not believe that the CIA or any other agency of the government had anything to do with Kennedy's murder, I do believe that they have drawn suspicion upon themselves by deliberately concealing and destroying vital evidence about Lee Harvey Oswald from becoming public. The ongoing efforts, even to the point of litigation, by *Washington Post* reporter Jefferson Morley to obtain the CIA files on George Joannides, the agency's contact man with the

Cuban Student Directorate and the man who received vital information about Oswald, has met with a degree of official stonewalling that makes the Nixon administration seem like a paragon of honesty and candor. In late January 2005, it was disclosed that the CIA still refuses to make public hundreds of thousands of pages of documentary material relating to U.S. relations with former Nazis after World War II—yet another example of the agency's disdain for maintaining the historical record. The continuing refusal by the Kennedy family to allow free public access to all of the autopsy records in the National Archives provides still another example of the continuing cover-up in the case.

In the opinion of many, the assassination of John Kennedy marked a watershed event in recent American history. Whatever his shortcomings, Kennedy inspired people as few other presidents have managed to do. The violence of the events in Dallas initiated a precipitous decline in national prestige. Kennedy's murder began, or so it seemed, a time of both domestic and foreign turmoil, symbolized by the growing militancy of the civil rights movement and of the counterculture, and by the morass in Vietnam. The major organs of the printed press and electronic media, already captivated by the Kennedy mystique, saw in Kennedy's assassination a representation of everything that was wrong with the country. Swallowing the Warren Commission story hook, line, and sinker, they unleashed a series of vicious attacks on those who believed that the facts proved a conspiracy.

The Warren Commission, established by Lyndon Johnson more to quell rumors and speculation than to conduct a full, free, and independent investigation, distorted the truth, concocted absurd interpretations like the single bullet theory, and deliberately suppressed much of its evidentiary base, only contributing to the growing suspicions of a cover-up of a conspiracy. Serious researchers easily exposed many of the commission's shortcomings and provided their readers and audiences with ample evidence of an assassination conspiracy. The opening up of millions of pages of long-suppressed documentary evidence in recent years has only served to add fuel to the suspicions, leading many to argue that the assassination cover-up reached to the highest levels of government.

The withholding of crucial evidence in the Kennedy assassination—the cover-up of the truth—stemmed, I believe, not from an effort to conceal the complicity of unnamed members of a military-industrial cabal behind the president's murder. Rather, it arose out of an understandable desire by individuals and agencies to hide their own shortcomings. As always, J. Edgar Hoover wanted to protect the image of the FBI, and he ordered agents investigating the assassination not to disclose anything that might tarnish that image. The CIA wanted to conceal evidence of its nefarious assassination plots against Fidel Castro, especially because they entailed an unholy alliance with organized crime. The Secret Service wanted to withhold evidence of its own failure to provide adequate protection for the president. The Kennedy family wanted to promote the Camelot image that blossomed quickly after John Kennedy's shocking death. Therefore, they wanted to suppress all evidence of presidential complicity in the Castro assassination plots and the negotiations with organized crime.

This coordinated campaign to cover up the whole truth about the Kennedy assassination was part of a continuing effort by government agencies and private individuals to withhold the truth from the public. Since the outbreak of World War II, it had become commonplace to classify materials whose public release might prove embarrassing. The onset of the cold war served to reinforce this propensity to suppress from the public any controversial materials under the umbrella of "national security." For two decades, the media and the public acquiesced in this arrangement. The Kennedy assassination, however, broke the tradition, for it coincided with an era of widespread public access to electronic sources of information, a new generation of highly educated Americans no longer willing to meekly accept all government pronouncements with absolute acceptance, and a group of dedicated researchers determined to bring the truth about the assassination to the public.

When all is said and done, I fully anticipate that the current impasse on the Kennedy assassination will continue. This case remains the greatest unsolved murder mystery in American history. A president of the United States—young, vital, just beginning to come to grips with the fearsome responsibilities of his office—was gunned down in one of the most shocking events of the twentieth century. The failure of two federal bodies, one appointed by the executive branch, the other by the legislative branch, to provide a satisfactory solution to the crime

has contributed to the continuing public distrust in the official pronouncements of their government. The massive cover-up and outright
destruction of evidence by the Secret Service, the FBI, the CIA, and
even the Kennedy family have generated in the citizens of this country
a degree of cynicism that remains high. We will never know the full
truth about what happened in Dallas that day, or who was responsible
for Kennedy's murder. I just hope that by presenting both sides of the
debate, I have contributed to a better understanding of the crime of
the century.

Notes

1. The Assassination and Its Aftermath

1. President's Commission on the Assassination of President Kennedy, *Report of the President's Commission on the Assassination of President John F. Kennedy* (Washington, 1964), 15 (hereafter cited as Warren Report).

2. Ibid. Gerald Posner, *Case Closed: Lee Harvey Oswald and the Assassination of JFK* (New York, 1993), 221–23.

3. Warren Report, 131–33.

4. Michael L. Kurtz, *Crime of the Century: The Kennedy Assassination from a Historian's Perspective*, 2nd ed. (Knoxville, 1993), 113–14; Harold Weisberg, *Whitewash: The Report on the Warren Report* (New York, 1965), 57–58.

5. Warren Report, 1–2.

6. Kurtz, *Crime of the Century*, 221–22.

7. Ibid., 222–31; Abraham Zapruder film of the assassination, frames Z189–Z335.

8. Mark Lane, *Rush to Judgment*, paperback ed. (New York, 1966), 33–38.

9. Posner, *Case Closed*, 242; Robert J. Groden, *The Killing of a President: The Complete Photographic Record of the JFK Assassination, the Conspiracy, and the Cover-up* (New York, 1993), 46, 50–51, 54–57, 60–61.

10. Warren Report, 149–55.

11. Charles A. Crenshaw, *Trauma Room One: The JFK Medical Coverup Exposed*, with J. Gary Shaw, D. Bradley Kizzia, Gary Aguilar, and Cyril H. Wecht (New York, 2001), 61–70; Warren Commission Exhibit 392; *Hearings before the President's Commission on the Assassination of President Kennedy* (Washington, 1964), 6:41, 48, 51, 61, 68 (hereafter cited as Warren Commission Hearings).

12. Commission Exhibit 392; Groden, *Killing of a President*, 86–88.

13. Warren Report, 157–63.

14. Robert R. Shaw interview, telephone, May 7, 1986; *Appendix to Hearings before the Select Committee on Assassinations of the U.S. House of Representatives*, 95th Cong., 2nd session (Washington, 1979), 325–29 (hereafter cited as HSCA Hearings).

15. Warren Report, 79, 81; Warren Commission Hearings, 6:128–34.

16. Warren Report, 163–64.

17. Ibid., 165; Dale K. Myers, *With Malice: Lee Harvey Oswald and the Murder of Officer J. D. Tippit* (Milford, MI, 1998), 55–57, 62.

18. Myers, *With Malice*, 67–74; Lane, *Rush to Judgment*, 171–72.

19. Warren Report, 79; Weisberg, *Whitewash*, 79–84, photograph section following 184; Gary Savage, *JFK: First Day Evidence* (Monroe, LA, 1993), 187–96.

20. Myers, *With Malice*, 63–187.

21. Roy Kellerman and William Greer interviews, telephone, January 16, 1984; Crenshaw, *Trauma Room One*, 88–90.

22. WFAA-TV, Dallas, film clips of assassination scenes; Warren Report, 199–200; Jesse Curry interview, telephone, March 18, 1984.

23. J. Edgar Hoover, summary of conversation with President Lyndon B. Johnson, November 22, 1963, Federal Bureau of Investigation Files on the Assassination of President John F. Kennedy, National Archives and Records Service, College Park, MD (hereafter cited as FBI Files); Robert I. Bouck interview, telephone, October 3, 1989.

24. Warren Report, 86; James W. Sibert and Francis X. O'Neill, Results of Autopsy on John F. Kennedy, 2, FBI files (hereafter cited as Sibert-O'Neill Report); James B. Livingston, "Statement of 18 November 1993," in James H. Fetzer, ed., *Assassination Science: Experts Speak Out on the Death of JFK* (Chicago, 1998), 162–63.

25. Deposition of John Stringer, July 16, 1996, Assassination Records Review Board Collection, National Archives and Records Service, College Park, MD (hereafter cited as ARRB Collection); deposition of Floyd A. Riebe, May 7, 1997, ibid.

26. Sibert-O'Neill Report, 3–5.

27. Ibid.

28. James J. Humes interview, telephone, March 18, 1997.

29. Ibid., Warren Report, 541.

30. Seth Kantor, *Who Was Jack Ruby?* (New York, 1978), 47; Seth Kantor interview, telephone, May 19, 1987.

31. Seth Kantor interview.

32. Crenshaw, *Trauma Room One*, 132–34; Nigel Turner, *The Men Who Killed Kennedy*, video, 1988.

33. Nicholas DeB. Katzenbach to William Moyers, November 24, 1963, FBI Files.

34. Max Holland, *The Kennedy Assassination Tapes* (New York, 2004), 153–59; 195–201.

35. Robert I. Bouck interview; David S. Lifton, *Best Evidence: Disguise and Deception in the Assassination of John F. Kennedy*, paperback ed. (New York, 1988), 703; HSCA Hearings, 8:23.

36. Douglas P. Horne, "Evidence of a Government Cover-up: Two Different Brain Specimens in President Kennedy's Autopsy," in James H. Fetzer, ed., *Murder in Dealey Plaza: What We Know Now that We Didn't Know Then about the Death of JFK* (Chicago, 2000), 299–310.

37. FBI Report on the Assassination of President John F. Kennedy, December 9, 1963, FBI Files; Transcript of Warren Commission Executive Session of January 22, 1963, Records of the President's Commission on the Assassination of President Kennedy, National Archives and Records Service, College Park, MD (hereafter cited as Warren Commission Records).

38. Arlen Specter, *Passion for Truth: From Finding JFK's Single Bullet to Questioning Anita Hill to Impeaching Clinton* (New York, 2000), 108–12.

39. Holland, *Kennedy Assassination Tapes*, 250.

2. Conflict: The Evidence

1. See Henry Lee and Jerry Labriola, *Famous Crimes Revisited: From Sacco-Vanzetti to O. J. Simpson, Including: Lindbergh Kidnapping, Sam Sheppard, John F. Kennedy, Vincent Foster, Jon Benet Ramsey* (Southington, CT, 2001), 265–66; David Owen, *Hidden Evidence: 40 True Crimes and How Forensic Science Helped Solve Them* (Willowdale, Ontario, Canada, 2000), 26; LeMoyne Snyder, *Homicide Investigation: Practical Information for Coroners, Police Officers, and Other Investigators*, 3rd ed. (Springfield, IL, 1977), 25–32; Henry M. Morris interview, Many, LA, March 14, 1982; Henry Lee conversation, Pittsburgh, November 21, 2003.

2. Snyder, *Homicide Investigation*, 33–36; Cyril H. Wecht, "A Critique of President Kennedy's Autopsy," in Thompson, *Six Seconds in Dallas*, 278–84; Charles G. Wilber, *Medicolegal Investigation of the President John F. Kennedy Murder* (Springfield, IL, 1978), 20–49; William Eckert interview, Gretna, LA, August 6, 1995.

3. Henry M. Morris interview, New Orleans, June 18, 1979; Jesse Curry interview, telephone, July 8, 1978; Roger D. Craig interview, May 5, 1972; Kurtz, *Crime of the Century*, 57; Groden, *Killing of a President*, 47–57, 60–64.

4. Warren Report, 139; Josiah Thompson, *Six Seconds in Dallas: A Micro-Study of the Kennedy Assassination* (New York, 1967), 141–45; Roger D. Craig interview, telephone, March 8, 1970; Jesse Curry interview.

5. Warren Report, 134–35; Savage, *JFK: First Day Evidence*, 77–82.

6. Wilber, *Medicolegal Investigation*, 102–4, 113, 128–29, 291–92; HSCA Hearings, 7:138–41; Warren Report, 93–94; Specter, *Passion for Truth*, 96.

7. Tomlinson testimony, Warren Commission Hearings, 6:129–32; Pool interview, HSCA Records, National Archives and Records Service, College Park, MD; Thompson, *Six Seconds in Dallas*, 155–58, 175–76.

8. Tomlinson testimony, Warren Commission Hearings, 6:129–31; Johnsen statement, ibid., 18:800; Frazier and Rowley statements, ibid., 3:428, 24:412.

9. FBI statement, ibid., 24:412; Thompson, *Six Seconds in Dallas*, 175–76. For a convincing refutation of the official version of the "identification" of Bullet 399 as the "stretcher bullet," see Gary Aguilar and Josiah Thompson, "The Magic Bullet: Even More Magical than We Knew?" available at http://history-matters.com/essays/frameup/EvenMoreMagical/EvenMoreMagical.htm, which cites recently declassified documents proving that neither Tomlinson nor Wright ever identified Bullet 399 as the one they saw and handled.

10. Tomlinson testimony, Warren Commission Hearings, 6:129–35; "Who Shot President Kennedy?" *Nova*, PBS, 1988; Arlen Specter insists that he did not try to put words into Tomlinson's mouth or ask him leading questions: Specter, *Passion for Truth*, 96–97, 120.

11. Warren Report, 95; Posner, *Case Closed*, 333–37.

12. See Gary L. Aguilar, "The Converging Medical Case for Conspiracy in the Death of JFK," in Fetzer, *Murder in Dealey Plaza*, 175–217; Mantik, "Paradoxes of the JFK Assassination: The Medical Evidence Decoded," ibid., 219–97; Horne, "Evidence of a Government Cover-up," 299–310.

13. Transcript of Press Conference with Drs. Malcolm Perry and Kemp Clark. November 22, 1963, 5, ARRB Collection; Commission Exhibit 392, Warren Commission Records; Hutton and Nelson testimony, Warren Commission Hearings, 6:46–47, 6:143–47.

14. Nicholas deB. Katzenbach to William Moyers, November 25, 1963, FBI Files; Outline of Warren Commission Inquiry, Warren Commission Records.

15. Vincent Palamara, "The Secret Service: On the Job in Dallas," in Fetzer, *Murder in Dealey Plaza*, 165; Perry testimony, Warren Commission Hearings, 3:373; St. Louis *Post-Dispatch*, December 1, 1963.

16. Milton Helpern interview, telephone, October 9, 1975; autopsy photograph in Lifton, *Best Evidence*, photographs following 682.

17. Milton Helpern interview; William Eckert interview, Gretna, LA, February 17, 1991; Robert R. Shaw interview; Robert Livingston interview, telephone, August 15, 1990; Claude Craighead interview, May 15, 1977; Orien Anthon interview, Springfield, LA, November 7, 1993; Edward Brown interview, Hammond, LA, May 5, 1991; Joseph Dolce interview, telephone, June 12, 1988.

18. Jenkins notes, Warren Commission Exhibit 392; Baxter notes, Warren Report, 523; Carrico testimony, Warren Commission Hearings, 6:51; Perry statement, Warren Commission Exhibit 392; Crenshaw, *Trauma Room One*, 67; Clark note, Warren Commission Exhibit 392; Jones testimony, Warren Commission Hearings, 6:53–56; Peters testimony, ibid., 71.

19. McClelland testimony, Warren Commission Hearings, 6:33–34; McClelland account, "Who Shot President Kennedy?" *Nova*, PBS, 1988.

20. Gary L. Aguilar and Cyril H. Wecht, "The Medical Case for Conspiracy," in Crenshaw, *Trauma Room One*, 193–208; Wilber, *Medicolegal Investigation*, 20–49; Milton Helpern interview; William Eckert interview.

21. HSCA Hearings, 7:37–39; Aguilar, "Converging Medical Case for Conspiracy," 197–200.

22. Aguilar, "Converging Medical Case for Conspiracy," 199.

23. Robert O. Canada interview, telephone, March 6, 1968; George G. Burkley interview, telephone, December 14, 1983; Henry Hurt, *Reasonable Doubt: An Investigation into the Assassination of John F. Kennedy* (New York, 1985), 49.

24. Godfrey McHugh interview, telephone, April 19, 1984; Horne, "Evidence of a Government Cover-up," 306.

25. Russell Fisher et al., "1968 Panel Review of Photographs, X-ray Films, Documents and Other Evidence Pertaining to the Fatal Wounding of President John F. Kennedy on November 22, 1963 in Dallas, Texas," National Archives and Records Service, College Park, MD (hereafter referred to as Clark Panel Report), 12; HSCA Hearings, 7:103–5, 126.

26. Robert I. Bouck interview; Roy Kellerman interview; Lifton, *Best Evidence*, 703.

27. "Chain of Custody of Materials Acquired during the Autopsy," HSCA Hearings, 7:23–24; Aguilar, "Converging Medical Case for Conspiracy," 209; ARRB interview of Joseph O'Donnell, February 28, 1997, ARRB Collection; ARRB interview of Saundra Spencer, June 7, 1997, ARRB Collection.

28. "Chain of Custody of Materials Acquired during the Autopsy," HSCA Hearings, 7:23–24.

29. Aguilar, "Converging Medical Case for Conspiracy," 210–11; ARRB interview of Floyd A. Riebe, May 7, 1997, ARRB Collection; ARRB interview of John T. Stringer, July 7, 1996, ARRB Collection.

30. Robert Dallek, *An Unfinished Life: John F. Kennedy, 1917–1963* (Boston, 2003), 76, 81, 105, 705.

31. Burke Marshall to Lawson G. Knott Jr., October 29, 1966, John F. Kennedy assassination collection, National Archives and Records Service, College Park, MD; "Report of Inspection by Naval Medical Staff on November 1, 1966 at National Archives of X-rays and Photographs of Autopsy of President John F. Kennedy," ibid.; "Chain of Custody of Materials Acquired during the Autopsy," HSCA Hearings, 7:23–33.

32. David W. Mantik, "The JFK Assassination: Cause for Doubt," in Fetzer, *Assassination Science*, 120–37.

33. Ibid.; William Eckert interview; Sidney Johnston interview, Hammond, LA, September 17, 1990.

34. Douglas Weldon, "The Kennedy Limousine: Dallas 1963," in Fetzer, *Murder in Dealey Plaza*, 135–36; Robert I. Bouck interview; Roy Kellerman interview; William Greer interview; FBI photographs of the limousine taken at the White House garage on the morning of November 23, 1963, reveal no bullet fragments, FBI Files; photos may be viewed at: http://www.jfklancer.com/LimoMarsh.html.

35. HSCA Hearings, 7:122–24; Mantik, "Paradoxes of the JFK Assassination: The Medical Evidence Decoded," 279–82.

36. Robert I. Bouck interview; HSCA Hearings, 7:123; Mantik, "Paradoxes of the JFK Assassination: The Medical Evidence Decoded," 279–82.

37. Aguilar and Wecht, "Medical Case for Conspiracy," 196–202.

38. Myers, *With Malice*, 150–55, 158–60, 162–64.

39. Ibid., 261–74.

40. Abraham Fortas interview, telephone, September 14, 1986; Leon Jaworski interview, telephone, September 16, 1986.

3. Conflict: The Case for the Lone Assassin

1. Warren Report, 21; *Report of the Select Committee on Assassinations*, U.S. House of Representatives, 95th Cong., 2nd Sess. (Washington, 1979), 95 (hereafter cited as HSCA Report).

2. See Specter, *Passion for Truth*, 122–25; Max Holland, "After Thirty Years: Making Sense of the Assassination," *Reviews in American History* 22 (1994): 208–9;

"The Key to the Warren Report," *American Heritage* (1995): 50–64. See also the comprehensive lone assassin Web site of John McAdams: http://mcadams.posc .mu.edu/home.htm.

3. Posner, *Case Closed*, 247–50; Jim Moore, *Conspiracy of One: The Definitive Book on the Kennedy Assassination*, rev. ed. (Fort Worth, 1992), 62.

4. Warren Report, 79–85.

5. Ibid., 18; Kurtz, *Crime of the Century*, 48–50.

6. Warren Report, 95–109.

7. FBI Report on assassination, December 9, 1963; Specter, *Passion for Truth*, 110.

8. Ibid.; Warren Report, 107.

9. Warren Report, 90–91; Report of the Forensic Pathology Panel, HSCA Hearings, 7:175, 179.

10. Kurtz, *Crime of the Century*, 56–60.

11. Warren Report, 107–9.

12. Warren Commission Hearings, 4:104–25; Posner, *Case Closed*, 337–39, 478–79, 481.

13. HSCA Hearings, 1:491–533; Kenneth A. Rahn, "Neutron Activation Analysis and the John F. Kennedy Assassination," March 2001, available at: http://karws .gso.uri.edu/JFK/Scientific_topics/NAA/NAA_and_assassination_II/NAA_and _assassination.html. See also Kenneth Rahn and Larry Sturdivan, "Neutron Activation and the JFK Assassination—Part 1: Data and Interpretation" and "Part 2: Extended Benefits," *Journal of Radioanalytical and Nuclear Chemistry* 262 (2004): 205–22.

14. "Who Shot President Kennedy?" *Nova*, PBS, 1988; "Who Killed JFK?" ABC News, 2003; Posner, *Case Closed*, 329–30; Clark Panel Report; HSCA Hearings, 7:179–80.

15. See Posner, *Case Closed*, 309–16.

16. Warren Report, 541.

17. See ARRB testimony of James J. Humes, February 13, 1996; J. Thornton Boswell, February 6, 1996; and Pierre A. Finck, May 27, 1996, ARRB Collection; autopsy photographs reproduced in Lifton, *Best Evidence*, photographic section following 682; Cyril H. Wecht and Robert P. Smith, "The Medical Evidence in the Assassination of President John F. Kennedy," *Forensic Science* 3 (1974): 105–28.

18. ARRB testimony of Humes, Boswell, and Finck, ARRB Collection.

19. HSCA Hearings, 7:103–15. Also see Daniel Sullivan, Rodrick Faccio, Michael Levy, and Robert G. Grossman, "The Assassination of President John F. Kennedy: A Neuroforensic Analysis—Part 1: A Neurosurgeon's Previously Undocumented Eyewitness Account of the Events of November 22, 1963," *Neurosurgery* 53 (2003): 1019–27; Michael L. Levy, Daniel Sullivan, Rodrick Faccio, Robert G. Grossman, "A Neuroforensic Analysis of the Wounds of President John F. Kennedy—Part 2: A Study of the Available Evidence, Eyewitness Correlations, Analysis, and Conclusions," *Neurosurgery* 54 (2004): E1–E22.

20. Ibid., 172–74; testimony of Larry Sturdivan, ibid., 1:383–427; Luis W. Alvarez, "A Physicist Examines the Kennedy Assassination Film," *American Journal of Physics* 44 (1976): 813–27. For a recent attempt to prove the scientific validity of

the lone assassin thesis, see Larry M. Sturdivan, *The JFK Myths: A Scientific Investigation of the Kennedy Assassination* (St. Paul, MN, 2005).

21. Testimony of Thomas Canning, HSCA Hearings, 1:490–567; Sturdivan testimony, HSCA Hearings, 1:383–427; HSCA Report, 50–51; Robert Grossman Lecture, *Into Evidence*, DVD of 40th anniversary of JFK Assassination, Cyril H. Wecht Institute of Forensic Science and Law, Duquesne University School of Law, Pittsburgh, PA, November 2003 (hereafter cited as *Into Evidence*).

22. Posner, *Case Closed*, 5–22.

23. Warren Report, 118–22.

24. Ibid., 122–24; Savage, *JFK: First Day Evidence*, 99–120.

25. Warren Report, 124–25.

26. Ibid., 125–28; HSCA Report, 53; Savage, *JFK: First Day Evidence*, 123–42.

27. Warren Report, 128–29.

28. Ibid., 129–30.

29. Ibid., 130–31; Posner, *Case Closed*, 220–23.

30. Warren Report, 131–34.

31. Ibid., 134–36; Gus Russo, *Live by the Sword: The Secret War against Castro and the Death of JFK* (Baltimore, 1998), 264–71.

32. Warren Report, 143.

33. Ibid., 62–63, 143–46.

34. Ibid., 63; WFAA-TV, Dallas, footage of Dealey Plaza, November 22, 1963.

35. Warren Report, 144–46; Posner, *Case Closed*, 247–50.

36. Warren Report, 68–71.

37. Ibid., 149–56.

38. Ibid., 154–55.

39. Ibid., 157–60; Posner, *Case Closed*, 266–67.

40. Warren Report, 161–63.

41. Ibid., 163–64; Posner, *Case Closed*, 268.

42. Posner, *Case Closed*, 273–74; Myers, *With Malice*, 69–72.

43. Warren Report, 166–67, 176–79.

44. Ibid., 161–76; Myers, *With Malice*, 71–72.

45. Warren Report, 171–72; Leon Jaworski interview.

46. Warren Report, 377–78; Posner, *Case Closed*, 5–10.

47. Warren Report, 378–82.

48. Ibid., 383–84.

49. Posner, *Case Closed*, 20–23.

50. Warren Report, 191–92, 384–86.

51. Posner, *Case Closed*, 32–34, 46–57.

52. Warren Report, 393–406.

53. Ibid., 404–12.

54. Posner, *Case Closed*, 156–57.

55. Russo, *Live by the Sword*, 191–206.

56. Ibid., 209–28.

57. Posner, *Case Closed*, 197–223.

58. Warren Report, 160–61.

59. Ibid., 20.

4. Conflict: The Case for Conspiracy

1. Zogby Poll, August 2001, reported in Associated Press release; see Kurtz, *Crime of the Century*, 238.

2. Jeff MacIntyre, "Brilliant Careers: Don DeLillo," October 23, 2001, available at: http://archive.salon.com/people/bc/2001/10/23/delillo/index.html?x.

3. See David W. Mantik, "Paradoxes of the JFK Assassination: The Silence of the Historians," in Fetzer, *Murder in Dealey Plaza*, 371–411.

4. See Daniel Patrick Moynihan, "The Paranoid Style in American Politics Revisited," *Public Interest* 81 (1985): 107–27; Mark Fenster, *Conspiracy Theories: Secrecy and Power in American Culture* (Minneapolis, 1999); Timothy Melley, *Empire of Conspiracy: The Culture of Paranoia in Postwar America* (Ithaca, NY, 2000); Patrick O'Donnell, *Latent Destinies: Cultural Paranoia and Contemporary U.S. Narrative* (Durham, NC, 2000).

5. Letter to the author, June 1995; JFK Assassination Symposium, Louisiana Tech University, Ruston, LA, 1993; Jim Marrs, *Rule by Secrecy: The Hidden History that Connects the Trilateral Commission, the Freemasons, and the Great Pyramids* (New York, 2000).

6. See Marrs, *Rule by Secrecy*; Michael L. Kurtz, "Conspiracy Theories in the Assassination of President Kennedy," paper presented at the annual meeting of the Southwestern Social Sciences Association, New Orleans, 1995.

7. In the Warren Report, 19, the Warren Commission asserted that "it is not necessary to any essential findings of the Commission to determine just which shot hit Governor Connally." However, even staunch defenders of the lone assassin theory agree that it is essential to determine just which shot hit Governor Connally. Furthermore, they agree that the single bullet theory is essential to the lone assassin theory. See David W. Belin, *November 22, 1963: You Are the Jury* (New York, 1973), 302–6; David W. Belin interview, Ruston, LA, November 18, 1993; J. Wesley Liebeler interview, telephone, November 18, 1993.

8. "Ford Alters Location of JFK Wound," CNN interactive news release, July 3, 1997, available at: http://www.cnn.com; Warren Report, 87–88; shirt photograph in Harold Weisberg, *Post Mortem: JFK Assassination Cover-up Smashed!* (Frederick, MD, 1975), 597; Philip Willis slide #5, in David R. Wrone, *The Zapruder Film: Reframing JFK's Assassination* (Lawrence, KS, 2003), photograph section following 84; autopsy photographs in Lifton, *Best Evidence*, photograph section following 682.

9. Dennis L. Breo, "JFK's Death: The Plain Truth from the MDs Who Did the Autopsy," *JAMA* 267 (May 27, 1992): 2794–803; Pierre A. Finck to Joseph M. Blumberg, February 1, 1965, quoted in HSCA Hearings, 7:101; Robert O. Canada interview.

10. Warren Report, 250; Warren Commission Hearings, 6:141–43; Robert O. Canada interview.

11. Warren Commission Hearings, 2:93; Sibert-O'Neill Report, 4; St. Louis *Post-Dispatch*, December 1, 1963; *New York Times*, December 6, 1963.

12. *New York Times*, January 26, 1964; Sylvia Meagher interview.

13. HSCA Hearings, 7:142–43; *Reasonable Doubt: The Single-Bullet Theory and the Assassination of John F. Kennedy*, White Star Productions, 1988; Robert R. Shaw interview.

14. FBI Report, December 9, 1963; transcript of Warren Commission Executive Session, January 27, 1964; Arlen Specter to J. Lee Rankin, April 30, 1964, Warren Commission Records.

15. *Reasonable Doubt*; Joseph J. Dolce interview, telephone, October 9, 1986; Robert Shaw interview.

16. Zapruder film; Henry M. Morris interview; William Eckert interview; Sidney Johnston interview; HSCA Report, 284; Eddie Adams photographs and film of execution of Viet Cong prisoner; Eddie Adams interview, telephone, October 20, 1988; CNN News film of shootout outside North Hollywood bank, November 1997.

17. David W. Mantik, "Special Effects in the Zapruder Film: How the Film of the Century Was Edited," in Fetzer, *Assassination Science*, 279–84; Wilber, *Medicolegal Investigation*, 221–22; Sidney Johnston interview.

18. Aguilar and Wecht, "Medical Case for Conspiracy," 285–86; Robert O. Canada interview.

19. Warren Report, 128–29.

20. Ibid., 140–46; Russo, *Live by the Sword*, 267–68.

21. Howard Roffman, *Presumed Guilty: Lee Harvey Oswald in the Assassination of President Kennedy* (Cranbury, NJ, 1975), 201–22.

22. Walt Brown, *Treachery in Dallas* (New York, 1995), 248; Bledsoe testimony, Warren Commission Hearings, 1:51–52, 6:409; Lane, *Rush to Judgment*, 161.

23. Lane, *Rush to Judgment*, 164–68.

24. Warren Report, 160–61.

25. Ibid.; Kurtz, *Crime of the Century*, 130–33; Roger D. Craig interview.

26. Warren Report, 163, 165; Roberts testimony, Warren Commission Hearings, 6:438, 443.

27. Russo, *Live by the Sword*, 307–8; Myers, *With Malice*, 64–65.

28. Benavides testimony, Warren Commission Hearings, 6:448–52; Bowley account, ibid., 24:202.

29. Myers, *With Malice*, 71–72; Lane, *Rush to Judgment*, 188–94.

30. Warren Report, 165; Leon Jaworski interview.

31. Myers, *With Malice*, 64–66; Russo, *Live by the Sword*, 307–8, 314–15.

5. Consensus: The Facts

1. Wrone, *Zapruder Film*, 9–37.

2. The sharpest version of the film available to the public is in *Image of an Assassination: A New Look at the Zapruder Film*, VHS/DVD, MPI Productions, 1998.

3. See Jack White, "Mysteries of the JFK Assassination: The Photographic Evidence from A to Z," in James H. Fetzer, ed., *The Great Zapruder Film Hoax:*

Deceit and Deception in the Death of JFK (Chicago, 2003), 45–112; David S. Lifton, "Pig on a Leash: A Question of Authenticity," ibid., 309–426.

4. See Vincent Palamara, "59 Witnesses: Delay on Elm Street," in Fetzer, *Murder in Dealey Plaza*, 119–28; Douglas P. Horne, "Interviews with Former NPIC Employees: The Zapruder Film in November 1963," ibid., 311–24; David W. Mantik, "Paradoxes of the JFK Assassination: The Zapruder Film Controversy," ibid., 325–60; Groden, *Killing of a President*, 86–88.

5. Roland Zavada, *Analysis of Selected Motion Picture Photographic Evidence* (Rochester, NY, 1998).

6. Ibid.; Roland J. Zavada, "The Zavada Summary: Dissecting the Zapruder Bell & Howell 8mm Movie Camera," in Fetzer, *Great Zapruder Film Hoax*, 447–55; Wrone, *Zapruder Film*.

7. See autopsy photographs in Lifton, *Best Evidence*, photograph section following 682.

8. Forensic Pathology Panel Report, HSCA Hearings, 7:135; Weston comments, *The Kennedy Assassination*, CBS, November, 1975; DiMaio comments, *Who Killed President Kennedy?* Discovery Channel, 1998; Posner, *Case Closed*, 337–38.

9. HSCA Report, 43–44; Alvarez, "A Physicist Examines the Kennedy Assassination Film."

10. Aguilar and Wecht, "Medical Case for Conspiracy," 196–202; Warren Report, 541.

11. Warren Commission Hearings, 3:368, 370; 6:6, 33, 42, 60.

12. Sidney Johnston interview; Henry M. Morris interview; Billy Abel interview, Hammond, LA, May 8, 1978.

13. See HSCA interview of Robert Knudsen, a White House photographer who claimed that he had taken autopsy photographs revealing images strikingly different from those depicted in the official set, HSCA document 014028, 38–39; HSCA Document 002198, 34–35, in Records of the House Select Committee on Assassinations, National Archives and Record Services, College Park, MD (hereafter cited as HSCA Records); ARRB testimony of Saundra Spencer, June 6, 1997, ARRB Collection.

14. Roffman, *Presumed Guilty*, 109–20; James H. Fetzer, "'Smoking Guns' in the Death of JFK," in Fetzer, *Murder in Dealey Plaza*, 6.

15. Author's personal collection of Mannlicher-Carcano ammunition; Sidney Johnston interview; Billy Abel interview.

16. Warren Report, 87; Joseph Dolce interview.

17. Specter, *Passion for Truth*, 110; HSCA Report, 45; "Who Shot President Kennedy?" *Nova*, PBS, 1988; Forensic Pathology Panel Report, HSCA Hearings, 7:179–80.

18. Testimony of Dr. Malcolm Perry, Warren Commission Hearings, 3:368; testimony of Dr. Alfred Olivier, ibid., 5:77–78; Warren Commission Exhibit 850, ibid., 17:846.

19. Summary of HSCA interview with Dr. Shaw, HSCA Hearings, 7:325–29; Robert R. Shaw interview.

20. Warren Report, 93; Robert R. Shaw interview.

21. Zapruder film, frames Z236–Z238; Robert R. Shaw interview; Charles F. Gregory interview, telephone, March 6, 1970.

22. Kurtz, *Crime of the Century*, 56–58.

23. Warren Report, 97–103.

24. Weisberg, *Whitewash*, 283–84; Zapruder film, frame Z255; Robert R. Shaw interview; Charles F. Gregory interview.

25. Posner, *Case Closed*, 321–23; Wrone, *Zapruder Film*, 191–92.

26. See Warren Report, 118–56.

27. Ibid., 139; Thompson, *Six Seconds in Dallas*, 141–46; Roffman, *Presumed Guilty*, 151–200.

28. Baker testimony, Warren Commission Hearings, 3:252, 263; Truly testimony, ibid., 225; Warren Report, 155–57.

29. William Eckert interview; Robert O. Canada interview.

30. ARRB testimony of Francis X. O'Neill, September 12, 1997, ARRB Collection; ARRB testimony of James W. Sibert, September 11, 1997, ibid.; Lifton, *Best Evidence*, 590–92; Thompson, *Six Seconds in Dallas*, 166–69.

31. Warren Report, 165; Myers, *With Malice*, 68–73, 86–87.

32. Myers, *With Malice*, 62, 64; Warren Report, 167–68, 176–80.

33. Warren Report, 171–76; Myers, *With Malice*, 364.

34. Warren Report, 172; Myers, *With Malice*, 269–73.

35. Courtland Cunningham testimony, Warren Commission Hearings, 3:474; Warren Report, 171–72.

36. See Lane, *Rush to Judgment*, 159–75; Myers, *With Malice*, 62–65; Russo, *Live by the Sword*, 307–8.

37. Markham testimony, Warren Commission Hearings, 3:310.

38. Aguilar and Wecht, "Medical Case for Conspiracy," 196–98, 200–201, 267–68, 285–86.

39. Lifton, *Best Evidence*, 703; "Chain of Evidence of Materials Acquired during the Autopsy," HSCA Hearings, 7:23–36.

40. Roy Kellerman interview; William Greer interview; Robert I. Bouck interview; Mantik, "Paradoxes of the JFK Assassination: The Medical Evidence Decoded," 273–79.

41. Horne, "Evidence of a Government Cover-up," 279–310.

42. Mantik, "The JFK Assassination: Cause for Doubt," 93–137, 153–60.

43. Mantik, "Paradoxes of the JFK Assassination: The Medical Evidence Decoded," 278; Horne, "Evidence of a Government Cover-up," 300, 310.

44. See New Orleans *Times-Picayune*, February 23, 25, 1967; Patricia Lambert, *False Witness: The Real Story of Jim Garrison's Investigation and Oliver Stone's Film "JFK"* (New York, 1998), 39–83.

45. Eric Norden, "Jim Garrison: A Candid Conversation with the Embattled District Attorney of New Orleans," *Playboy*, October 1967, 59–60, 62, 64, 66, 68, 70, 72, 74, 156–63, 165–68, 170–72, 174–76, 178; Lambert, *False Witness*, 123; James DiEugenio, *Destiny Betrayed: The Kennedy Assassination and the Garrison Trial* (New York, 1992); Joan Mellen, *A Farewell to Justice: Jim Garrison, JFK's Assassination, and the Case that Should Have Changed History* (Washington, DC, 2005); Dave

Reitzes, "Who Speaks for Clay Shaw?" available at: http://mcadams.posc.mu .edu/shaw1.htm.

46. Lambert, *False Witness*, 53–83.

47. The trial transcripts are in *State of Louisiana v. Clay L. Shaw*, Criminal District Court, Parish of Orleans, Case No. 198-059.

48. For sympathetic views of Garrison, see DiEugenio, *Destiny Betrayed*; and William Davy, *Let Justice Be Done: New Light on the Jim Garrison Investigation* (Reston, VA, 1999).

49. "Who Shot President Kennedy?" *Nova*, PBS, 1988; "The Kennedy Assassination—Beyond Conspiracy" ABC News, 2003; *JFK Reloaded*, downloadable video game, available at: http://www.gamespot.com/pc/action/jfkreloaded/.

50. See Posner, *Case Closed*, 479; Warren Report, 91–109; HSCA Report, 45–46, 48–51; *The Assassination of President Kennedy*, Discovery Channel, 2004.

51. William Eckert interview; Alvarez, "A Physicist Examines the Kennedy Assassination Film," 813–27; Luis Alvarez interview; Kurtz, *Crime of the Century*, 102–3.

52. *Into Evidence*, 2004; Mantik, "Paradoxes of the JFK Assassination: The Silence of the Historians," in Fetzer, *Murder in Dealey Plaza*, 379.

53. See "Cover: The Warren Report: How the Commission Pieced Together the Evidence: Told by One of Its Members," *Life*, October 2, 1964; "The Warren Commission Report," *Time*, October 2, 1964, 45–50, 55; "Unraveling the Mystery of the Assassination of John F. Kennedy: The Official Story," *U.S. News and World Report*, October 5, 1964, 35–42, 70–71, 96–97.

54. Lane, *Rush to Judgment*; Weisberg, *Whitewash*; Edward Jay Epstein, *Inquest* (New York, 1966), 58; Cyril H. Wecht, "Critique of President Kennedy's Autopsy," 278–84; Clark Panel report; John K. Lattimer, "The Kennedy-Connally One Bullet Theory: Further Circumstantial and Experimental Evidence," *Medical Times* 36 (November 1974): 33–56; Alan Stang, "They Killed the President," *American Opinion* 19 (February 1976): 1–8, 67.

55. Commission on CIA Activities within the United States, *Report of the Commission on CIA Activities within the United States* (Washington, 1975); David W. Belin interview.

56. HSCA Report, 41, 65.

57. See Robert R. Artwohl, "JFK's Assassination: Conspiracy, Forensic Science, and Common Sense," *JAMA* 269 (March 24–31, 1993): 1540–43; Aguilar, "Converging Medical Case for Conspiracy," 175–219; Harold Weisberg, *Case Open: The Unanswered JFK Assassination Questions* (New York, 1994), 57–80.

58. Henry Lee lecture, *Into Evidence*, 2004.

6. Lee Harvey Oswald

1. Posner, *Case Closed*, 5–21.

2. Warren Report, 380–81.

3. Posner, *Case Closed*, 10–14; see Marguerite Oswald's testimony, Warren Commission Hearings, 1:234–36, 262.

4. Warren Report, 384–86; Posner, *Case Closed*, 18–19.

5. Hurt, *Reasonable Doubt*, 199–201; Edward Jay Epstein, *Legend: The Secret World of Lee Harvey Oswald*, paperback ed. (New York, 1978), 55–85.

6. Epstein, *Legend*, 86–88; Posner, *Case Closed*, 30–32.

7. Posner, *Case Closed*, 34–46; Warren Report, 690; HSCA Report, 211.

8. Hurt, *Reasonable Doubt*, 209–10; Posner, *Case Closed*, 50–52.

9. Michael Beschloss, *Mayday: The U-2 Crisis: The Untold Story of the Greatest U.S.-U.S.S.R. Spy Scandal*, paperback ed. (New York, 1987), 236; Posner, *Case Closed*, 49; John Newman, *Oswald and the CIA* (New York, 1995), 43–46. See also Anthony Summers, *Not in Your Lifetime*, updated ed. (New York, 1998), 92–93, 101–2.

10. Warren Report, 392–93; Posner, *Case Closed*, 24, 70, 120.

11. Richard Helms interview, telephone, October 3, 1994; Richard Bissell interview, telephone, November 6, 1991; Posner, *Case Closed*, 35–46; Summers, *Not in Your Lifetime*, 129–35; HSCA Report, 101–2.

12. Richard Helms interview; Richard Bissell interview.

13. Richard Helms interview; Richard Bissell interview; Epstein, *Legend*, 107–16.

14. Epstein, *Legend*, 134–56; Summers, *Not in Your Lifetime*, 123–28.

15. Richard Helms interview; Hunter C. Leake interview, telephone, March 15, 1981; Hamilton Johnson interview, New Orleans, June 8, 1984.

16. Hurt, *Reasonable Doubt*, 218–20; Epstein, *Legend*, 177–89.

17. Summers, *Not in Your Lifetime*, 154–60; Newman, *Oswald and the CIA*, 276–79; Hunter C. Leake interview; Richard Bissell interview.

18. Warren Report, 118–22, 172–74; Posner, *Case Closed*, 104–6.

19. Warren Report, 182–87; Posner, *Case Closed*, 115–16; Summers, *Not in Your Lifetime*, 161–64.

20. Warren Report, 183–87; *Dallas Morning News*, April 11, 12, 1963; HSCA Report, fn. On 98; Billy Abel interview; Henry M. Morris interview; Robert A. Maurin Sr. interview, Hammond, LA, May 7, 1983; Sidney Johnston interview; Jesse Curry interview.

21. Sylvia Meagher, *Accessories after the Fact: The Warren Commission, the Authorities, and the Report* (Indianapolis, 1967), 282–93. Posner, *Case Closed*, 116–17.

22. Posner, *Case Closed*, 116–18, 264.

23. Hurt, *Reasonable Doubt*, 215–16; Summers, *Not in Your Lifetime*, 163–65; HSCA Hearings, 11:126–27; Warren Report, 128.

24. Warren Report, 186–87; HSCA Report, 60–61; Jesse Curry interview.

25. See John H. Davis, *Mafia Kingfish: Carlos Marcello and the Assassination of John F. Kennedy*, paperback ed. (New York, 1989), 135–37; 248–49; G. Robert Blakey and Richard N. Billings, *Fatal Hour: The Assassination of President Kennedy by Organized Crime* (New York, 1992), 368–72; David E. Scheim, *Contract on America: The Mafia Murder of President John F. Kennedy* (New York, 1988), 64–65, 257.

26. Warren Report, 286–92; Posner, *Case Closed*, 126–30, 148–63.

27. U.S. Senate, Select Committee to Study Governmental Operations with Respect to Intelligence Activities, Interim Report, *Alleged Assassination Plots In-*

volving Foreign Leaders, 94th Cong. 1st Sess., Report No. 94-465 (Washington, 1975), 134–69; U.S. Senate, Select Committee to Study Governmental Operations with Respect to Intelligence Activities, Final Report, *The Investigation of the Assassination of President John F. Kennedy: Performance of the Intelligence Agencies*, book 5 (Washington, 1976), 10–13; Hunter C. Leake interview; Richard Bissell interview.

28. Hunter C. Leake interview; Henry M. Morris interview; William George Gaudet interview, telephone, July 17, 1985; HSCA Report, 145–46; author's personal observations.

29. Consuela Martin interview, telephone, August 18, 1973.

30. Newman, *Oswald and the CIA*, 309; Consuela Martin interview; Warren Hinckle and William W. Turner, *The Fish Is Red: The Story of the Secret War against Castro* (New York, 1981), 208; Henry Mason interview, New Orleans, October 8, 1988; Henry "Hank" Kmen interview, New Orleans, September 6, 1972.

31. Hunter Leake interview; Russo, *Live by the Sword*, 141–44; Consuela Martin interview; William George Gaudet interview.

32. William George Gaudet interview; Hunter C. Leake interview; Anthony Summers, *The Assassination of John F. Kennedy: What We Know Now that We Didn't Know Then*, VHS, Witness Productions, 1978.

33. Hunter C. Leake interview. In an interview, Richard Helms neither confirmed nor denied Leake's story.

34. HSCA Report, 133–34, 143–44; Russo, *Live by the Sword*, 3–85, 155–90.

35. Henry C. Morris interview; Samuel Wilson interview, Many, LA, March 18, 1981; Bernard "Ben" Eble interview, Many, LA, March 18, 1981; Hunter C. Leake interview.

36. Andrews testimony, Warren Commission Hearings, 11:325–31; Santos Miguel Gonzalez interview, New Orleans, April 16, 1983; Hamilton Johnson interview; Posner, *Case Closed*, 142–48; Summers, *Not in Your Lifetime*, 236–39.

37. Summers, *Not in Your Lifetime*, 250–52, 280–82, 370–71; Consuela Martin interview; William George Gaudet interview; Santos Miguel Gonzalez interview.

38. Deborah Schillace conversation, Hammond, LA, April 19, 1989; Posner, *Case Closed*, 180–94; Summers, *Not in Your Lifetime*, 261–81.

39. William George Gaudet interview; Richard Bissell interview.

40. Warren Report, 321–24; HSCA Report, 137–39.

41. Warren Report, 322–24; HSCA Report, 139.

42. Warren Report, 159; Bledsoe testimony, Warren Commission Hearings, 400–427.

7. The Intelligence Connection

1. Edward Lopez and Dan Hardaway, "Oswald in Mexico City," HSCA Staff Report 180-10110-10484 (hereafter cited as Lopez Report), HSCA Records, National Archives and Records Service, College Park, MD.

2. Holland, *Kennedy Assassination Tapes*, 72.

3. Ibid., 159–60.

4. FBI Legat[ion] to Director, April 6, 1964, FBI Files; Lopez Report, 123–24; CIA Mexico City Station to Director, October 8, 1963, CIA Files; photographs in Summers, *Not in Your Lifetime,* photograph section following 172.

5. Director, CIA, to McGeorge Bundy [Presidents Kennedy and Johnson's national security advisor], November 26, 1963, CIA Files.

6. Richard Helms interview; Richard Bissell interview; Hunter C. Leake interview.

7. Richard Helms interview; Bernard Fensterwald interview, Washington, DC, May 15, 1972; Richard Bissell interview.

8. Richard Helms interview.

9. Russo, *Live by the Sword,* 13–84; Richard M. Bissell, *Reflections of a Cold Warrior* (New Haven, CT), 196–203; Summers, *Not in Your Lifetime,* 182–89.

10. HSCA Report, 130–37; Santos Miguel Gonzalez interview; Consuela Martin interview.

11. Richard Helms interview; Richard Bissell interview; Bissell, *Reflections of a Cold Warrior,* 201.

12. Russo, *Live by the Sword,* 61–62; Summers, *Not in Your Lifetime,* 177–78.

13. Select Committee to Study Governmental Operations with Respect to Intelligence Activities, *Alleged Assassination Plots Involving Foreign Leaders,* 139–48, 181–89; Richard Helms interview; Richard Bissell interview; Hunter C. Leake interview.

14. Select Committee to Study Governmental Operations with Respect to Intelligence Activities, *Alleged Assassination Plots Involving Foreign Leaders,* 74–85; Summers, *Not in Your Lifetime,* 184–89.

15. House Select Committee on Assassinations, Staff Report, "The Evolution and Implications of the CIA-Sponsored Assassination Conspiracies against Fidel Castro," HSCA Hearings, 10:167–76.

16. Tad Szulc interview; Jack Anderson, "Were Trujillo, Diem, CIA Targets, Too?" syndicated article, January 20, 1971; Select Committee to Study Governmental Operations with Respect to Intelligence Activities, *Alleged Assassination Plots Involving Foreign Leaders,* 130–35.

17. Summers, *Not in Your Lifetime,* 188; Richard Helms interview; Hunter C. Leake interview; Richard Bissell interview.

18. Hunter C. Leake interview; Richard Helms interview.

19. HSCA Report, 127; Summers, *Not in Your Lifetime,* 303–6.

20. Summers, *Not in Your Lifetime,* 306; HSCA Report, 111–14; Russo, *Live by the Sword,* 242–45; Richard Helms interview; Richard Bissell interview.

21. Manuel Artime interview, telephone, August 23, 1987; Hunter C. Leake interview; HSCA Report, 137–39.

22. HSCA Report, 135–37; Summers, *Not in Your Lifetime,* 250–52, 370–71.

23. HSCA Report, 135–36; Summers, *Not in Your Lifetime,* 250–52, 370–71.

24. HSCA Report, 136–37; House Select Committee on Assassinations Staff Report, "Anti-Castro activities and Organizations and Lee Harvey Oswald in New Orleans," HSCA Hearings, 10:37–52.

25. Richard Helms interview; Richard Bissell interview; Hunter C. Leake interview.

26. Hunter C. Leake interview; Richard Helms interview; Henry M. Morris interview; Samuel Wilson interview; Bernard Fensterwald interview, Washington, DC, May 17, 1972.

27. Hunter C. Leake interview; Henry M. Morris interview; Hamilton Johnson interview.

28. Hamilton Johnson interview.

29. Hunter C. Leake interview.

30. Consuela Martin interview; Henry Mason interview; Henry "Hank" Kmen interview.

31. Consuela Martin interview; William George Gaudet interview; Henry "Hank" Kmen interview; Henry M. Morris interview.

32. William George Gaudet interview; Henry M. Morris interview.

33. Henry M. Morris interview.

34. Hunter C. Leake interview.

35. Hunter C. Leake interview; William George Gaudet interview; Richard Helms interview; Summers, *Not in Your Lifetime*, 262.

36. House Select Committee on Assassinations Staff Report, "Anti-Castro Activities and Organizations and Lee Harvey Oswald in New Orleans," HSCA Hearings, 10:19–32.

37. Ibid.; William George Gaudet interview; Richard Helms interview.

38. CIA teletype, October 10, 1963; Summers, *Not in Your Lifetime*, 270.

39. Lopez Report, HSCA Records; Russo, *Live by the Sword*, 237–72.

40. Associated Press account of Fidel Castro interview, September 7, 1963.

41. Richard Bissell interview; Richard Helms interview.

42. Russo, *Live by the Sword*, 242–48.

43. HSCA Report, 129; Richard Bissell interview.

8. The Organized Crime Connection

1. Ruby testimony, Warren Commission Hearings, 5:194–96; Scheim, *Contract on America*, 192–98.

2. Warren Commission Hearings, 5:190–94; Meagher, *Accessories after the Fact*, 452–53.

3. Warren Report, 780–85; Kantor, *Who Was Jack Ruby?* 98–102.

4. Warren Report, 790–93; Warren Commission Exhibit 1753; Henry M. Morris interview; Seth Kantor interview, telephone, September 6, 1985.

5. Warren Report, 790; HSCA Report, 149–51; Henry M. Morris interview.

6. Scheim, *Contract on America*, 121–38; HSCA Report, 154–56.

7. Warren Commission Exhibits 2266, 2267, 2274, 2384; HSCA Hearings, 9:334–64; Seth Kantor interview; Jesse Curry interview.

8. Warren Report, 335–37; Tice account, Warren Commission Hearings, 15:285–87, 392–94; Kantor, *Who Was Jack Ruby?* 40–44. It took Secret Service agent Forrest Sorrels only twenty to twenty-five minutes to return to Dealey Plaza from Parkland Hospital, Warren Report, 52.

9. Warren Commission Hearings, 15:348–52; Warren Report, 340–42.

10. "The Assassination of President Kennedy: What We Know Now that We Didn't Know Then"; Warren Commission Hearings, 13:204–12.

11. Seth Kantor interview; HSCA Report, 169, 173; Davis, *Mafia Kingfish*, 101–19; Henry M. Morris interview.

12. HSCA Report, 164–66; Hawk Daniels interview, Baton Rouge, LA, November 12, 1985; Henry M. Morris interview.

13. HSCA Report, 176–77; Edward Grady Partin interview, Baton Rouge, LA, July 7, 1985.

14. HSCA Report, 176–77; Edward Grady Partin interview; Hawk Daniels interview; "The Assassination of President Kennedy: What We Know Now that We Didn't Know Then"; Blakey and Billings, *Fatal Hour*, xii–xiii.

15. Blakey and Billings, *Fatal Hour*, 314–15; HSCA Hearings, 9:172–78; Warren Commission Exhibit 1689; "The Assassination of President Kennedy: What We Know Now that We Didn't Know Then."

16. Peter Dale Scott, *Deep Politics and the Death of JFK* (Berkeley, 1993), 171–81; Richard Helms interview; Richard Bissell interview; Henry M. Morris interview.

17. HSCA Report, 161; Summers, *Not in Your Lifetime*, 186, 196–97; Scott, *Deep Politics*, 181.

18. HSCA Report, 172–76; Aleman testimony, HSCA Hearings, 5:301–7.

19. HSCA Hearings, 301–7; Summers, *Not in Your Lifetime*, 197.

20. HSCA Report, 171; Summers, *Not in Your Lifetime*, 200–202; Henry M. Morris interview; Hunter C. Leake interview.

21. HSCA Report, 171–72; Davis, *Mafia Kingfish*, 11–15; 342–43; 579–82.

22. Warren Commission counsel David Slawson tried to persuade chief counsel J. Lee Rankin to call Martino as a witness to testify before the commission, but Rankin, never eager to open potential cans of worms, refused. Memo, W. David Slawson to J. Lee Rankin, April 1, 1964, Warren Commission Records; Summers, *Not in Your Lifetime*, 325–28. For a discussion of the CIA's notorious "Bayo-Pawley" affair, see Hinckle and Turner, *The Fish Is Red*, 168–73; and Scott, *Deep Politics*, 113–17.

23. William George Gaudet interview; Consuela Martin interview; Henry M. Morris interview; Hamilton Johnson interview.

24. Allen "Black Cat" Lacombe interview, New Orleans, September 3, 1985; Henry M. Morris interview; Bernard "Ben" Eble interview; Bernard Fensterwald interview; Lou Russell interview.

25. Summers, *Not in Your Lifetime*, 328, 372–73; Hunter C. Leake interview; Henry M. Morris interview.

26. Summers, *Not in Your Lifetime*, 327–28; Henry M. Morris interview.

27. Russo, *Live by the Sword*, 393–95; Jack Anderson presentation, Louisiana Tech University, 1993.

28. Summers, *Not in Your Lifetime*, 188–89; Richard Bissell interview; Richard Helms interview; Bernard Fensterwald interview.

29. Hunter C. Leake interview; Henry M. Morris interview; Samuel Wilson interview.

30. "The Assassination of President Kennedy: What We Know Now that We Didn't Know Then"; Richard Bissell interview.

31. HSCA Report, 133–34; Russo, *Live by the Sword*, 185; Scott, *Deep Politics*, 329–30; Larry Hancock, *Someone Would Have Talked: What We Know about the JFK Assassination after 40 Years* (Southlake, TX, 2003), 65–70; Scheim, *Contract on America*, 218.

32. Blakey and Billings, *Fatal Hour*, 194–99; Henry M. Morris interview.

33. Henry M. Morris interview; Richard Helms interview; Hunter C. Leake interview. Blakey and Billings, *Fatal Hour*, 280–81; Scheim, *Contract on America*, 83–86; Davis, *Mafia Kingfish*, 445–46; Edward Grady Partin interview, Baton Rouge, LA, June 17, 1984.

34. Blakey and Billings, *Fatal Hour*, xi–xvii; Edward Grady Partin interview; Hawk Daniels interview, Baton Rouge, LA, June 6, 1986.

35. Blakey and Billings, *Fatal Hour*, xiv.

36. Henry M. Morris interview; Morey Sear interview, telephone, August 12, 1989, New Orleans, December 7, 1986; Henry Mentz interview, New Orleans, December 7, 1986.

37. Blakey and Billings, *Fatal Hour*, 7–8; Summers, *Not in Your Lifetime*, 308–9; Scott, *Deep Politics*, 49–51.

38. Henry M. Morris interview; Samuel Wilson interview; Hawk Daniels interview.

39. Bernard "Ben" Eble interview; Samuel Wilson interview; Henry M. Morris interview.

40. Clem Sehrt interview, New Orleans, January 10, 1971; Henry M. Morris interview.

41. Blakey and Billings, *Fatal Hour*, 397–432; Richard Bissell interview; Richard Helms interview.

42. "The Assassination of President Kennedy: What We Know Now that We Didn't Know Then"; Hancock, *Someone Would Have Talked*, 136.

43. Quoted in Summers, *Not in Your Lifetime*, 341.

Selected Bibliography

Primary Sources

Government Documents

Central Intelligence Agency. John F. Kennedy Assassination Records. National Archives and Records Service, College Park, MD.

Federal Bureau of Investigation. John F. Kennedy Assassination Files. National Archives and Records Service, College Park, MD.

Records of the Assassination Records Review Board. National Archives and Records Service, College Park, MD.

Records of the President's Commission on the Assassination of President Kennedy. National Archives and Records Service, College Park, MD.

Government Reports

Assassination Records Review Board. *Final Report of the Assassination Records Review Board.* Washington, DC, 1998.

Commission on CIA Activities within the United States. *Report of the Commission on CIA Activities within the United States.* Washington, DC, 1975.

House of Representatives, Committee on Governmental Information and Individual Rights, Subcommittee on Governmental Operations. *National Archives-Security Classification Problem Involving Warren Commission Files and Other Records.* 94th Congress, 1st Session. Washington, DC, 1976.

House of Representatives, Select Committee on Assassinations. *Investigation of the Assassination of President John F. Kennedy: Appendix to Hearings before the* Select *Committee on Assassinations of the U.S. House of Representatives.* 95th Congress, 2nd Session. 7 volumes. Washington, DC, 1979.

House of Representatives, Select Committee on Assassinations. *Investigation of the Assassination of President John F. Kennedy: Hearings before the Select Committee on Assassinations.* 95th Congress, 2nd Session. 5 volumes. Washington, DC, 1979.

House of Representatives, Select Committee on Assassinations. *Report of the Select Committee on Assassinations.* 95th Congress, 2nd Session. Washington, DC, 1979.

President's Commission on the Assassination of President Kennedy. *Hearings before the President's Commission on the Assassination of President Kennedy.* 26 volumes. Washington, DC, 1964.

President's Commission on the Assassination of President Kennedy. *Report of the President's Commission on the Assassination of President Kennedy.* Washington, DC, 1964.

Senate, Select Committee to Study Governmental Operations with Respect to Intelligence Activities. *Alleged Assassination Plots Involving Foreign Leaders.* Interim Report. 94th Congress, 1st Session. Washington, DC, 1975.

Senate, Select Committee to Study Governmental Operations with Respect to Intelligence Activities. *The Investigation of the Assassination of President John F. Kennedy: Performance of the Intelligence Agencies.* Book V, Final Report. 94th Congress, 2nd Session. Washington, DC, 1976.

Other Primary Sources

John F. Kennedy Assassination Collection. Center for Southeast Louisiana Studies, Linus Sims Memorial Library. Southeastern Louisiana University, Hammond, LA.

Kurtz, Michael L. Personal collection of JFK Assassination materials.

Secondary Sources

Personal Interviews

Notes, tapes, and transcripts of all interviews will be deposited at a later date in the John F. Kennedy Assassination Collection, Center for Southeast Louisiana Studies, Linus A. Sims Memorial Library, Southeastern Louisiana University, Hammond, LA. Interviews were conducted in person, and by telephone, e-mail, and letter.

Abel, Billy
Adams, Eddie
Aguilar, Gary L.
Alvarez, Luis
Anthon, Orien
Artime, Manuel
Bissell, Richard
Bouck, Robert I.
Brown, Edward
Burkley, George G.
Canada, Robert O.
Craig, Roger D.
Craighead, Claude
Curry, Jesse
Daniels, William Hawk
Dolce, Joseph
Eble, Bernard
Eckert, William
Fensterwald, Bernard
Fisher, Russell S.
Fortas, Abraham
Gaudet, William George

Gonzalez, Miguel Santos
Greer, William
Gregory, Charles F.
Griffith, Michael
Guinn, Vincent
Helms, Richard
Helpburn, Milton
Humes, James J.
Jaworski, Leon
Johnson, Hamilton
Johnston, Sidney
Kantor, Seth
Kellerman, Roy
Kmen, Henry
Lacombe, Allen
Leake, Hunter C.
Liebeler, J. Wesley
Livingston, Robert B.
Mantik, David W.
Martin, Consuela
Mason, Henry
Maurin, Robert A., Sr.

McCone, John
Meagher, Sylvia
Morris, Henry M.
Nelson, Charles
Partin, Edward Grady

Rusk, Dean
Russell, Louis
Sehrt, Clem H.
Shaw, Robert R.
Szulc, Tad

Books

Associated Press. *The Torch Is Passed: The Associated Press Story of the Death of a President*. New York, 1963.

Belin, David W. *Final Disclosure*. New York, 1988.

———. *November 22, 1963: You Are the Jury*. New York, 1973.

Belzer, Richard. *UFOs, JFK, and Elvis: Conspiracies You Don't Have to Be Crazy to Believe*. New York, 1999.

Beschloss, Michael R. *The Crisis Years: Kennedy and Khrushchev, 1960–1963*. New York, 1991.

———. *Mayday: The U-2 Affair: The Untold Story of the Greatest U.S.-U.S.S.R. Spy Scandal*. New York, 1987.

———. *Taking Charge: The Johnson White House Tapes, 1963–1964*. New York, 1997.

Bishop, James A. *The Day Kennedy Was Shot*. New York, 1968.

Bissell, Richard M. *Reflections of a Cold War Warrior*. New Haven, CT, 1996.

Blakey, G. Robert, and Richard Billings. *The Plot to Kill the President*. New York, 1981.

Brener, Milton E. *The Garrison Case: A Study in the Abuse of Power*. New York, 1969.

Brown, Walt. *The Guns of Texas Are upon You*. Williamsport, PA, 2005.

———. *People vs. Lee Harvey Oswald: History on Trial*. New York, 1992.

———. *Referenced Index Guide to the Warren Commission*. Wilmington, DE, 1995.

———. *Treachery in Dallas*. New York, 1995.

———. *The Warren Omission: A Micro-Study of the Methods and Failures of the Warren Commission*. Wilmington, DE, 1996.

Crenshaw, Charles, et al. *Trauma Room One: The JFK Medical Coverup Exposed*. New York, 2001.

Curry, Jesse. *The JFK Assassination File*. Dallas, 1969.

Dallek, Robert. *An Unfinished Life: John F. Kennedy, 1917–1963*. Boston, 2003.

———. *Flawed Giant: Lyndon Johnson and His Times*. New York, 1998.

Davis, John H. *The Kennedy Contract*. New York, 1993.

———. *The Kennedys: Dynasty and Disaster*. 2nd ed. New York, 1992.

———. *Mafia Kingfish: Carlos Marcello and the Assassination of John F. Kennedy*. 2nd ed. New York, 1989.

Davison, Jean. *Oswald's Game*. New York, 1983.

Davy, William. *Let Justice Be Done: New Light on the Jim Garrison Investigation*. Reston, VA, 1999.

DiEugenio, James. *Destiny Betrayed: JFK, Cuba, and the Garrison Case*. New York, 1992.

Eddowes, Michael. *The Oswald File.* New York, 1977.

Epstein, Edward Jay. *Inquest: The Warren Commission and the Establishment of Truth.* New York, 1966.

———. *Legend: The Secret World of Lee Harvey Oswald.* New York, 1978.

Evica, George Michael. *And We Are All Mortal: New Evidence and Analysis in the John F. Kennedy Assassination.* West Hartford, CT, 1978.

Fenster, Mark. *Conspiracy Theories: Secrecy and Power in American Culture.* Minneapolis, 1999.

Fetzer, James H., ed. *Assassination Science: Experts Speak Out on the Death of JFK.* Chicago, 1998.

———. *The Great Zapruder Film Hoax: Deceit and Deception in the Death of JFK.* Chicago, 2003.

———. *Murder in Dealey Plaza: What We Know Now that We Didn't Know Then about the Death of JFK.* Chicago, 2000.

Fonzi, Gaeton. *The Last Investigation.* New York, 1993.

Frewin, Anthony, comp. *The Assassination of John F. Kennedy: An Annotated Film, TV, and Videography, 1963–1992.* Westport, CT, 1993.

Galanor, Stewart. *Cover-up.* New York, 1998.

Garrison, Jim. *A Heritage of Stone.* New York, 1970.

———. *On the Trail of the Assassins: My Investigation and Prosecution of the Murder of President Kennedy.* New York, 1988.

Groden, Robert J. *The Killing of a President.* New York, 1993.

Hancock, Larry. *Someone Would Have Talked: What We Know about the JFK Assassination after 40 Years.* Southlake, TX, 2003.

Hersch, Seymour M. *The Dark Side of Camelot.* Boston, 1997.

Hinckle, Warren, and William Turner. *The Fish Is Red: The Story of the Secret War against Castro.* New York, 1981.

Holland, Max. *The Kennedy Assassination Tapes.* New York, 1984.

Hosty, James. *Assignment Oswald.* New York, 1996.

Hurt, Henry. *Reasonable Doubt: An Investigation into the Assassination of John F. Kennedy.* New York, 1987.

James, Rosemary, and Jack Wardlaw. *Plot or Politics? The Garrison Case and Its Cast.* New Orleans, 1967.

Joesten, Joachim. *Oswald: Assassin or Fall Guy?* New York, 1964.

Kaiser, David. *American Tragedy: Kennedy, Johnson, and the Origins of the Vietnam War.* Cambridge, MA, 2000.

Kantor, Seth. *Who Was Jack Ruby?* New York, 1978.

Kirkwood, James. *American Grotesque: An Account of the Clay Shaw–Jim Garrison Affair in the City of New Orleans.* New York, 1970.

Kornbluh, Peter, ed. *Bay of Pigs Declassified: The Secret CIA Report on the Invasion of Cuba.* New York, 1998.

Kurtz, Michael L. *Crime of the Century: The Kennedy Assassination from a Historian's Perspective.* 2nd ed. Knoxville, 1993.

Lambert, Patricia. *False Witness: The Real Story of Jim Garrison's Investigation and Oliver Stone's Film "JFK."* New York, 1998.

Lane, Mark. *A Citizen's Dissent: Mark Lane Replies.* New York, 1968.

———. *Plausible Denial: Was the CIA Involved in the Assassination of JFK?* New York, 1991.

———. *Rush to Judgment: A Critique of the Warren Commission's Inquiry into the Murder of President John F. Kennedy, Officer J. D. Tippit, and Lee Harvey Oswald.* New York, 1966.

Lattimer, John K. *Kennedy and Lincoln: Medical and Ballistic Comparison of Their Assassinations.* New York, 1980.

Law, William Matson. *In the Eye of History: Disclosures in the JFK Assassination Medical Evidence.* Southlake, TX, 2005.

Lawrence, Lincoln. *Mind Control, Oswald and JFK: Were We Controlled?* Edited by Kenn Thomas. Kempton, IL, 1997.

Lee, Henry, and Jerry Labriola. *Famous Crimes Revisited: From Sacco-Vanzetti to O. J. Simpson, Including: Lindbergh Kidnapping, Sam Sheppard, John F. Kennedy, Vincent Foster, Jon Benet Ramsey.* Southington, CT, 2001.

Lifton, David S. *Best Evidence: Disguise and Deception in the Assassination of John F. Kennedy.* New York, 1988.

Mahoney, Richard D. *Sons and Brothers: The Days of Jack and Bobby Kennedy.* New York, 1999.

Mailer, Norman. *Oswald's Tale: An American Mystery.* New York, 1995.

Mallon, Thomas. *Mrs. Paine's Garage and the Murder of John F. Kennedy.* New York, 2002.

Marcus, Raymond. *The Bastard Bullet: A Search for Legitimacy for Commission Exhibit 399.* Los Angeles, 1966.

Marrs, Jim. *Crossfire: The Plot that Killed Kennedy.* New York, 1989.

———. *Rule by Secrecy: The Hidden History that Connects the Trilateral Commission, the Freemasons, and the Great Pyramids.* New York, 2000.

McClellan, Barr. *Blood, Money and Power: How LBJ Killed JFK.* New York, 2003.

McKnight, Gerald D. *Breach of Trust: How the Warren Commission Failed the Nation and Why.* Lawrence, KS, 2005.

McMillan, Priscilla Johnson. *Marina and Lee.* New York, 1977.

Meagher, Sylvia. *Accessories after the Fact: The Warren Commission, the Authorities, and the Report.* Indianapolis, 1967.

Mellen, Joan. *A Farewell to Justice: Jim Garrison, JFK's Assassination, and the Case that Should Have Changed History.* Washington, DC, 2005.

Melley, Timothy. *Empire of Conspiracy: The Culture of Paranoia in Postwar America.* Ithaca, NY, 2000.

Menninger, Bonar. *Mortal Error: The Shot that Killed JFK.* New York, 1992.

Moore, Jim. *Conspiracy of One: The Definitive Book on the Kennedy Assassination.* 2nd ed. Fort Worth, 1992.

Myers, Dale K. *With Malice: Lee Harvey Oswald and the Murder of Officer J. D. Tippit.* Milford, MI, 1998.

Newman, John. *Oswald and the CIA.* New York, 1995.

O'Donnell, Patrick. *Latent Destinies: Cultural Paranoia and Contemporary U.S. Narrative.* Durham, NC, 2000.

Oglesby, Carl. *The Yankee and Cowboy War*. Kansas City, MO, 1976.

O'Leary, Bradley S., and Edward Lee. *The Deaths of the Cold War Kings: The Assassinations of Diem and JFK*. Baltimore, 2000.

Popkin, Richard. *The Second Oswald*. New York, 1966.

Posner, Gerald. *Case Closed: Lee Harvey Oswald and the Assassination of JFK*. New York, 1993.

Rappleye, Charles, and Edward Becker. *All-American* Mafioso: *The Johnny Roselli Story*. New York, 1991.

Rhodes, Richard. *Why They Kill: The Discoveries of a Maverick Criminologist*. New York, 1999.

Roberts, Charles. *The Truth about the Assassination*. New York, 1967.

Roffman, Howard. *Presumed Guilty: Lee Harvey Oswald in the Assassination of President Kennedy*. Rutherford, NJ, 1975.

Russo, Gus. *Live by the Sword: The Secret War against Castro and the Death of JFK*. Baltimore, 1998.

Savage, Gary. *JFK: First Day Evidence*. Monroe, LA, 1993.

Scheim, David E. *Contract on America: The Mafia Murders of John and Robert Kennedy*. New York, 1988.

Schotz, E. Martin. *History Will Not Absolve Us: Orwellian Control, Public Denial, and the Murder of President Kennedy*. Brookline, MA, 1996.

Scott, Peter Dale. *Deep Politics and the Death of JFK*. Berkeley, CA, 1993.

Scott, Peter Dale, Paul L. Hoch, and Russell Stetler, eds. *The Assassinations: Dallas and Beyond: A Guide to Cover-ups and Investigation*. New York, 1976.

Scott, William E. *November 22, 1963: A Reference Guide to the JFK Assassination*. Lanham, MD, 1999.

Shaw, J. Gary, and Larry R. Harris. *Cover-up*. Austin, 1976.

Simon, Art. *Dangerous Knowledge: The JFK Assassination in Art and Film*. Philadelphia, 1996.

Smyth, Frank. *Cause of Death: The Story of Forensic Science*. New York, 1980.

Sneed, Larry A. *No More Silence: An Oral History of the Assassination of President Kennedy*. Dallas, 1998.

Snyder, Lemoyne. *Homicide Investigation: Practical Information for Coroners, Police Officers, and Other Investigators*. 3rd ed. Springfield, IL, 1977.

Specter, Arlen. *Passion for Truth: From Finding JFK's Single Bullet to Questioning Anita Hill to Impeaching Clinton*. New York, 2000.

Stone, Oliver, and Zachary Sklar. *JFK: The Book of the Film*. New York, 1992.

Sturdivan, Larry M. *The JFK Myths: A Scientific Investigation of the Kennedy Assassination*. St. Paul, MN, 2005.

Summers, Anthony. *Not in Your Lifetime*. Updated ed. New York 1998.

Theoharis, Athan G., ed. *A Culture of Secrecy: The Government Versus the People's Right to Know*. Lawrence, KS, 1998.

Thomas, Evan. *Robert Kennedy: His Life*. New York, 2000.

Thompson, Josiah. *Six Seconds in Dallas: A Micro-Study of the Kennedy Assassination*. New York, 1967.

Toplin, Robert Brent, ed. *Oliver Stone's USA: Film, History, and Controversy.* Lawrence, KS, 2000.

———. *Reel History: In Defense of Hollywood.* Lawrence, KS, 2002.

Trask, Richard B. *National Nightmare on Six Feet of Film.* Danvers, MA, 2005.

———. *Pictures of the Pain: Photography and the Assassination of President Kennedy.* Danvers, MA, 1994.

Twyman, Noel. *Bloody Treason: On Solving History's Greatest Murder Mystery: The Assassination of John F. Kennedy.* Rancho Santa Fe, CA, 1997.

Waldron, Lamar, with Thom Hartman. *Ultimate Sacrifice: John and Robert Kennedy, The Plan for a Coup in Cuba, and the Murder of JFK.* New York, 2005.

Weisberg, Harold. *Case Open.* New York, 1994.

———. *Never Again.* New York, 1995.

———. *Oswald in New Orleans: A Case for Conspiracy with the CIA.* New York, 1967.

———. *Post Mortem.* Frederick, MD, 1975.

———. *Whitewash: The Report on the Warren Report.* New York, 1966.

Wilber, Charles G. *Medicolegal Investigation of the President John F. Kennedy Murder.* Springfield, IL, 1978.

Winks, Robin W., ed. *The Historian as Detective: Essays on Evidence.* New York, 1968.

Wrone, David R. *The Zapruder Film: Reframing JFK's Assassination.* Lawrence, KS, 2003.

Zavada, Roland. *Analysis of Selected Motion Picture Photographic Evidence.* Rochester, NY, 1998.

Zelizer, Barbie. *Covering the Body: The Kennedy Assassination, the Media, and the Shaping of Collective Memory.* Chicago, 1992.

Fictional Works

Condon, Richard A. *The Manchurian Candidate.* New York, 1959.

———. *Winter Kills.* New York, 1974.

DeLillo, Don. *Libra.* New York, 1988.

Ellroy, James. *American Tabloid.* New York, 1995.

Garrison, Jim. *The Star Spangled Contract.* New York, 1976.

LaFountaine, George. *Flashpoint.* New York, 1976.

Tannenbaum, Robert K. *Corruption of Blood.* New York, 1995.

Journal Articles

Abrahamsen, David. "A Study of Lee Harvey Oswald: Psychological Capability of Murder." *Bulletin of the New York Academy of Medicine* 43 (1967): 861–88.

Alvarez, Luis W. "A Physicist Examines the Kennedy Assassination Film." *American Journal of Physics* 44 (1976): 813–27.

Appleton, Sheldon. "Assassinations." *Public Opinion Quarterly* 64 (2000): 495–522.

Artwohl, Robert. "JFK's Assassination: Conspiracy, Forensic Science, and Common Sense." *JAMA* 269 (March 24–31, 1993): 1540–43.

Ball, Moya Ann. "The Phantom of the Oval Office: The John F. Kennedy Assassination's Impact on Lyndon B. Johnson, His Key Advisers, and the Vietnam Decision-Making Process." *Presidential Studies Quarterly* 24 (1994): 105–19.

Banta, Thomas J. "The Kennedy Assassination: Early Thoughts and Emotions." *Public Opinion Quarterly* 28 (1964): 216–24.

Breo, Dennis L. "JFK's Death—The Plain Truth from the MDs Who Did the Autopsy." *JAMA* 267 (May 27, 1992): 2794–803.

———. "JFK's Death, Part 2—Dallas MDs Recall Their Memories." *JAMA* 267 (May 27, 1992): 2804–7.

———. "JFK's Death, Part 3—Dr. Finck Speaks Out: 'Two Bullets from the Rear'" *JAMA* 268 (October 7, 1992): 1748–54.

Cook, Andrew. "Lone Assassins." *History Today* 53 (2003): 25–31.

Costigliola, Frank C. "Like Children in the Darkness: European Reaction to the Assassination of John F. Kennedy." *Journal of Popular Culture* 20 (1986): 115–24.

DeCurtis, Anthony. "An Outsider in This Society: An Interview with Don DeLillo." *South Atlantic Quarterly* 89 (1990): 281–304.

DerDerian, James. "The CIA, Hollywood, and Sovereign Conspiracies." *Queen's Quarterly* 100 (1993): 329–47.

Feighery, Glen. "The Warren Report's Forgotten Chapter: Press Response to Criticism of Kennedy Assassination Coverage." *American Journalism* 20 (2003): 83–101.

Fetzer, James H. "Disinformation: The Use of False Information." *Mind and Machines* 14 (2004): 231–40.

Freese, Paul L. "The Warren Commission and the Fourth Shot: A Reflection on the Fundamentals of Forensic Fact Finding." *New York University Law Review* 40 (1965): 424–65.

Gibson, Donald E. "The Creation of the Warren Commission." *Mid-America* 79 (1997): 203–54.

Greene, A. C. "The Sixth Floor: A Personal View." *Southwestern Historical Quarterly* 94 (1990): 171–77.

Griffin, Leland M. "When Dreams Collide: Rhetorical Trajectories in the Assassination of President Kennedy." *Quarterly Journal of Speech* 70 (1984): 111–31.

Hall, Kermit L. "JFK's Assassination in an Age of Open Secrets." *OAH Newsletter* 25 (1997): 1, 6–8, 10.

Hamilton, Geoff. "Oswald's Wake: Representations of JFK's Alleged Assassin in Recent American Literature." *University of Toronto Quarterly* 7 (2002): 651–64.

Hamilton, James W. "Some Observations on the Motivations of Lee Harvey Oswald." *Journal of Psychohistory* 14 (1986): 43–54.

Harrison, Albert A., and James Moulton Thomas. "The Kennedy Assassination, Unidentified Flying Objects, and Other Conspiracies: Psychological and Organizational Factors in the Perception of 'Cover-up.'" *Systems Research and Behavioral Science* 14 (2000): 113–28.

Holland, Max. "After Thirty Years: Making Sense of the Assassination." *Reviews in American History* 22 (June 1994): 191–209.

———. "A Cold War Odyssey: The Oswald Files." *Cold War International History Project Bulletin* 14–15 (2003–2004): 410–18.

———. "The Demon in Jim Garrison." *Wilson Quarterly* 25 (2001): 10–17.

Kaplan, John. "The Assassin." *Stanford Law Review* 19 (1967): 1110–51.

Keener, John F. "Biography, Conspiracy, and the Oswald Enigma." *Biography* 20 (1997): 302–30.

Keller, James R. "Oliver Stone's *JFK* and the 'Circulation of Social Energy' and the 'Textuality of History.'" *Journal of Popular Film and Television* 21 (1993): 72–78.

Kurtz, Michael L. "The Assassination of John F. Kennedy: A Historical Perspective." *Historian* 45 (1982): 1–19.

———. "Lee Harvey Oswald in New Orleans: A Reappraisal." *Louisiana History* 21 (1980): 7–22.

Lattimer, John K. "Additional Data on the Shooting of President Kennedy." *JAMA* 269 (March 24–31, 1993): 1544–47.

———. "Experimental Duplication of the Important Physical Evidence of the Lapel Bulge of the Jacket Worn by Governor Connally when Bullet 399 Went through Him." *Journal of the American College of Surgeons* 178 (1994): 517–22.

———. "Observations Based on a Review of the Autopsy Photographs, X-rays and Related Materials of the Late President John F. Kennedy." *Resident and Staff Physician Medical Times* 34 (May 1972): 34–63.

Lattimer, John K., and Jon Lattimer. "The Kennedy-Connally Single Bullet Theory: A Feasibility Study." *International Surgery* 50 (1968): 524–32.

Lattimer, John K., Jon Lattimer, and Gary Lattimer. "An Experimental Study of the Backward Movement of President Kennedy's Head." *Surgery, Gynecology and Obstetrics* 142 (1976): 246–54.

———. "Could Oswald Have Shot President Kennedy: Further Ballistics Studies." *Bulletin of the New York Academy of Medicine* 53 (1977): 280–90.

Lentricchia, Frank. "*Libra* as Postmodern Critique." *South Atlantic Quarterly* 89 (1990): 431–53.

Levy, Michael L., Daniel Sullivan, Rodrick Faccio, and Robert G. Grossman. "A Neuroforensic Analysis of the Wounds of President John F. Kennedy: Part 2—A Study of the Available Evidence, Eyewitness Correlations, Analysis, and Conclusions." *Neurosurgery* 54 (June 2004): E1–E22.

Morales, Frank, and Paul DiRienzo. "Interview with Zachary Sklar, Co-Writer of the Movie *JFK*." *Shadow* (March 1992): 12–18.

Nelson, Anna K. "JFK Assassination Review Board, OAH, Foster Release of Top Secret Documents." *OAH Newsletter* 26 (February 1998): 5, 8, 10.

———. "Operation Northwoods and the Covert War against Cuba." *Cuban Studies* 32 (2001): 145–54.

———. "The Outsider as Insider: Reflections on the Kennedy Assassination Records Review Board." *Public Historian* 21 (1999): 57–62.

Nichols, John. "Assassination of President Kennedy." *Practitioner* 211 (1973): 625–33.

———. "The Wounding of Governor Connally of Texas, November 22, 1963." *Maryland State Medical Journal* 26 (October 1977): 58–77.

Norton, Linda E., and Vincent J. M. DiMaio. "The Exhumation and Identification of Lee Harvey Oswald." *Journal of Forensic Sciences* 29 (1984): 19–38.

Noya, Jose Liete. "Naming the Secret: Don DeLillo's *Libra*." *Contemporary Literature* 45 (2004): 239–75.

Ogg, E. Jerald. "*Life* and the Prosecution of Clay Shaw: A More Curious Silence." *Louisiana History* 45 (2004): 133–49.

Olson, Don, and Ralph F. Turner. "Photographic Evidence and the Assassination of President John F. Kennedy." *Journal of Forensic Sciences* 16 (1971): 399–419.

Parrish, Timothy L. "The Lesson of History: Don DeLillo's Texas Schoolbook, *Libra*." *Clio* 30 (2000): 1–23.

Pinsker, Sanford. "America's Conspiratorial Imagination." *Virginia Quarterly Review* 68 (1992): 605–25.

Pratt, Roy. "Theorizing Conspiracy." *Theory and Society* 32 (2003): 255–71.

Rabbe, Stephen G. "After the Missiles of October: John F. Kennedy and Cuba, November 1962 to November 1963." *Presidential Studies Quarterly* 30 (2000): 714–26.

Rahn, Kenneth, and Larry Sturdivan. "Neutron Activation and the JFK Assassination—Part 1: Data and Interpretation." *Journal of Radioanalytical and Nuclear Chemistry* 262 (2004): 205–13.

———. "Neutron Activation and the JFK Assassination—Part 2: Extended Benefits." *Journal of Radioanalytical and Nuclear Chemistry* 262 (2004): 215–22.

Raskin, Marcus. "*JFK* and the Culture of Violence." *American Historical Review* 97 (1992): 487–99.

Rogin, Michael. "*JFK:* The Movie." *American Historical Review* 97 (1992): 500–505.

Rosenstone, Robert A. "*JFK:* Historical Fact/Historical Fiction." *American Historical Review* 97 (1992): 506–11.

Schuyler, Michael. "The Bitter Harvest: Lyndon B. Johnson and the Assassination of John F. Kennedy." *Journal of American Culture* 8 (1985): 101–9.

———. "Ghosts in the White House: LBJ, RFK, and the Assassination of JFK." *Presidential Studies Quarterly* 17 (1987): 503–18.

Sullivan, Daniel, Rodrick Faccio, Michael L. Levy, and Robert G. Grossman. "The Assassination of President John F. Kennedy: A Neuroforensic Analysis—Part 1: A Neurosurgeon's Previously Undocumented Eyewitness Account of the Events of November 22, 1963." *Neurosurgery* 54 (2003): 1019–27.

Thomas, D. B. "Echo Correlation Analysis and the Acoustic Evidence in the Kennedy Assassination Revisited." *Science and Justice* 41 (2001): 21–32.

Trujillo, Nick. "Interpreting November 22: A Critical Ethnography of an Assassination Site." *Quarterly Journal of Speech* 79 (1993): 447–66.

Vogt, Allen R. "The Kennedy Assassination and the History Teacher." *History Teacher* 20 (1986): 7–26.

Wecht, Cyril H. "A Critique of the Medical Aspects of the Investigation into the Assassination of President Kennedy." *Journal of Forensic Sciences* 2 (1966): 300–317.

———. "New Evidence Rekindles Old Doubts: JFK Assassination: 'A Prolonged and Willful Cover-up.'" *Modern Medicine* 42 (October 28, 1974): 40X–40FF.

————. "Pathologist's View of JFK Autopsy: An Unsolved Case." *Modern Medicine* 40 (November 27, 1972): 28–32.

————. and Robert P. Smith. "The Medical Evidence in the Assassination of President John F. Kennedy." *Forensic Science* 3 (April 1974): 105–28.

Wilber, Charles G. "The Assassination of the Late President John F. Kennedy: An Academician's Thoughts." *Journal of Forensic Medicine and Pathology* 7 (1986): 52–58.

Willman, Skip. "Art after Dealey Plaza: DeLillo's *Libra*." *Modern Fiction Studies* 45 (1999): 621–40.

Wolske, J. Alan. "Jack, Judy, Sam, Bobby, Johnny, Frank . . . : An Investigation into the Alternate History of the CIA-Mafia Collaboration to Assassinate Fidel Castro, 1960–1967." *Intelligence and National Security* 15 (2000): 104–30.

Zelizer, Barbie. "The Kennedy Assassination through a Popular Eye: Towards a Politics of Remembering." *Journal of Communication Inquiry* 16 (1992): 21–36.

Other Articles

Ambrose, Stephen. "Writers on the Grassy Knoll: A Reader's Guide." *New York Times Book Review*, February 2, 1992, 1, 23–25.

Ansen, David. "A Troublemaker for Our Times." *Newsweek*, December 23, 1991, 50.

Anson, Robert Sam. "The Shooting of *JFK*." *Esquire*, November 1991, 93–102, 174–76.

"The Assassination of President Kennedy." *Life*, November 29, 1963, 23–38.

Auchincloss, Kenneth. "Twisted History." *Newsweek*, December 23, 1991, 46–49.

Belin, David W. "The Big Lies of *JFK*." *New York Times Magazine*, February 17, 1992, 24–27.

————. "The Warren Commission: Why We Still Don't Believe It." *New York Times Magazine*, November 20, 1988, 74–80.

Bickel, Alexander. "The Failure of the Warren Report." *Commentary*, October 1966, 31–39.

Boyles, Peter. "Fear and Loathing on the Assassination Trail." *Denver Magazine*, November 1980, 36–41, 100–101.

Carter, Hodding. "'JFK' Stonewalls History." Newspaper Enterprise Association Column, January 13, 1992.

Cohen, Jacob. "Conspiracy Fever." *Commentary*, October 1975, 33–42.

————. "Yes, Oswald Alone Killed Kennedy." *Commentary*, June 1992, 32–40, 94; November 1992, 10–12, 14–15, 17–21.

Corliss, Richard. "Who Killed JFK?" *Time*, December 23, 1991, 66–70.

"The Crime of the Century." *Pitt Magazine*, November 1988, 36–38.

DeSantis, Vincent P. "Who Killed JFK?" *Notre Dame Magazine*, Autumn 1988, 51–55.

Epstein, Edward Jay. "The Second Coming of Jim Garrison." *Atlantic Monthly*, March 1993, 89–92.

————. "Shots in the Dark." *New Yorker*, November 30, 1992, 47–55.

Fein, Arnold L. "JFK in Dallas: The Warren Report and Its Critics." *Saturday Review*, October 22, 1966, 36–38, 43–47.

Grichot, Jack. "Cyril Wecht: Coroner and Skeptic." *Medical Dimensions*, March 1975, 24–28.

Groden, Robert. "A New Look at the Zapruder Film." *Rolling Stone*, April 24, 1975, 24–36.

Grunwald, Lisa. "Why We Still Care." *Life*, December 1991, 34–46.

Hamil, Pete. "JFK: The Real Thing." *New York*, November 28, 1988, 44–51.

Hennelly, Robert, and Jerry Policoff. "JFK: How the Media Assassinated the Real Story." *Village Voice*, March 31, 1992, 33–39.

Holland, Max. "The Assassination Tapes." *Atlantic Monthly*, June 2004, 82–94.

Houts, Marshall. "Dr. Milton Helpern: World's Greatest Expert on Gunshot Wounds Speaks Out: 1. Warren Commission Botched the Kennedy Autopsy; 2. Warren Commission One-Bullet Theory Exploded." *Argosy*, July 1967, 21–22, 108–16.

Jackson, Donald. "The Evolution of an Assassin." *Life*, February 21, 1964, 68–80.

Janos, Leo. "The Last Days of the President." *Atlantic Monthly*, July 1973, 35–41.

Lardner, George. "Dallas in Wonderland: Oliver Stone and JFK's Assassination." *Washington Post*, national weekly ed., May 27–June 2, 1991.

———. "Zapruder Film of JFK Assassination Is Public Record." *Washington Post*, April 25, 1998.

Lewis, Anthony. "Stone's Fantasy." *New York Times* News service column, January 13, 1992.

Morley, Jefferson. "November 22, 1963: Why We Need the Real History of the Kennedy Assassination." *Washington Post*, November 24, 1996.

Morley, John. "The Entangling Kennedy Myths." *Nation*, December 12, 1988, 646–53.

Nidiry, Rosemary. "The Assassination Archivist." *National Journal*, June 13, 1992, 14–24.

Norden, Eric. "Jim Garrison: A Candid Conversation with the Embattled District Attorney of New Orleans." *Playboy*, October 1967, 59–60, 62, 64, 66, 68, 70, 72, 74, 156–63, 165–68, 170–72, 174–76, 178.

"November 22: Twenty Years Later." *Dallas Morning News* special issue of November 20, 1983.

Parshall, Gerald. "The Man with a Deadly Smirk." *U.S. News and World Report*, August 30–September 6, 1993, 62–72.

Posner, Gerald. "Case Closed—Part 1: The Sniper's Nest; Part 2: The Magic Bullet." *U.S. News and World Report*, August 30–September 6, 1993, 74–98.

Rosenbaum, Ron. "Taking a Darker View." *Time*, January 13, 1992, 38–40.

Rowland, Mark. "Stone Unturned." *American Film*, March 1991, 41–43.

Salholz, Eloise. "Did the Mob Kill JFK?" *Newsweek*, January 27, 1992, 26–27.

Sidey, Hugh. "A Shattering Afternoon in Dallas." *Time*, November 28, 1988, 45.

Snyder, Lemoyne. "Lee Oswald's Guilt: How Science Nailed Kennedy's Killer." *Popular Science*, April 1965, 68–73.

Specter, Arlen. "Overwhelming Evidence Oswald Was the Assassin." *U.S. News and World Report*, October 10, 1966, 48–50, 53–59, 62–63.

Thomas, Evan. "Bobby Kennedy's War on Castro." *Washington Monthly*, December 1995, 24–30.

———. "Who Shot JFK?" *Newsweek*, September 6, 1993, 14–17.

Thompson, Josiah. "The Crossfire that Killed President Kennedy." *Saturday Evening Post*, December 2, 1967, 27–31, 46, 50–55.

Zoglin, Richard. "More Shots in Dealey Plaza." *Time*, June 10, 1991, 64–66.

Theses, Dissertations, and Other Papers

Brossman, Brent Gene. "Rhetorical Hermeneutics and Oliver Stone's *JFK*: A Method and an Application." Ph.D. dissertation, University of Kansas, 1995.

Brown, Robert S. "Football as a Rhetorical Site of National Reassurance: Managing the Crisis of the Kennedy Assassination." Ph.D. dissertation, Indiana University, 1996.

Dvorak, Andrew Lee. "Rendezvous with Death: The Assassination of President Kennedy and the Question of Conspiracy." Ph.D. dissertation, Illinois State University, 2003.

Hall, Richard A. "Beyond a Reasonable Fact: The Role of Historians in the Study of the Assassination of President John F. Kennedy." M.A. thesis, Texas A&M International University, 2004.

Igbal, Zaryab, and Christopher Zorn. "The Political Economy of Assassination." Paper presented at the annual meeting of the Midwest Political Science Association, 2000.

Kurtz, Michael L. "Conspiracy Theories in the Kennedy Assassination." Paper presented at the Annual Meeting of the Southwestern Social Sciences Association, 1997.

Love, Ruth L. "Television and the Death of a President: Network Decisions in Covering Collective Events." Ph.D. dissertation, Columbia University, 1969.

McCaffrey, Raymond Aloysius. "Assassination of American Presidents: An Analysis of the Literature." Ph.D. dissertation, Fordham University, 1982.

Ralston, Ross Frank. "The Media and the Kennedy Assassination: The Social Construction of Reality." Ph.D. dissertation, Iowa State University, 1999.

Reynolds, Michael Louis. "Suspicious Narrative: The Assassination of JFK and American Ways of Not-Knowing." Ph.D. dissertation, University of Southern California, 2001.

Robins, Robert, and Jerrold M. Post. "Political Paranoia as Cinematic Motif: Stone's *JFK*." Paper presented at the annual meeting of the American Political Science Association, 1997.

Seay, Theresa Margaret Carroll. "The Warren Commission and Beyond: The Question of Conspiracy in the Assassination of President John F. Kennedy." Ph.D. dissertation, University of Connecticut, 2002.

Simon, Arthur. "The Site of Crisis: Representation and the Assassination of JFK." Ph.D. dissertation, New York University, 1993.

Stone, Nancy. "A Conflict of Interest: The Warren Commission, the FBI, and The CIA." Ph.D. dissertation, Boston College, 1987.

Tagg, Carl Francis. "Fidel Castro and the Kennedy Assassination." M.A. thesis, Florida Atlantic University, 1982.

Zelizer, Barbie. "'Covering the Body': The Kennedy Assassination and the Establishment of Journalistic Authority." Ph.D. dissertation, University of Pennsylvania, 1990.

Audiovisual Materials

The Assassination Films. New Frontier Productions, 1995.
*The Assassination of President Kennedy: What We Know Now That We Didn't Know Then.*Witness Productions, 1978.
Best Evidence: The Research Video. Rhino Home Video, 1990.
CBS News Inquiry: The Warren Commission Report. 1967.
CBS Reports Inquiry: The American Assassins: Lee Harvey Oswald and John F. Kennedy. 1975.
Four Days in November. MGM/UA Home Video, 1988.
He Must Have Something: The Real Story of Jim Garrison's Investigation into the Assassination of JFK. NOVAC, 1992.
Image of an Assassination: A New Look at the Zapruder Film. MPI Home Video, 1998.
JFK: The Assassination, the Cover-up, and Beyond. James H. Fetzer, 1994.
The JFK Assassination: The Jim Garrison Tapes. Vestron Video, 1992.
JFK, Hoffa and the Mob. PBS Home Video, 1993.
The Kennedy Assassination: Beyond Conspiracy. ABC News, 2003.
The KGB Oswald Files. MPI Home Video, 1991.
The Men Who Killed Kennedy. 5 parts. A&E Home Video, 1995.
NBC News White Paper: The JFK Conspiracy: The Case of Jim Garrison. 1967.
The Plot to Kill JFK: Rush to Judgment. MPI Home Video, 1988.
Reasonable Doubt: The Single-Bullet Theory and the Assassination of John F. Kennedy. White Star, 1988.
The Trial of Lee Harvey Oswald. ABC, 1977.
The Trial of Lee Harvey Oswald. BBC, 1978.
The Trial of Lee Harvey Oswald. Ian Hamilton, director. 1986.
Who Killed JFK? Facts, Not Fiction. CBS Video, 1992.
"Who Shot President Kennedy?" *Nova*, PBS, 1988.
"Who Was Lee Harvey Oswald?" *Frontline*, PBS, 1993.

Motion Pictures

Executive Action. David Miller, director. Executive Action Enterprises. 1973.
Flashpoint. William Tannen, director. Home Box Office. 1984.
JFK. Oliver Stone, director. Warner Brothers. 1991.
The Parallax View. Alan J. Pakula, director. Paramount. 1974.
Ruby. John Mackenzie, director. Propaganda Films. 1992.
Winter Kills. William Richert, director. Winter Gold Productions, 1979.

Internet Sources

The Academic JFK Assassination Site. Kenneth Rahn. http://karws.gso.uri.edu/JFK/JFK.html.
ClintBradford.com. Clint Bradford. http://jfk-info.com/index2.html.

JFK Assassination Web Page. Michael T. Griffith. http://ourworld-top.cs.com/ mikegriffith1/id35.htm.

JFK Assassination Records. National Archives and Records Service. http://www .archives.gov/research/jfk/.

JFK Lancer. Debra Conway. http://jfklancer.com/index.html.

The Kennedy Assassination Home Page. John McAdams. http://mcadams.posc .mu.edu/home.htm.

Secrets of a Homicide. Dale Myers. http://www.jfkfiles.com/jfk/html/intro.htm.

Index